ETHNICITY AND WAR

* * * * *

VOLUME III

**ETHNICITY AND
PUBLIC POLICY**
SERIES

ETHNICITY
AND WAR

WINSTON A. VAN HORNE
EDITOR

THOMAS V. TONNESEN
MANAGING EDITOR

UNIVERSITY OF WISCONSIN SYSTEM
AMERICAN ETHNIC STUDIES COORDINATING
COMMITTEE/ URBAN CORRIDOR CONSORTIUM

University of Wisconsin System American Ethnic Studies
Coordinating Committee/Urban Corridor Consortium
P. O. Box 413, Milwaukee, WI 53201

International Standard Book Number ISBN 0-942672-04-6 (cloth)
International Standard Book Number ISBN 0-942672-05-4 (paper)
Library of Congress Catalog Card Number: 84-50655

UNIVERSITY OF WISCONSIN SYSTEM AMERICAN ETHNIC STUDIES COORDINATING COMMITTEE

DR. WINSTON A. VAN HORNE
University of Wisconsin–Milwaukee
Chairperson, AESCC

DR. PETER J. KELLOGG
University of Wisconsin–Green Bay

DR. LIONEL A. MALDONADO
University of Wisconsin–Parkside

DR. WILLIAM J. MURIN
Director, Urban Corridor Consortium

DR. MELVIN C. TERRELL
University of Wisconsin–Oshkosh

MR. THOMAS V. TONNESEN
Program Coordinator, AESCC (ex officio)

The University of Wisconsin System American Ethnic Studies Coordinating Committee (AESCC) wishes to acknowledge the contributions of its former members, as well as those of the Urban Corridor Consortium Steering Committee and the University of Wisconsin System American Ethnic Studies Advisory Committee.

PREFACE

At first glance one might wonder how the combination of ethnicity and war falls under the parameters of public policy. Yet there can be little argument that issues related to domestic dissent and intolerance, foreign policy, the military and, ultimately, armed conflict are some of the most crucial ones decided upon by governments and their citizenry. War is definitely a facet, albeit an abhorrent one, of public policy, and ethnicity has surely played, plays, and foreseeably will continue to play a central role in nearly all wars, foreign and civil.

The collection of essays written and assembled for this volume was designed to touch upon an array of topics and ethnic groups. Surely few if any ethnic groups have been immune to war or the issues that surround and spawn it, and the chapters that follow give evidence to this fact. The reader will find essays that concern themselves with Jewish Americans, blacks, American Indians, Japanese Americans, German Americans, Irish Americnas and Indochinese. Although the various selections deal specifically with this assorted collection of groups, the issues discussed are in a very real sense "trans-ethnic"—that is, the lessons to be drawn from the chapters have relevance that transcends ethnic boundaries. Surely the experiences of German Americans during World War I and the plight of Japanese Americans during World War II have implications for us all. On the same note, the distinction developed between political loyalty and cultural loyalty in the chapter by Lawrence Fuchs on ethnic group influence on foreign policymaking is one which has a place in the experiences of all groups comprising this nation.

Neither those readers on the political left nor those on the political right will find themselves totally at ease with all the chapters in this volume. A concerted effort has been made throughout the duration of our *Ethnicity and Public Policy* series to include selections from various points on the political spectrum. This practice has been continued in *Ethnicity and War*. Perhaps coincidentally, along with the nation's growing interest in the circumstances confronting Vietnam veterans has been a burgeoning revisionist outlook on the United States' participation in the conflict. For better or for worse, the political winds are gusting from a different direction than they were in the Vietnam-Watergate era, and it should come as no surprise that this type of change affects how we interpret the past. The chapter by Stephen Young on the Vietnam War will rankle many, for it makes important observations that place it directly within this revisionist school. On a similar note, those who view the Irish Republican Army in a romantic, freedom-fighter sense will find discomfort in the chapter by Thomas Hachey.

All of this is not to say that the essays in this volume can only be embraced by those who, fairly or unfairly, are viewed as to the right of center. The chapter by Lane and James Hirabayashi places the forced relocation of Japanese Americans during World War II within a theoretical framework of racism, and the selection by Frank Zeidler poses weighty questions about our nation's ability to tolerate dissent in matters related to foreign policy and war. One will also find a penetrating study by Donald Fixico of the cultural and psychological devices used by agents of the federal government in their treaty relations with American Indian nations, as well as a straightforward assessment by Alvin Schexnider of the embroilment surrounding the numbers of blacks in the United States' armed forces. In summation, we feel that the volume presents a broad cross section of perspectives on specific topics related to ethnicity, war and public policy, and that this is in keeping with the charge given to academia to allow all opinions to flower. We hope that you agree.

With the publication of *Ethnicity and War*, we see our *Ethnicity and Public Policy* series as having rounded a significant corner. Just as many conferences which are billed as "Annual" are never held a second time, so too was the danger of launching a "series" that would never produce a second volume. Doing something once or even twice can be considered a fluke, but being able to do it a third time puts one well on the way toward establishing one's reputation. We have reached that point with the release of this volume, and for this we have many to thank. One of the first who comes to mind is Sharon Gutowski, whose indefatigable work as the organizer of colloquium logistics starts us on the path toward the next volume. We must also give recognition to Joanne Brown, whose considerable copy editing skills allow us to bring cohesiveness to the collection. Finally, and most importantly, we owe a huge debt of gratitude to Linda Krueger. Her patience is unsurpassable, and her careful nurturing of the volumes through the labyrinths of editing, design and publication has been indispensable to the entire *Ethnicity and Public Policy* series. To these individuals, and to all who lend support to the varied activities of the University of Wisconsin System American Ethnic Studies Coordinating Committee, a tip of our cap.

Thomas V. Tonnesen

CONTENTS

INTRODUCTION

Winston A. Van Horne   W. Werner Prange

University of Wisconsin-Milwaukee   *University of Wisconsin-Green Bay*

And I looked, and behold a pale horse: and his name that sat on him was Death, and Hell followed with him. And power was given unto them over the fourth part of the earth, to kill with sword, and with hunger, and with death, and with the beasts of the earth.

Revelation 6:8.

War is the highest form of struggle for resolving contradictions, when they have developed to a certain stage, between classes, nations, states, or political groups . . . "War is the continuation of politics." In this sense *war is politics* and *war itself is political action* . . . . But war has its own particular characteristics and in this sense it cannot be equated with politics in general. "War is the continuation of politics by other means." . . . *(P)olitics is war without bloodshed while war is politics with bloodshed.* (Our italics.)

Quotations from Chairman Mao Tse-tung.

(P)eace is the end sought for by war. For every man seeks peace by waging war, but no man seeks war by making peace . . . . For even those whom (men) make war against they wish to make their own, and impose on them the laws of their own peace.

St. Augustine, *The City of God*, XIX, 12.

Mind and emotion are stirred by the passages above. War kills, and death is the antithesis of life. One feels the foulness, meanness, wretchedness and brutality of death as it consumes life insatiably in the rage of war. Death and war are the negation of life and peace, yet, intriguingly, life and peace ground the ultimate purpose of death and war. Indeed, St. Augustine believes "even those who take pleasure in exercising their warlike nature in command and battle" do so "with the desire for peace," in the hope that by imposing upon the enemy "the laws of their own peace," they may lead more secure and commodious lives.

War entails struggle—struggle in which Death and Hell serve political interests and purposes. The struggle of war is not an end in itself but a means to secure the ends of peace that cannot be realized through peaceful struggle. War and peace are opposites but struggle is common to both, and politics gives form and substance to the struggle of each. Struggle in peace is conceptually and empirically distinguishable and separable from struggle in war, yet struggle in both peace and war that sets classes, nations and states against one another emanates from a common substratum, politics.

Politics entails the creation, maintenance and persistence of an environment in which authoritative decisions, binding upon all, structure the form and content of impure competitive struggle to procure, order and allocate things that are of value and/or are valued in a particular society. It structures human relationships, which evince different forms and contents in peace and war, even though these relationships share a range of common elements grounded in the defining attributes of politics.

War is a means; peace is an end. If the structure of relationships at which politics aims cannot be secured by struggle in peace, struggle in war becomes a means towards its realization. The politics of struggle in war and the politics of struggle in peace are thus two species of one genus, politics. These two species of politics, which we shall call war-politics and peace-politics, are differentiated by the nature of the struggle that gives each its distinctiveness.

Struggle in war-politics is marked by the degradation of human life and bloodshed; struggle in peace-politics is marked by regard for the intrinsic value of human life and the absence of bloodshed. The line of demarcation that separates struggle in war-politics from struggle in peace-politics is not hard, fast and impregnable, but moveable, diffuse and penetrable. The open texture of the line accommodates the degeneration of struggle in peace-politics into struggle in war-politics just as readily as it does the regeneration of struggle in war-politics into struggle in peace politics. It is the recognition of the continuity between degenerative and regenerative political struggle that led Karl von Clausewitz to his insight that war is the continuation of politics by other means, which has withstood the test of time by grounding two species of politics in one genus. What, then, are the defining attributes of war-politics and peace-politics?

Perhaps the most compelling attribute of war-politics is the molding and nurturing of an undifferentiated mass social psychology that inclines and impels individuals to perceive common mortal foes, and feel a strong, maybe even overpowering, inner need either to destroy them physically or render them impotent if they cannot be killed. This attribute of war-politics excites one's consciousness, and perchance even scandalizes one's mind, in Frank Zeidler's chapter, as well as in the one by Lane and James Hirabayashi.

The Hirabayashis ground their presentation in one unambiguous, evocative and potent sentence. They write, ". . .the case of the Japanese Americans indicates that when a group (1) is identifiable physically, (2) has suffered from a history of racial stereotypes and actions, and (3) is targeted as a scapegoat or a suspected enemy in a national crisis, racist and discriminatory sentiments can be *formalized, legalized, and implemented as public policy*." (Our italics.) James Hirabayashi knows firsthand, and Lane Hirabayashi through familial agony occasioned by trauma inflicted by the state, the chilling consequences of the impact of physiognomy upon an undifferentiated mass social psychology that blurs the distinction between friend and foe to a point where everyone who is identifiable through the sharing of a set of physical attributes is designated "the enemy." This is an emotion-laden observation that might readily incline one to infer that a one-to-one correspondence obtains between racism and war-politics, such that whenever and wherever war-politics is observed, always and without exception, racism is also observed. The empirical reality of both racism and war-politics would be grossly distorted by such an inference— which, incidentally, the Hirabayashis do *not* make. The social psychology of racism grounded the political economy of slavery in the United States, but it cannot really be said that war-politics obtained between masters and slaves—in spite of the repeated slave revolts—until, perhaps, the time of the Civil War. The masters' social psychology neither inclined nor impelled them to perceive their slaves, whom they discerned to be both their biological and social inferiors, to be enemies. The slaves no doubt perceived their masters as enemies, but since rigid controls prevented them from engaging in political activity, they stood outside the bounds of war-politics. The critical point here is that the social psychology of war-politics *may* tap racist sentiments in order to destroy or render impotent those who are innocent, but are nonetheless perceived to be enemies. And it is the ease with which such emotions are mobilized that makes war-politics so dangerous to civil rights and civil liberties which are taken for granted, particularly in liberal democracies.

The mobilization of emotions—without the racism of which the Hirabayashis speak so painfully, passionately and eloquently—is portrayed starkly and vividly by Zeidler. The ethnic identity of German Americans made them the object of emotions mobilized by the flames of war-politics during the First World War. Zeidler quotes Dean Wittke, who writes, ". . .the war precipitated an hysterical effort to eradicate everything of German origin from American civilization. The anti-German campaign was directed by extremists, but many Americans approved the patriotic drive against 'Teutonism' and the 'Hun.' German books, music, church services, newspapers, singing societies, German in the schools, and many other features of American life that could somehow be traced to a German origin came under the ban." And Zeidler himself writes,

> The effect of the war for control of American public opinion through propaganda was to cause everything German in the United States to be "regarded as part of an organized propaganda of the German government to make the United States an appendage of the Kaiser's empire. Hyphen hunting became a popular pastime among American superpatriots. . . ." The daily excitement of the war news from Europe tended to polarize the American population between friends of the Central Powers, particularly friends of Germany, and people of British heritage. . . . The issue grew to be one of *loyalty*. The pressure on the German community and German-speaking people became immense. . . . It was widely thought that in this struggle for the mind of America, the President and those around him were committed to the Allied cause by virtue of their ethnic backgrounds, and President Wilson, even though he at first sought to keep the United States neutral, and been converted to the idea of intervention by the spring of 1916. Supporters of the Allies had started a successful "preparedness" movement which was designed to prepare Americans to enter the war on the side of the Allies. Literature and motion pictures were used to stir up opposition to Germany. President Wilson joined this movement in 1916 with a series of speeches. Thus the *psychological groundwork* for war hysteria was prepared by the time war was actually declared. Even before the declaration of war the animus toward things German had become so great that any opposition to joining the conflict, including that of non-Germans, brought down bitter condemnation. Thus, Theodore Roosevelt could suggest that Senator Robert M. LaFollette, Sr., not of German extraction, but an opponent of the war, was a "Hun within our gates." (Our italics.)

This insightful passage by Zeidler makes a number of critical points in relation to the mobilization of emotions by the social psychology of war-politics.

First, emotions mobilized and harnessed by war-politics in the undifferentiated and hysterical mass social psychology of a substantial portion of the populace are most corrosive of rational discourse. Reasoned and reasonable arguments tend to dissolve into vapors before those whose psyches and emotions have been mobilized. Temperance, one of Plato's four cardinal virtues, is crushed by the weight of unreason as the sort of intemperate utterance of Theodore Roosevelt becomes a commonplace.

Second, the sharing of common physiognomic attributes is not in itself a sure and certain shield against the socially and morally brutalizing effects of hysterical emotions that have been mobilized by warpolitics. German Americans resembled Anglo Americans physiognomically, but the sharing of common physiognomic attributes was not empirically sufficient to undo the force of ethnic hatred in the emotions that had been mobilized by the social psychology of war-politics. German Americans could have hidden behind their physiognomy—as many of them did—in order to escape what Zeidler terms ". . . wartime hysteria . . . directed against ethnics and aliens in the United States." Put differently, German Americans were confronted with a cruel dilemma: they could shed the outward and visible manifestations of their ethnic identity and difference and become invisible by hiding behind physiognomic sameness; or they could shun the security of physiognomic invisibility in defense of the integrity of their ethnic identity and difference. No grouping of human beings should be presented with this dilemma, yet this is the sort of untenable choice with which war-politics has confronted individuals and groups down through the ages. One final point here. The German Americans had the option of hiding behind physiognomic sameness; the Japanese Americans did not. Thus, if war-politics makes ethnic differentiation and identification deadly, particularly in wartime, it makes the coupling of racial and ethnic differentiation and identification absolutely lethal. Zeidler recognizes the empirical force of this point when he writes, ". . . the hysteria against the Japanese Ameicans did not die quickly after the war. The treatment of Japanese Americans led to something far worse than that which resulted from the German-American experience. The Japanese-American experience led to the Emergency Detention Act of 1950," which permits the detention of individuals whom are deemed likely to " 'commit or conspire to commit espionage or sabotage.' A precedent has been established for future concentration camps for those American citizens who dare dissent from the policies of a headstrong national authority." The act did not target specific racial/ethnic groups, but racial differentiation and identification certainly eases the task of detention if those who are to be detained cannot hide physiognomically in the majority population of a multi-racial/multiethnic society.

Third, the social psychology of war-politics tends to conflate dissent and disloyalty. Zeidler observes that the "issue grew to be one of loyalty" for German Americans during the First World War. Given the unreason and intemperance that are such a commonplace in war-politics, when dissent is conjoined with a socially salient difference, for example, race and/or ethnicity, there tends to be a presumption of disloyalty. German Americans who embrace "Germanic culture" must be disloyal to the symbols summed by the American flag, otherwise they would not do so; Japanese-Americans who are steeped in American culture but do not bear the physiognomy of the Occident must be disloyal given the physical features they share with the Japanese who are the enemy; Jews who are acculturated in American values but support the interests of a sovereign Israel are questioned about their loyalty to America—so the unreason goes. But as Lawrence Fuchs notes, "(p)olitical disloyalty to the United States has never been predominantly a result of immigrant-ethnic old country ties . . . . Opposition to American wars has been common enough, but not a property of other-nation loyalties . . . . Opposition to war, especially after it has begun, has not come primarily from immigrant-ethnic groups with strong other-nation loyalties." Fuchs' essay demonstrates clearly that opposition to war is not in itself incontrovertible evidence of disloyalty, for "(d)ual or even multiple loyalties do not constitute disloyalty to the United States as far as the American Constitution is concerned."

If Fuchs is correct, dual or even multiple loyalties are not constitutionally infirm; nonetheless, they are abjured by the social psychology of war-politics, which places a premium on conformity. Behaviors that do not fit within bounds demarcated by war-politics are repugnant; physical features that set one apart from the dominant group make one suspect; oppresive conformity becomes the litmus test of loyalty and the bedrock of security. But nature itself limited the scope of conformity by the Japanese Americans, and the German Americans conformed only through an act of denial—the denial of their ethnic identity. Savage, then, were the demands of loyalty as they were felt by both German Americans and Japanese Americans, and this is made plain by Zeidler as well as the Hirabayashis.

Fourth, war-politics uses emotions that have been mobilized to breach, if not obliterate, established limits to particular forms of conduct. What was heretofore repugnant, abhorrent and impermissible becomes a commonplace. One only has to watch the evening news on television and observe the carnage and barbarism of the vile, nasty, brutal and murderous regional wars around the world that light the blackened sky with wicked tracer bullets and fill the turbulent night air with the groans of dying men, the wailing of widowed women, and the cries of orphaned children to be conscious of the significance of this point. In his chapter entitled "Irish Republicanism Yesterday and Today," Thomas Hachey observes that "the Irish, who have always had scruples about going against the priest and bishop, surmount that scruple by concentrating on the fact that British rule in Ireland is unjust." From this

> developed the myth of the gunman, "the freedom fighter," a man committed to the simple ideal of freeing his country from its oppressors, seeking no glory other than martyrdom, *faithful in his own way* to a church that did not understand him. His blood, and the blood of those who have gone before, will water the seed of freedom which will sprout from the ground and bloom at the moment least expected. Such is the myth and mystique of the IRA . . . . (Our italics.)

The moral limits of the church are set aside as IRA gunmen, in their own way, shed blood in order to rid Ireland of British rule. And so, in the mobilization of emotion, terror becomes an instrument of war-politics; for it is the abandonment of established, recognized and accepted limits of fighting that makes terror so abhorrent.

Finally, the mobilization of emotions by war-politics is designed to supercharge the populace about the evils of the enemy. Evil abounds, and the enemy is evil incarnate. Accordingly, the enemy must either be destroyed or rendered impotent. Jews are enemies of the Reich, thus they must be destroyed; Japanese Americans share the physiognomy of the enemy with whom they must be sympathetic, hence they must be interned; German Americans participate in Germanic (a foreign) culture, thus their activities must be circumscribed; this is the sort of perverse reasoning that is a commonplace where emotions have been mobilized by war-politics in relation to a purported enemy. And it is without scruple or refined human sentiment that uncivil, and sometimes downright barbarous, acts are inflicted upon those who are perceived to be the enemy.

The social psychology of war-politics is reinforced by the "we/they" dichotomizing of the world. We are good and they are evil; we are noble and they are ignoble; we are honorable and they are dishonorable; we are trustworthy and they are untrustworthy; we are humane and they are inhumane; and so on and so forth. In depicting Soviet communism as an "evil empire" that was implacably hostile to the cardinal values of Western democracy and unrelenting in its determination to dominate the whole world, President Ronald Reagan dichotomized the world neatly between the good "we" and the evil "they." If they are evil and determined to dominate us, common sense, not to mention prudence and good judgment, requires that we should be prepared to fight. Here one observes a central feature of war-politics, namely, the trumpeting of preparedness in a dichotomous world in order to thwart the design(s) of an evil enemy. Zeidler calls attention to this point in his presentation on the confluence of events and actions that brought the United States into the First World War on the side of the Allies.

It is well that a people, nation or country should be prepared to fight to defend their/its values and interests, but neat dichotomies of complex social phenomena are fraught with troublesome risks and incalculable dangers. Stephen Young informs us that "(w)ar results from willfulness . . . . Individuals stand ready to assert their willfulness when their identities are challenged. A state of war is not far away from this state of mind . . . This gives ethnicity its power to provoke a state of war." And so "(c)oncerns for ethnicity can provoke the individual to use force in order (1) to assert the status needs of the group or (2) resist denigration of the group in his or her own eyes. In this way ethnicity can set the stage for the conflict of wills, for the use of force and so, for war."

Divergent conceptions of the self and perceptions of belonging may impel ethnic groups to fight one another in defense of "group traditions." But they may also fight together in defense of common national values to which they both subscribe. Thus "(i)n World War II ethnic Japanese and ethnic Germans fought under the American flag against an alliance of all Germans and Japanese." Japanese Americans fought valiantly against the Japanese even though large numbers of their ethnic group were interned in what Zeidler calls "concentration camps." Neat dichotomies of good and evil that are so appealing in war-politics and so useful in the mobilization of emotion usually obfuscate the complexity of the moral universe and the social phenomena of ethnicity. Recognizing the importance of this point, the Hirabayashis write, "(t)he Japanese American case illustrates the fact that an attack on one is a threat to all racial/ethnic minorities. Racism could become overt and institutionalized again with the outbreak of an international event, crisis or war. A concerted effort is still needed to rout out the ideology and practice of racism in the United States, for in and of itself it threatens the principles and procedures of a truly democratic society." Whether it is racism, sexism, ethnocentrism, nationalism, communism, capitalism or whatever *ism* it might be that provides the fulcrum in war-politics for the drawing of sharp and rigid lines of demarcation between virtue and vice, good and evil, with "we" being the sum of virtue and good and "they" the archetype of vice and evil, the psychological stage is set for the acting out of behaviors that would otherwise numb the sensibilities and scandalize the mind.

But there is a certain romance in neat dichotomies. All things become clear, distinct, simple and straightforward. And since there is no romance without passion, it is easier to stimulate passionate, maybe even mindless, behaviors where the objects of those behaviors are sharp, clear and distinct, and not beclouded by ambiguity and confusing patterns. War-politics thus imbues war with a measure of romance. It excites the passions, tantalizes the spirit with the prospect of *victory*, and glorifies sacrifice, courage, loyalty, honor and heroism. There is no romance without excitement, and war-politics creates *fascination* and *excitement*. The excited passions of the populace impel some to dream dreams of glory, others to see visions of doom, and still others to prophesy an admixture of calamity and hope. This aspect of war-politics is hinted at repeatedly by Young, and one wishes that he had developed it more fully in the intriguing conceptual framework that he presents.

One cannot miss the passion in Colin S. Gray's words as he writes in volume one of the two invaluable volumes on *U.S. Defense Policy in the 1980s* that *Daedalus* published in the fall of 1980 and the winter of 1981:

> Soviet thought on the military dimensions of statecraft, what loosely can be called "strategic theory," is distinguished by its rarity. Soviet writings tend to focus on efficient force preparation and implementation—generically *operational* (Gray's italic) matters—or on grand strategic, highly politicized topics . . . . Today, the U.S. defense community has to grapple with the implications of the hypothesis that Soviet military ideas and activities are deeply rooted in local soil . . .(in) *a Russian national political character marked by cunning, brutality, and submissiveness* . . . and hence are very likely to endure . . . . In the half-light of the growing appreciation of the *alien character* of Soviet strategic culture, U.S. policymakes have to reassess the relevance, and prudence, of the strategic ideas that have held intellectual and declaratory . . . sway for the past fifteen years. . . .
>
> Despite the evidence accumulating on Russian/Soviet strategic culture and the military-program momentum implications of that culture, Western commentators continue to deny, implicitly, that *stability* is a condition describing a military-politicial relationship. "Stability," as it pervades much of American theorizing about deterrence questions, is essentially static and absolute. It tends to lack a sense of competition . . . (Stability) reflects a belief that nuclear war would mean the end of history. The assumed certainty of unrestrained escalation and mutual destruction leads easily to the conclusion that there can be no intelligent way of *preparing for* or *waging nuclear war* . . . . An important reason U. S. strategic commentators have focused so heavily on deterrence, as opposed to military operational questions, is that they realize American society is profoundly unwilling to contemplate,

or *debate coolly, the prospect of losing tens of millions of people*
. . . . American society and even the defense community have
shown little inclination to think beyond prewar deterrence, let
alone to invest large resources in a capability to *prevail in, survive,
and recover from nuclear war* . . . (Thus the United States) has no
real plans for timely mobilization or for postwar recovery . . . it
has no convincing story to tell vis-à-vis war aims and the *political
character of a postwar international order.* (pp. 139, 138, 139-141,
143-144. Our italics.)

The romance of the idea of victory in the preceding passage is coun-
tered by Sidney D. Drell, who writes in the same volume:

Nuclear war would be so great an extrapolation of the scale of
disaster in human experience, and so great a physical disturbance
of our environment and ecosphere, that the unknowns of a nuclear conflict clearly far outweigh the knowns or predictables. Yet
there appear more and more detailed calculations that describe
how hundreds of millions of people will behave in all-out conflict,
when deadly radioactive rain will fall for many months. These
calculations also predict casualty levels and recovery times with
incredible precision. The *fascination* with these calculations reminds me of the exchange in George Bernard Shaw's *Major
Barbara* between Lomax, a young man-about-town, and Andrew
Undershaft, a millionaire munitions manufacturer. To Lomax's
comment, "Well, the more destructive war becomes, the sooner it
will be abolished, eh?", Undershaft retorts: "Not at all. *The more
destructive war becomes the more fascinating we find it.*"

Keep this in mind when you hear claims made on the basis of
calculations as to how much civil defense will contribute to the
survival of how many people, and thereby to an ultimate victory,
in a nuclear war for *a nation that will suffer only 20 million fatali-
ties while killing 60 million of their enemy!* It is also well to keep in
mind how rapidly individual units of society descend to chaos and
fall apart at much lower levels of stress—just remember what
happens during sudden blackouts. It makes you wonder how societies will react after just one thermonuclear weapon has hit—
much less a hundred or several thousand. (pp. 183-184. Our italics.)

Drell is most sensitive to the dangers inherent in the fascination and
excitement of the idea of victory that is all too often romanticized by
war-politics. He is conscious of the potency of fascination and excitement in romance. And so he sounds a strong note of caution, knowing
well the element of blindness in romance and the grief it oftentimes
occasions.

Still, as chilling as one might find Gray's passage, one should not perceive only gloom and doom here. Romance is a powerful instrument for mobilizing emotions. If the United States is disadvantaged militarily in relation to the Soviet Union, if this endangers its values and security, and if the populace is made fully conscious of this state of affairs, will the people not respond by making the sacrifices necessary to secure their democracy. In a very real sense Gray uses the idea of victory in a nuclear war as one means of mobilizing emotions behind a greater military effort and the redirection of American military strategy and tactics in peacetime. In this way Gray hopes that if America were forced to fight a nuclear war it would win it. The romance of victory thus becomes an instrument for the redirection of attitudes.

Military service was once viewed "as both a civic duty and a rite of passage," Alvin Schexnider informs us. This served to imbue a substantial portion of the populace with the sentiments and consciousness of the citizen-soilder. The Vietnam War and the accompanying anti-war protests had a profound impact on this tradition. Indeed, as Schexnider states, "among the residual effects of the anti-war protest is a noticeable shift in attitudes regarding military service. As the Defense Manpower Commission noted in its final report, 'The effect of the shifts in the attitudes of young men and women regarding military service is not subject to quantification, but major changes could profoundly alter the prospects for sustaining DOD manpower requirements in the next decade.' (T)he acknowledgement of this singular fact has led to a renewed discussion of the merits of conscription or some form of compulsory national service."

The change of which Schexnider speaks no doubt troubles Gray, and it is precisely this sort of attitudinal shift that Gray hopes to redirect by engaging the national consciousness in the idea of military victory. Today the Department of Defense has no trouble meeting its manpower needs. The troubled economy and the material benefits offered by the military have no doubt contributed to this; however, one cannot but wonder about the potency of the romance of military life that has been used so heavily in the recruitment process. (The psychological effect and emotional appeal of excitement, adventure, duty, victory and fascination with warfare in the decision of young men and women to join the armed forces no doubt occupy a good portion of the time of those who are charged with the responsibility of satisfying the military's manpower needs.)

The romance of victory, fuelled by a sense of mission, makes war-politics highly combustible. Young observes that "Americanism rests on an acknowledgement of mission, of civic responsibility. Grace is received by the nation and by its citizens as long as the duties of the chosen moral calling are fulfilled . . . .(As) Senator Albert Beveridge said as the frontier closed: 'God . . . has marked the American people to finally lead in the redemption of the world. This is the divine mission of America . . . . We are the trustees of the world's progress, guardians of its righteous peace'." It was the historic power of this very American sense of mission and trusteeship of progress that propelled Presidents Eisenhower, Kennedy, Johnson, Nixon and Ford to sacrifice American lives in Vietnam. Each was sensitive to "the logic of Americanism" in relation to Vietnam, and, like Kennedy, they all recognized "(o)ur special calling required of us as a duty sacrifices on behalf of a far away people. To shoulder their burden would be to improve the world and remain faithful to our chosen course in human history." The ideas of grace, calling, duty and mission ground Young's concept of Americanism that was tested in the Vietnam war.

Although Young does not say so explicitly, one senses strongly that he believes the United States could, and should, have been victorious in the war. As President Johnson's "claim that the Vietnam war was a fitting undertaking for the American sense of mission" came under increasing attack both at home and abroad—but especially at home— "(p)rudential arguments that the war effort could not succeed had a deep impact on the average American as the cost of the war mounted . . . ." Young disdains the "self-righteous moralism" of McGovern and those anti-war leaders whose activities undermined the American sense of mission and handed South Vietnam to Hanoi and Cambodia to Pol Pot's Khmer Rouge. Victory was denied by the unrelenting assault of the anti-war forces that occasioned the decomposition of emotions mobilized by war-politics.

Young's treatment of the Indochina War demonstrates how flammable war-politics are when emotions split apart over mission and victory. Of what significance is this for American ethnicity? Young observes that "(i)t may be only coincidential, but as the belief of our articulate elite in Americanism waned in the late 1960s, the hyphenated Americans of Polish, Irish, and Italian descent discovered more importance in the non-American half of their ethnic heritages." As disputes raged over the meaning of "Americanism" and the purpose of "the American sense of mission," ethnic identity provided a measure of cultural belonging and continuity. The sense of mission of which Young speaks, though secular, is fortified by the religious precepts of grace and calling, and underpins a strong cultural monism. Ethnicity does not thrive in cultural monism. Thus, as the secular and religious bonds of the mission of Americanism unraveled, the ascendancy of cultural monism was superceded by that of cultural pluralism and renewed pride in ethnic differentiation and identification. This was not a unique development of the 1960s, for there has been a constant tug and pull between cultural monism and cultural pluralism—the tug of uniformity and sameness contra the pull of diversity and difference. The war-politics of the Vietnam era—set against the background of the civil rights struggle—fostered serious questioning of America's mission both at home and abroad. One consequence of this was a reassessment of the value of cultural pluralism and ethnic identity in the context of the symbols of Americanism and shared national purpose.

The romance of victory was tarnished by the failure of the mission in Indochina. The failure was one of will, not arms; the defeat was political, not military. War-politics at home proved incapable of the sustained effort needed to win in Indochina. One unintended consequence of this at home has been, what is known in some circles as, "the blackening of the combat arms." We have already called attention to Schexnider's observation concerning "the growing disinclination toward military service on the part of American youth." But these are, for the most part, white youth, not black youth. Blacks find the military to be attractive for a variety of reasons—difficulty in securing employment in the civilian economy, career mobility, greater racial tolerance, self-respect and self-esteem, et cetera—and since 1972 are twice as likely to reenlist as whites. This has led to a substantial black presence in the armed forces, particularly the combat arms, and has raised questions concerning black overrepresentation. Schexnider finds this to be "an ironic twist for hundreds of thousands of black youth who, when they too had the opportunity to flee to Canada, elected instead to bear arms in defense of their country."

War-politics did not drive the wedge between black youth and the military that it did in the case of white youth. This may be due in part to the different cultures in which black youth and white youth are socialized, and the different life chances that they perceive for themselves as they enter adulthood. That which whites oftentimes find unattractive represents opportunity for blacks and other racial minorities, and this is true of military service. The overrepresentation of blacks in the combat arms is thus the product of a structure of opportunity that war-politics helped to create.

The end of war is peace, but there is an inherent tension between the imperatives of war-politics and the pursuit of liberal, democratic values. One purpose of war-politics is to prepare for war, win it when it does come, restore the peace and prepare for the next war, ad infinitum. The circularity here is obvious, and it tends to belie the claim that the end of war-politics is peace-politics. Still, war-politics does not merely aim at an interlude between wars which is designated peace, it seeks to bring into being a social order in which it itself is undone. But this is

impossible, given the circularity of its own logic. It thus exists cotermi-
nously with peace-politics over historical time, and each plays a greater
or lesser role in structuring the behavior of the social order as war either approaches or recedes in time.

Niccolò Machiavelli understood well the art of war-politics. In *The
Prince* he writes:

> . . . how we live is so far removed from how we ought to live, that
> he who abandons what is done for what ought to be done, will
> rather learn to bring about his own ruin than his preservation. A
> man who wishes to make a profession of goodness in everything
> must necessarily come to grief among *so many who are not good*.
> Therefore it is necessary for a prince, who wishes to maintain
> himself, to learn how not to be good, and to use this knowledge
> and not use it, according to the necessity of the case . . . There-
> fore, a prudent ruler ought not to keep faith when by so doing it
> would be against his interest, and when the reasons which made
> him bind himself no longer exist. If men were all good, this pre-
> cept would not be a good one; *but as they are bad*, and would not
> observe their faith with you, so you are not bound to keep faith
> with them. (Chs. 15 and 18. Our italics.)

War-politics is grounded in this conception of human nature and the
necessities of a world in which there are "so many who are not good
. . . but are bad." In a world where so many are bad, war-politics
makes the keeping of faith contingent on self-interest. The breaking of
agreements is a measure of prudence when the self-interested reason(s)
that led one to bind oneself no longer exist(s) in one's own judgment.
(Many advocates of setting aside the anti-ballistic missile treaty with
the Soviet Union are obviously persuaded by this argument.) Moreover, secrecy, lying, deception, suspiciousness and faithlessness are
useful in dealing with those who are not good—the enemy—even as the
appearance of openness, truthfulness, faithfulness, integrity and humanity is manifested. This puts war-politics squarely at odds with the
values of peace-politics in a liberal democracy which places a premium
on not only the appearance, but the reality of openness, trust, truthfulness, faithfulness, integrity and humanity in relationships that are
given form and substance by political activity. This is the "inherent
tension" of which we spoke a moment ago—a tension that occasioned
high drama as knowledge of President Richard Nixon's "secret war" in
Cambodia became widespread.

There are those who perceived Machiavellianism—evil—in Nixon's
action. But this is most unfortunate; for just as Machiavelli's prescriptions are not in themselves evil, given the bounds of the context in
which they are made, Nixon's action in particular, and war-politics in

general, are not intrinsically evil, given certain assumptions about self-interest and the enemy. In a very real sense, then, there are separable and distinguishable sets of proper behavior in war-politics and peace-politics, and innumerable problems arise when the imperatives of one set are transposed to the other.

These observations are particularly compelling as one reflects on the chapter by Donald Fixico. The treaty-making process, and the treaties themselves, between Indians and the United States demonstrate graphically the inherent tension between war-politics and peace-politics—especially when one of the parties is not fully conscious of the species of politics in which the other is engaged. Machiavelli observed that given the nature of man and the art of ruling, a prince "must imitate the fox and the lion, for the lion cannot protect himself from traps, and the fox cannot defend himself from wolves. One must therefore be a fox to recognize traps, and a lion to frighten wolves." Fixico perceives this in the behavior of the United States towards the Indians. He writes:

During the early stages of Federal-Indian relations, each side treated the other as a sovereign people. The Indian nations clearly held an advantage in military strength, causing American officials to negotiate cautiously with the tribes . . . . The young republic's weak military status called for careful strategy in defending its national interests . . . . United States government agents negotiated treaties with Indian nations asking them to recognize the young republic as a sovereign nation . . . . Smaller, more vunerable tribes like the Delaware could be negotiated with easily; larger and more warlike tribes . . . presented a potential threat. Secretary of War Henry Knox suggested to Governor Arthur St. Clair of the Western Territory in 1790 that the Indians on the Wabash River and west end of Lake Erie could be put in awe of the whites by the construction of military posts. Exhibitions of troops would impress the Indians, insuring peace in the area . . . The need for increased military strength and careful strategy in dealing with the neighboring tribes grew as American settlers began trespassing more and more on Indian lands . . . . American officials approached Indian leaders in a *peaceful, but shrewd, manner.* By utilizing the kinship term 'Brother,' they attempted to show the Indians that they came as friends . . . . The Indian nations (whom whites, for the most part, regarded as enemies) lost the exercise of liberty when they were defeated by the United States military . . . . The Indians' defeat subjected them to the standards of American culture and hampered their efforts to live in harmony with all things and to continue to live like their ancestors. (Our italics.)

This is an awfully poignant passage, for in it Fixico captures vividly the substance of war-politics. The whites perceived the Indians to be their mortal enemies—obstacles in their struggle to create a sovereign, peaceful nation for themselves. When they were weak militarily, they employed the craft and cunning of the fox to manipulate the languages, signs and symbols of the Indians in order to seduce them into making treaties in which they parted with their lands and recognized the sovereignty of the whites.

Fixico points out that whites used the "jargon of kinship terms," for example, "Elder Brother" and "Great Father," as well as "fundamental concepts" of Indian theologies and philosophies such as "Great Spirit," "Mother Earth" and "Father Sun," to create the impression of friendship and bonds of kinship between themselves and the Indians. Recognizing the significance of "the Indian cultural concept of *dependency* on the Great Spirit" (our italic), and the complex norms of dependency around which much of Indian life was structured, whites shrewdly manipulated Indians into becoming dependent upon them, and "substituted the Great White Father image of the President of the United States for the Great Spirit." The structure of relationships—friendship, kinship, dependency—that whites organized brought them time to increase their military prowess.

Fixico observes that "(d)uring early negotiations in the late 1700s and early 1800s, treaties were a legal means to obtain land; but as Indian military strength decreased and U.S. military strength increased, the government began placing restrictions upon Indian nations." The shift in the correlation of forces emboldened whites to rely less on the craft and cunning of the fox and more on the power and majesty of the lion in their relations with the Indians. Thus, Lieutenant Colonel James Wilkinson could warn the tribes living on the Wabsh River that "the arms of the United States are again exerted against you and your towns are in flames, and your wives and children made captives; again you are cautioned to listen to the voice of reason, to sue for peace, and submit to the protection of the United States, who are willing to become your friends and fathers, but, at the same time, are determined to punish you for every injury you may offer to their children." A formerly poor and landless people, grasping, and with an insatiable appetite for land, now stood lionlike as majestic conquerers over those whom they had ensnared with foxlike cunning while calling them "Brothers." The Indians, conquered psychologically by whites with the cunning of the fox and militarily with the power of the lion, were to suffer the indignities, humiliation and subjugation of a vanquished people, whom their conquerers perceived to be inferior by race, culture and civilization.

Indians smoked the cermonial tobacco in the belief that it "sealed all that was said and agreed upon, . . . white officials politely participated in the smoking of the pipe (but) did not view it as the sealing of the agreement or treaty," observes Fixico. The ceremonial pipe had two clear and distinct sets of meaning and purpose in the context of peace-politics contra war-politics. In peace-politics it meant trust, veracity, integrity, dignity and communion with the Great Spirit for the purpose of ratifying what was agreed upon to the end of peaceful relations. In war-politics is meant subterfuge, playing along and buying time to increase military preparedness for the purpose of subjugating the believers in the Great Spirit. In the treaty-making process, the values of peace-politics disadvantaged the Indians as much as the imperatives of war-politics advantaged the whites. We are thus impelled to conclude that a people or nation risk(s) their/its independence and sovereignty by mistranslating the behavior of an adversary and acting in conformity with the values of peace-politics at the very time that the adversary is acting according to the dictates of war-politics.

We have said much about war-politics, and little about peace-politics, due to the fact that the essays in this volume lend themselves more readily to a discussion of the former than the latter. We should, however, be remiss if we were to end without saying a few words about the attributes of peace-politics.

In reflecting upon peace-politics, we find the respect for the dignity and worth of the individual to be its most compelling attribute. One of us recalls well the profound impact of the words of the former Secretary General of the United Nations, U Thant, on him when, as a young nineteen year old, he heard him say, "I believe in the inherent dignity and worth of the individual," and continued to observe that the inviolability of this principle formed the cornerstone of true peace. Yet, it is precisely this principle that war-politics violates in the name of securing it. Sometimes the reasons for the violation are sound and good, at other times they are weak and dubitable, and at still other times they are downright wrong and perverse. The preeminence of the intrinsic value of the individual human being limits the sorts of behaviors that are permissible. Behaviors that injure, damage or harm the individual—in his person and/or property—intentionally, deliberately and consciously are outside the bounds of the permissible. This is a tough standard of conduct which, perhaps, is satisfiable only in the New Jerusalem. Nonetheless, it does provide a measure here on Earth for the fullness of peace.

In positing the inherent dignity and worth of the individual as the fundamental principle, and its protection as the ultimate end, of peace-politics, we are not unmindful of the empirical reality of a world in which there are friends and foes. Obviously, our enemies are not our friends, yet Machiavelli was correct when he observed that every foe is a potential friend and every friend a potential foe. This is true in consequence of a range of attributes that are shared by friend and foe alike. One element in this range is the inherent dignity and worth of the individual. It is not easy, nay, it is downright difficult for most of us to act in conformity with the imperatives of this principle in relation to those whom we perceive to be our enemies. If our enemies are not good, if they are bad, if they are beasts and not men, they have no inherent dignity and worth, and are outside the limits of behaviors that are morally impermissible in relation to individuals. Subterfuge, deception, faithlessness and brutality become permissible without feelings of violation. But this is precisely what peace-politics abhors and strives to avoid by extending to individuals who are foes the same inherent dignity and worth that friends have. This does not transform foes into friends; it does, however, make possible a measure of civility, orderliness and humanity in the relations between friends and foes.

The sacrosanctity of the dignity and worth of the individual makes the willful shedding of blood, particularly innocent blood, abhorrent to peace-politics. If God is the ultimate measure of all things in the universe, man is the ultimate measure of all things on Earth, thus the willful destruction of men troubles the mind greatly in peace-politics. Still, peace-politics is not synonymous with pacifism, and sometimes it recognizes the necessity of giving way to war-politics in the short run in order that its own values may be made more secure in the long run. Wise men engaged in peace-politics lament the necessity of this, but they do so nonetheless, recognizing that just wars are fought for the sake of defending and protecting cherished values, the most sacrosanct of which is the inherent dignity and worth of the individual. Thus, in spite of their lamentable horrors, war-politics and war that are just are empirically necessary extensions of peace-politics and peace in a world where so many are not good. There is, then, no real irony in the preparation for war in peace, as long as the preparation itself does not do violence to the dignity and worth of the individual and the war itself is just.

If all men were truly good and just, political activity would cease and politics would disappear from human society—as is true of Plato's Republic that is set up in the heavens, as well as in Augustine's eternal City of God and Marx's communist utopia. But many, perhaps most, are neither truly good nor truly just, and so innumerable and endless are the conflicts that mark the human condition.

Thomas Hobbes informs us in the *Leviathan* that in the state of nature men evince an insatiable appetite for power that ends only in death; and Augustine tells us in *The City of God* that the evil regard the good with "diabolical, envious hatred . . . for no other reason than because they are good while themselves are evil." Envy, jealousy, greed, hatred, fear and, yes, just plain misunderstanding often engender conflict in everyday life. Conflicts do not arise only between those who are good and those who are not good, they also arise between those who are deemed to be good and just, for few are truly good and just. Recognizing the pervasiveness of human conflict, Plato, Augustine and Hobbes each turn to law—man-made law—to place limits on it. Note, they seek to limit conflict, to place it within permissible bounds, not to end it. We cannot discuss here the arguments advanced by each of these theorists of a distinctive tradition in Western political philosophy; suffice it to say that they help us to discern clearly the empirical fact that peace-politics arises in the context of placing limits on human conflict, and law serves as an instrument for demarcating the bounds of the permissible and the impermissible.

As the force of law in peace-politics decreases, the propensity to lawlessness in war-politics increases. Law guides and constrains behavior by morals and punishment which are related inversely. As the restraint of morals increases, the necessity of punishment decreases; as the restraint of morals decreases, the necessity of punishment increases. This is a universal law of human society. Peace-politics thus places a premium on the restraint of morals over the constraint of punishment. Moral conviction is, however, a double-edged sword. It may move men either to willing obedience or willing disobedience of the law. Where they obey willingly by conviction, punishment is rare; where they disobey willingly by conviction, punishment is a commonplace. A congruence between the restraint of morals and the prescriptions and proscriptions of law is thus essential if punishment is to be little used in society. Peace-politics aims at this state of affairs which is, perhaps, empirically impossible to realize in a society of large size and diverse cultures.

We have just spoken of moral conviction, but there is also moral indifference which is the absence of belief or feeling concerning the precepts of right and wrong, good and evil. Here, as is true where conviction fosters willful disobedience, the fear of punishment becomes critical in securing obedience to the law. This is most undesirable for, over time, obedience elicited by the fear of punishment only increases the propensity to lawlessness which, in turn, stimulates war-politics. Peace-politics thus strives to limit lawlessness by discouraging moral indifference, as well as by either redirecting strong beliefs that foster behaviors contrary to the law or by changing the law to conform with the principles of those beliefs. If these cannot be done within the bounds of what is lawful, then lawlessness and war-politics suggest themselves as a means of effecting social change.

Much ground has been covered, and we should like to conclude with the following observations. First, the social efficacy of cultural loyalty conta political loyalty in promoting the interests of racial/ethnic groups varies inversely with the degree of dominance of war-politics over peace-politics. Put differently, in a political society where war-politics is dominant in a given cross section of time, cultural loyalty is less efficacious than political loyalty in promoting the interests of racial/ethnic minorities. Second, Thucydides was correct when he observed that "in peace and prosperity both states and individuals are actuated by higher motives, because they do not fall under the domination of imperious necessities; but *war*, which takes away the comfortable provision of daily life, *is a hard master*, and tends to assimilate men's characters to their conditions." (iii. 82, Jowett. Our italics.) War-politics sanctions the abridgement of constitutionally guaranteed privileges, immunities and rights of racial/ethnic minority groups when the latter are perceived to be threatening to the culture of the majority, capable of outnumbering the majority over time, and thought to be of uncertain loyalty. Finally, the tendency towards cultural hegemony is directly proportional to the dominance of war-politics over peace-politics, and inversely proportional to the dominance of peace-politics over war-politics. The tendency towards cultural pluralism, on the other hand, is directly proportional to the dominance of peace-politics over war-politics, and inversely proportional to the dominance of war-politics over peace-politics. If we are correct in this belief, racial/ethnic groups that believe strongly in the value of cultural pluralism have a substantial interest in activities that maximize the possibilities of peace-politics.

ETHNICITY AND THE INDOCHINA WAR: REASONS FOR CONFLICT

Stephen B. Young

Dean, Hamline University School of Law

Before considering the Indochina war, let us reflect on the perverse affinity between group perceptions of ethnic identity and the state of human affairs known as war.

Clausewitz defined war as "an act of violence intended to compel our opponent to fulfill our will."[1] He added, "the compulsory submission of the enemy to our will is the ultimate object in war."[2] There cannot be war without a clash of wills. Fighting to disarm the enemy and so to preclude him from further resistance becomes only a means toward the final objective of political mastery.

War is called forth by political motives. We can say it is created by those political conditions which contribute to the emergence of ambitions, fears, desires, interests and value systems. Thus Clausewitz concluded that war is but political activity using special means.[3]

Further understanding of war can be gained from the English social contract theorists, Thomas Hobbes and John Locke. For Hobbes, war is the absence of a ruling law to compel obedience. It is a state of unbridled will.[4] Men may impose their values on others or else resist the imposition on themselves of the goals held by others. When persuasion and peaceful incentives fail, force must be used to disarm opposing wills and to establish the primacy of one's ego.

For Locke, war exists whenever political relations become overbearingly in favor of one party who thus gains a dispositive power over the moral will of another. "[H]e who attempts to get another man into his absolute power does thereby put himself into a state of war with him."[5] "It is the use of force only that puts a man into the state of war."[6] Resort to force presumes a clash of wills and the need to invoke power whether or not the intended object of the power accepts the legitimacy of its use. Resort to force without color of right implies that no restraint on the dispositive will is recognized by the actor. Where a higher judicial power or the rule of law can constrain the one who seeks absolute dominion, then no state of war exists between that person and others affected by the limited power because the powerful are under constraint and the weak are correspondingly protected.

Slavery is thus beyond the law and is the perpetuation of a state of war where one is placed under the arbitrary power of another and so is justified in the use of force against such repression. As the master is free to use his will, so the slave is not bound to accept the dictates of that will. But a contract which limits the master's power and gives the subordinate some rights can convert slavery into the drudgery of bonded servitude, a condition of legitimate submission.[7] Where the will is held in check, there is no state of war. War results from willfulness.

Locke argues for a right of revolution. "Wherever law ends, tyranny begins," he wrote.[8] Without law, there is only unrestrained will, which is the definitive mark of a tyrant. Tyranny is the imposition of one's preferences on another without benefit of a law to do so. Tyranny is selfishness run beyond fixed limits; it is making use of the power anyone has in his hands, not for the good of those who are under it but for one's own private advantage.[9] Thus whenever rules make themselves or any portion of the community the "masters or arbitrary disposers of the lives, liberties, or fortunes of the people . . . they put themselves into a state of war with the people."[10]

Thus is war a moral phenomenon, reducing the power of a rival moral vision in order to elevate the efficacy of one's own will. A declaration of war announces an end to patience, a rejection of the other's claim that we should submit before his values and place restraints upon ourselves in his favor.

Ethnicity and The Urge to War

Ethnicity, ideology and religion, each in its own way, provide sharp incentives to war. Ideology and religion create in the believer a conviction of righteousness. The accepted cosmology of the adherent legitimates only a fixed value scheme. At one stroke, persuasive reasons to seek the certain ends chosen by the value system are available and, more importantly, these reasons argue for rejection of moral claims made by others.

Ideology and religion are cultural constructs.[11] They give us a sense of place and are quickly incorporated into our self-image. Ethnicity works in a similar fashion, though it is less a scheme of meaning and more a perception of belonging. But personal acceptance of belonging to a group gives the individual self-confidence to use the values legitimated by group traditions and processes. As Harold Isaacs has reminded us, Francis Bacon long ago pointed out that the idols of the tribe which take their hold over the human mind sink their roots into the foundation of human nature itself. Individuals need to belong to some social context more encompassing than their own egos, and such ties to a collective through assumption of a group identity become emotionally compelling psychological drives.[12] Isaacs refers to a basic group identity as a set of "holdings"—moorings, really, in the psychosocial ocean of possible individual meanings. With ethnicity and other group identifications, people know where they stand.

Freud spoke only once of "identity" in his writings. Significantly, it was to formulate his link to the Jewish people.[13] Ethnicity, then, rests on what Erikson calls "an identity of something in the individual's core with an essential aspect of a group's inner coherence."[14]

Isaacs pointed out that ethnicity has much to do with the quality of a person's self-esteem. This gives ethnicity its power to provoke a state of war. When our ethnicity is called into question we feel a sharp blow to our own sense of worth. Either we resist and assert our sense of ourselves or we submit, to then feel, at best, the blues, and at worst that sense of nothingness so deep that we live beyond hope and fear and according to base instincts and passions—in a caricature of slaves.

Henry Stack Sullivan's interpersonal theory of psychiatry offers a developmental approach to human motivation which ties the individual to a social world through the self-image developed to reduce anxiety. For Sullivan, any individual person was to a large degree a composite of the feelings, fears and aspirations of others, especially the mothering and fathering figures so important in childhood. The individual directs his or her energies as guided by the emotive symbols absorbed from others. The symbols are brought into the personality in order to reduce feelings of personal anxiety.

Anxiety for Sullivan is a state of restlessness arising whenever the self feels a loss of control, a submergence under more powerful forces, a falling away from the succor and sense of mastery once provided for the ego in the womb when the person was as yet undifferentiated from nature. Absence of anxiety Sullivan describes as euphoria, a telling phrase. The infant organizes what Sullivan calls a self-system or repetitive ways of living with significant people in order to avoid or minimize the incidence of anxiety.[15] The self-system, for example, is *not* an identity with the mothering one but a definition of "me" in response to, among other things, the mothering one's desires. Then, as the child learns language, language behavior brings about a fusion into a coherent personality of the different ideas and values already implicit in the self-system. Thus ethnic culture and ethnic identity quickly enter into the very core of the young person's self-definition, to rest at the well-spring of drives and energies eager to reduce anxiety and achieve euphoria.

A stable ego identity provides the individual with a sense of mastery over fate, an ability to accept life. This state of mind releases creative energies ready for deployment in conjunction with the work of others in society. But if the ego identity is threatened, anxiety increases and energy is accordingly diverted to the task of restoring one's sense of integrity. One's ability to secure the objects of one's will is called into question whenever ego identity is threatened, so the will is a highly sensitive variable for the sense of self-esteem. Individuals stand ready to assert their willfulness when their identities are challenged. A state of war is not far away from this state of mind. In extreme cases of identity anxiety, fear arises to stimulate an unthinking and spasmodic release of violent force.

Thus we can suggest a close tie between personal identity, group identity or ethnicity, and the preconditions for war. Concerns for ethnicity can provoke the individual to use force in order to: (1) assert the status needs of the group or; (2) resist denigration of the group in his or her own eyes. In this way ethnicity can set the stage for a conflict of wills, for the use of force and so, for war.

Ethnicity and the Indochina War

Two ways will be examined in which ethnic identity has entangled the United States in the destiny of the various Indochinese. First, aspects of the American identity commanded our participation in the war to preserve South Vietnam as a non-communist community. Second, aspects of the Vietnamese identity caused large numbers of South Vietnamese to resist the communists, creating the certainty of war, and then, when the communists won, to flee to the United States.

The American Identity

Speaking of an American identity is perhaps foolish. In the last decade or so we have rediscovered the ethnics among us. Jews, Poles, Italians, Irish and, of course, blacks did not melt away and become indistinguishable parts of an Anglo-Saxon, Protestant mainstream. Similarly, we would be foolish to expect our Hispanic, Vietnamese, Hmong, Lao and Cambodian newcomers to do so in the future.

Yet America is more than an alliance of disparate ethnic enclaves. While there is no unitary culture arising from a perception of consanguinal affinity as there is in modern European nation-states which rest on nineteenth century assertions of peoplehood, the country is not a thin political superstructure resting lightly over fixed tribal communities as is the case in sub-Saharan Africa. Nor is America like the Islamic polities of the Middle East where religious demands for fidelity to Allah often create an undercurrent of dissatisfaction with secular power and give rise to recurring aspirations for a Pan-Islamic social union of the faithful.

The seminal America experience as a community was its foundation in an act of violent revolution. That act of war-making asserted not the values of an existent people, but rather the racially-neutral political scheme of liberty and limited government demanded by a particular moral vision—that of secular Calvinism. The scheme, once called into being, could serve as the core identity of a new people. The civil religion, as Robert Bellah calls it, issuing from the revolution and embodied in the Constitution, can be identified as Americanism.[16] It is symbolized by the documents and other symbols of reverence associated with traditional Fourth of July celebrations.

Surprisingly, that vision of a political order of checked power has cross-cultural validity just as its parent doctrine of convenantal Christiantity can aspire to win converts from every branch of the human family. Americanism, once created, can be incorporated into the identities of converts. Thus the "hyphenated" citizen—the Irish American, for instance—came into being. In World War II ethnic Japanese and ethnic Germans fought under the American flag against an alliance of Germany and Japan, an alliance proclaiming the supreme rights of all Germans and Japanese. Americanism has a power to win the loyalty of persons not born to the community. It is a non-ascriptive kind of ethnicity.

Americanism rests on an acknowledgement of mission, of civic responsibility. Grace is received by the nation and by its citizens as long as the duties of the chosen moral calling are fulfilled. Toward the end of World War II, Walter Lippmann, born Jewish, made this point with his noted graceful style:

> For America is now called to do what the founders and the pioneers always believed was the American task: to make the new world a place where the ancient faith can flourish anew, and its eternal promise at last be redeemed. To ask whether the American nation will rise to this occasion and be equal to its destiny is to ask whether Americans have the will to live. We need have no morbid doubts about that.
>
> The American idea is not an eccentricity in the history of mankind. It is a hope and a pledge of fulfillment. The American idea is founded upon an image of man and of his place in the universe, of his reason and his will, his knowledge of good and evil, his hope of

a higher and a natural law which is above all governments, and indeed all particular laws . . ."[17]

Tuveson notes that the American sense of mission placed in opposition the innocence of the new world and the corruption of the old. Americans believed that "Providence, or history, has put a special responsibility on the American people to spread the blessings of liberty, democracy, and equality to others throughout the earth, and to defeat, if necessary by force, the sinister powers of darkness."[18] The American identity is an expectation of utopia, of the City of God made real on earth. As a "nationalistic theology" it has formed the cosmological basis for a unique American ethnicity.[19]

In 1766 John Adams envisioned "America" (not the colonies) as "the opening of a grand scene and design in providence."[20] In 1771 Yale-educated Timothy Dwight wrote of America in poetry: "Hail land of light and joy! Thy power shall grow far as the seas, which round thy regions flow."[21] In 1850 Herman Melville wrote in the novel *White Jacket*: "And we Americans are the peculiar, chosen people. The Israel of our time: we bear the ark of the liberties of the world."[22] Here liberty becomes the touchstone for the creation of a new people—the Americans.

Lincoln saw the issue of the Civil War in terms of Americanism. He told the special session of the Congress on July 4, 1861, that ". . . this issue embraces more than the fate of these United States. It presents to the whole family of man the question whether a constitutional republic or democracy—a government of the people by the same people—can or cannot maintain its territorial integrity against its own domestic foes."[23]

The American sense of manifest destiny did not die with the closing of the frontier. Merk has defined the American sense of mission in the nineteenth century as a mixture of Republicanism, democracy, freedom of religion and Anglo-Saxonism.[24] Yet Merk saw in the American spirit a drive other than imperialist expansionism. This he called "mission," an idealistic, self-denying hopefulness seeking divine favor for material aspirations.[25] Its language was that of dedication, of response to emergencies and ordeals, the very language later used by Walter Lippmann in 1944 and quoted previously.

Senator Albert Beveridge said as the frontier closed: "God . . . has marked the American people to finally lead in the redemption of the world. This is the divine mission of America . . . We are the trustees of the world's progress, guardians of its righteous peace."[26] President Woodrow Wilson believed that "America had the infinite privilege of fulfilling her destiny and saving the world."[27]

In the 1950s and the 1960s Americanism would carry the United States into war over the defense of South Vietnam, a war seen as one of duty and not of conquest. The young American senator, John F. Kennedy, said in September 1956 of America's stake in South Vietnam that: (1) Vietnam was a keystone to the arch of secure liberties in Asia—the finger in the dike against a communist sea; (2) Vietnam was a proving ground for democracy—an experiment we should help to success; and (3) Vietnam was a test of American responsibility and determination in Asia.[28] The country was our offspring and we could not abandon it in face of the perils of communism, political anarchy or poverty. Kennedy here applied the logic of Americanism to the situation in Vietnam. Our special calling required of us as a duty sacrifices on behalf of a far away people. To shoulder their burden would be to improve the world and remain faithful to our chosen course in human history.

Earlier in 1953 the secretary of state who actually authored our commitment to South Vietnam, John Foster Dulles, had said:

> Seeking first the Kingdom of God and His righteousness, many material things were added to us. We developed here an area of spiritual, intellectual and material richness, the like of which the world has never seen. What we did caught the imagination of men everywhere and became known everywhere as 'the Great American experiment' . . . Be proud of your association with U.S. power, which is indispensable in the world today; but remember that that power is worthy only as it is the shield behind which moral values are invigorated and spread their influence; and accept, as citizens, the obligation to preserve and enhance those moral values. They are the rich heritage that has been bequeathed us. It must be our ambition that future generations shall look back upon us, as we look back upon those who preceded us, with gratitude for the gift to our Republic of the qualities that made it noble, so that men call it blessed.[29]

Notions of a just international order—the moral purposes of Americanism defended for the entire human family—crept as well into President Eisenhower's concern for the defense of South Vietnam. He sought to prevent further expansion of despotic systems bent on using force to get their way. Vietnam in his mind was only the first in a row of dominoes. In May 1957, while advocating foreign aid, he said the "American people" would fight "hostile and aggressive despotisms" whenever the barriers of freedom were attacked.[30] The image was not of imposing our ways on others in traditional patterns of colonial acculturation but of assuming the burdens of an obligation, of sacrificing in order to advance the claims of a moral undertaking. Thus President Eisenhower invoked the lesson of having defended Greece and Turkey from Soviet designs in 1947 and urged that we make a similar effort in

South Vietnam. Communist aggression around the world was to be re-sisted in large part because a certain way of life—the values abstracted from Americanism—would otherwise come under pressure to change and modify its virtues. Such change threatened our identity by belit-tling our role in the world and our self-esteem as a chosen people.

Under the Kennedy administration, support for South Vietnam in-creased. President Kennedy was committed to defeating a new kind of warfare—covert aggression waged through deceit, subversion and destabilization:

> We dare not fail to see the insidious nature of this new and deeper struggle. We dare not fail to grasp the new concepts, the new tools, the new sense of urgency we will need to combat it . . . The complacent, the self-indulgent, the soft societies are about to be swept away with the debris of history. Only the strong, only the industrious, only the determined, only the courageous, only the visionary . . . can possibly survive. No greater task faces this country or this administration. No other challenge is more de-serving of our every effort and energy.[31]

At stake for Kennedy was the American self-image. If we were to succeed then we had to assume the challenge created by guerrilla wars, proving to ourselves above all others that we had not grown compla-cent, self-indulgent and soft. Only through action could we display our virtue and so be fit inheritors of the American mission. The torch of freedom had been passed to a new generation of Americans. The com-munist threat to South Vietnam could not be ignored if Kennedy meant what he said in his inaugural.

In mid-May 1961, the new administration said of its support for South Vietnam that "the United States is also conscious of its responsi-bility and duty, in its own self-interest as well as in the interest of other free peoples, to assist a brave country in the defense of its liberties against unprovoked subversion and communist terror. It has no other motive than the defense of freedom."[32] That same month Kennedy himself said "We stand, as we have always stood from our earliest be-ginnings, for the independence and equality of all nations. This nation was born of revolution and raised in freedom. And we do not intend to leave an open road for despotism."[33]

In April 1965 President Lyndon Johnson repeated these themes. America would stay the course in South Vietnam to strengthen world order by giving to all confidence in the value of an American commit-ment, to stifle the appetite of aggression, and because we had a "re-sponsibility for the defense of freedom." He said "Our objective is the independence of South Vietnam and its freedom from attack. We want nothing for ourselves . . ."[34]

In June of that year as pressure built on him to escalate the American commitment, Johnson reflected on the American calling:

> In the 1930s we made our fate not by what we did but what we Americans failed to do. We propelled ourselves and all mankind toward tragedy, not by decisiveness but by vacillation, not by determination and resolution but by hesitation and irresolution, not by action but by inaction. The failure of free men in the 1930s was not of the sword but of the soul. And there just must be no such failure in the 1960s.[35]

In Johnson's eyes we were not just another nation, but one having a special bearing on the course of human history. We were a fiduciary of higher purposes, holding power in order to do right.

When he finally agreed to commit American combat battalions to the fight in late July 1965, President Johnson said, "We did not choose to be the guardians of the gate, but there is no one else."[36] To leave South Vietnam in mid-1965 under the pressure of military victory for the aggressor was for Johnson inconsistent with American self-esteem: "We just cannot now dishonor our word, or abandon our commitment, and leave those who believed us and who trusted us to the terror and repression and murder that would follow. This my fellow Americans is why we are in Vietnam."[37]

The Anti-War Critique

That the American commitment to South Vietnam was the logical result of the moral premises behind American ethnicity can be further shown through consideration of arguments advanced in opposition to the war. While many points were advanced by anti-war leaders, a good number of these arguments were designed to counter Johnson's claim that the Vietnam war was a fitting undertaking for the American sense of mission. Prudential arguments that the war effort could not succeed had a deep impact on the average American as the cost of the war mounted, but such arguments relied more on their appeal to common sense than on any attack on the premises of Americanism.

Vogelgesang's study of anti-war writings among intellectuals from 1965 to 1968 concluded that the war was used as an "ideal other." "It was the catalyst. It galvanized discontent and exposed contradictions throughout the political system."[38] The war provided intellectuals, long estranged from Americanism, with a point of attack on the most basic assumptions about America, assumptions held by the ordinary citizen and reflected in established political leadership. Trained to value a more elitist, European Enlightment tradition of highbrow disdain for mid-cult and lowbrow patriotism, college-educated professionals and white-collar workers rejected the premises standing behind American sacrifices in Vietnam. Lionel Trilling was discovering in the 1960s that intellectuals were pursuing their own adversary culture, out of step with the norms of Americanism.

It may be only coincidental, but as the belief of our articulate elite in Americanism waned in the late 1960s, the hyphenated Americans of Polish, Irish and Italian descent discovered more importance in the non-American half of their ethnic heritages.

Vogelgesang described the "fundamental undercurrent" of the anti-war movement in these words: "More important than the potential long-range realignment of domestic forces and the readjustment of foreign policy was—and is—the intellectuals' obsessive quest after their meaning as Americans and the validity of the American dream and their hunt for a new America."[39] Charles Reich in the *Greening of America* could hope that a prophetic minority might reshape the consciousness of a nation. This radicalism reflected Rousseauist notions of starting society anew through recognition of a new general will.[40] As Norman Mailer said at the Berkeley teach-in of 1965: "America is a country which has never decided its true nature."[41] Mailer was wrong of course; Americanism had long been defined but he did not like its contents.

The motivational core of the teach-ins were references to the "soul of America."[42] Susan Sontag wrote in the *New York Review* that there was now a need for "a more emotional kind of appeal and attempt at re-educating America."[43] She continued:

> Most Americans are possessed by a profound chauvinism that is existential rather than ideological: they really do not believe that other countries, other ways of life, exist—in the way that they, and theirs do . . . Whatever challenges this chauvinism, which is the basis of American consensus on foreign policy, is good—however simplified and unelaborated.[44]

In 1966 she said to a rally in New York City: "America has become a criminal, sinister country—swollen with priggishness, numbed by affluence, lowered by the monstrous conceit that it has the mandate to dispose of the destiny of the world, of life itself, in terms of its own interests and jargon."[45]

The target of protest was really not an isolated foreign war but the source of established power to define what was legitimate about America. The anti-war movement rejected what Sontag called the "consensus" on chauvinism and sought: (1) to discredit spokesmen for Americanism like Lyndon Johnson and Richard Nixon and (2) to replace the consensus with a new idea of what it means to be an American.

In 1967 Howard Zinn called for a unilateral American withdrawal from Vietnam. Zinn argued that the perspective of Americanism was not sacrosanct. Rather, communism too had a valid claim to participate in building a just world:

> Right now, for Vietnam, a communist government is probably the best avenue available to that whole packet of human values which make up the common morality of mankind today; the preservation of human life, self-determination, economic security, the end of race and class oppression, and that freedom of speech and press which an educated population begins to demand.[46]

Zinn began from a personal perspective that America was a morally flawed society.[47] The war was wrong for him partially because it was an *American* war and America was wrong. Zinn's premises contradicted the sense of mission articulated by the national political leaders who had committed this nation to the defense of South Vietnam in order to echo the deepest sense of identity of their constituents.

In 1970 the Committee of Concerned Asian Scholars published their version of Indochinese history calling for a communist victory and American withdrawal. "The demand for total, immediate, unilateral withdrawal should be put forward as a part of an effort to build a new America. It should be a call for a changed political consciousness."[48] The scholars wanted America to begin a "massive scaling-down of its position in Asia and Latin America," recognizing that such a policy would "entail profound changes in [American] outlooks and institutions."[49]

The end for the scholars was an America willing to let revolutionary—generally communist—cliques come to power around the world. Here was explicit rejection of a special American mission in the world. The scholars advocated more than a new isolationism: They saw America in a way new for American citizens, as an unexceptional country undeserving of unusual loyalty and special honor.

They were as naive about left revolution in Indochina as Reich had been about changing the American identity. The scholars said the logic of American policy was "genocide."[50] In fact, the only genocide in Indochina was brought about by one of their vaunted revolutionary leaders—Pol Pot.

In 1972 George McGovern, stepping out of the Adlai Stevenson "egghead" tradition, continued the anti-war crusade for a new America by campaigning against "the Establishment Center":

> Most Americans see the Establishment Center as an empty decaying void that commands neither their confidence nor their love. It is the Establishment Center that has led us into the stupidest and cruelest war in all history. That war is a moral and

political disaster—a terrible cancer eating away the soul of the
nation . . . The Establishment Center has constructed a vast
military colossus based on the paychecks of the American worker
. . . I want this nation we all love to turn away from cursing and
hatred and war to the blessings of hope and brotherhood and love
. . . [51]

McGovern's rhetorical theme was "Come home America."

In his self-righteous moralism McGovern misread the American
people. They were already home without the benefit of his crusade.
Two million men had served as called in Vietnam; only fourteen thousand had answered a contrary call and escaped service. The numbers
were for Richard Nixon.[52] Americanism—"peace with honor"—was
still far more powerful with the electorate in 1972 than was the intellectuals' alternative. In 1980 the same point would be made again with
Ronald Reagan as the political beneficiary.

A major line of intellectual attack on the American war policy focused on the government's assertion that the war resulted from aggression by North Vietnam. If that premise held, then the war policy
showed some consistency with traditional American undertakings. The
Munich analogy as applied by Johnson to Vietnam had persuasive validity in the context of Americanism. Thus in 1965 George Kahin
sought to establish that the National Liberation Front in South Vietnam was an autonomous political movement brought into being by
Ngo Dinh Diem's repression in the South, and not by North
Vietnamese conniving. The South Vietnamese should therefore be left
free to work out their own accommodation, he felt. In this approach
the American academic followed the lead of two French colonial jour-
nalists, Phillipe Devillers and Jean Lacoture.

Frances FitzGerald followed in 1972 with her extension of another
Frenchman's theory to argue in *Fire in the Lake* that the Vietnamese
needed revolution to restore a cultural harmony broken by the modern-
ization and Western acculturation introduced by colonialism. For Fitz-
Gerald there was no aggression from North Vietnam, only the inevitable tides of revolution at work in South Vietnam. Given that
understanding of the facts, she could argue that Americanism had no
role to play in the Vietnamese struggle. In fact, it could even be seen as
a willful evil, imposing a war on people who otherwise had no reason to
fight.

Both Kahin and FitzGerald, and others, further argued that communism in Vietnam was subordinated to nationalism; in a word, that
Ho Chi Minh was only an Asian "Tito." Thus a communist victory in
Vietnam would not extend either Moscow's or Peking's power deeper
into Southeast Asia. Since an objective of Americanism was to prevent

such growth of communist power, the anti-war movement could now assert with this benign image of Ho Chi Minh in their minds that Americanism need not respond to the defense of South Vietnam because Hanoi and the NLF posed no threat to our role in the world nor to our sense of self-esteem.

Another line of attack on the war adopted a premise of Americanism and turned it against the governing establishment. This was the theme of war crimes and wanton destruction wrought by American forces. The American sense of self depends for moral justification on an assumption of purity in American motives and actions. Napalm, My Lai, search and destroy, free-fire zones—all called that assumption into question as far as the Vietnam war was concerned. Jonathan Schell's description of relocating the village of Ben Suc disturbed even Robert McNamara, architect of the attrition strategy. In 1972 Anthony Lewis could write that America was the most dangerous and destructive power *in the world*.

In a Senate speech on March 2, 1967, when Robert Kennedy broke with Lyndon Johnson over the war, he enjoined Americans to visualize the "horror" of the war. It was each American's responsibility, he said, that we sent chemicals to scorch children and bombs to level villages. *We*, he asserted, had turned Vietnam into a "night of death," "an unending crescendo of violence, hatred and savage fury." Kennedy's unstated premise was that doing so was un-American. He even said Johnson's policy was to "destroy Vietnam and its people."[53]

The next year he said to an audience of Catholic girls, "Don't you understand that what we are doing to the Vietnamese is not very different than what Hitler did to the Jews?"[54] And he asked in the best puritan tradition, "Are we like the God of the Old Testament that we can decide in Washington, D.C., what cities, what towns, what hamlets in Vietnam are going to be destroyed?"[55] Since we fought in Vietnam not as the highest ideals of Americanism demanded, the war should end, argued Kennedy, in order to save our sense of self-esteem. This argument was using Americanism against itself as Kennedy sought the presidency in 1968. However, American participation in the Vietnam war cannot be divorced from the power over the popular mind held by traditional Americanism, our ethnic heritage.

Vietnamese Nationalism: The Origins of Conflict

American soldiers did not fight alone in Vietnam. Hundreds of thousands of South Vietnamese opposed with arms the communist desire to rule that country. After American troops left, some two million

South Vietnamese soldiers, policemen and self-defense militia kept to their positions until Thieu's failures as a military commander and American failures to provide sufficient aid made further struggle futile. Ethnic nationalism motivated these Vietnamese to oppose the communists.

To date, no accurate study of Vietnamese ethnicity has appeared in the West. As I have pointed out elsewhere, works presenting the modern history of Vietnam are infected with misconceptions rooted in colonial narrow-mindedness.[56] The French did not perceive an ethnic nationalism in Vietnam, preferring to see the society as divided into a small upper class and a large rural peasantry, ruled by the former. French colonial policy was to rule the villages through the assistance of the local elite. Some colonial administrators sought to co-opt the traditional mandarins who led the village councils. Other administrators sought to replace that traditional, neo-Confucian native ruling class with a new one trained in Western ways. This latter plan to build French schools to train selected Vietnamese and favor their graduates in employment and with economic advantage was an attempt to implement France's mission to civilize the unruly. The *mission civilisatrise* of those Frenchmen who would Westernize the Vietnamese gave honor to an otherwise quite grubby exploitation of less well-armed peoples.

The legitimacy of France's work in Vietnam—either of colonial exploitation or of cultural assimilation—would have been less evident had the Vietnamese been credited with strong national loyalties. Succeeding waves of Frenchmen stricken with *"la malaise jaune"* (the yellow inquietude) all insisted that ordinary Vietnamese *("les annamites")* would willingly accept rule by an effective elite of bureaucratic managers. The French could then say in good conscience and with fervor that France had a bona fide role to play in Vietnam, a role which even the Vietnamese themselves would appreciate.

Thus anti-French secret societies were dismissed by Georges Coulet in the 1920s as nothing more than bands of morose malcontents seeking to take property away from the rich. The nationalism of the peasants was overlooked. When a nationalist party organized a revolt in 1930, French papers presented the disturbances as the work of class-agitating communists. Communism, because it also existed in the metropole itself, was *less* threatening to the French colonial enterprise than was nationalism. The advance of communism, in a strange way, even represented a success for French policies. After all, Ho Chi Minh had learned his Leninism in Paris, not in Vietnam's villages. Communism was a Western ethic brought to Vietnam as a consequence of colonial acculturation. Nationalism, on the other hand, denied the moral supremacy of French ways, language and culture. It was an obstinate refusal to acknowledge the progressive role of French civilization.

Paul Mus has written that:

> On many occasions in Vietnam, newcomers from France were surprised to realize that they were closer to the communist Vietnamese than to other local political groups when talking about the nature of society. These communists spoke the French language of society, even though it was in a Marxist dialect . . . [57]

Thus the French misunderstood the Vietnamese they ruled. Sadly, many American writers have followed where the French have led to perpetuate the colonial misconceptions. Other Americans, like those on the Committee of Concerned Asian Scholars, who have adopted Hanoi's neo-colonialist Marxist analysis of modern Vietnamese history, have similarly overlooked the reality of Vietnamese nationalism. The war in Vietnam grew out of the conflict beween communist values and the patterns of life associated with Vietnamese ethnic identity. As Ho and his colleagues forced their views on their countrymen, there ensued a clash of wills leading to war.

The first party founded by the Vietnamese communists was a supranational Indochinese party, part of Stalin's Comintern organization. Nationalism was a cover for the communists and not their heart and soul. A Vietnamese workers party did not appear until 1951 when a war for national independence was well under way. Thus we can almost see the inevitability of Hanoi's 1978 decisions to join COMECON, to enter into a defensive alliance with the Soviet Union, and to conquer Cambodia. Ideological fidelity to Leninist principles was a stronger pull on policymakers than the need to accommodate the powerful Chinese neighbor.[58]

The communist party in Vietnam has always recognized the primacy of nationalism over communism as a Vietnamese political force. When the Japanese surrender came suddenly in August 1945, the tiny communist party stepped into a power vacuum. Its leadership was accepted in large part because of rumors about American support for Ho Chi Minh. Vietnamese were told that since Ho had American patronage, he could use Washington to keep Paris from restoring the French empire in Indochina. Support for Ho was presented to the people as a way to advance ethnic interests. Nothing was said of communism. When American support for Ho proved not to be the case within a few months, Ho disbanded the communist party to minimize the growing opposition to his rule. His dearest ideological principles held no appeal for his countrymen. In March of 1946 Ho then betrayed his people by bringing French colonial forces back to North Vietnam when

his forces were too weak to seize it under their own power. Ho needed
the French to help him crush his nationalist rivals. Paul Mus, who had
noted the sympathetic bonds between the French and the communists
via-à-vis the nationalists, advocated reaching this understanding with
Ho in order to recognize him as the paramount Vietnamese with whom
the French would deal.

Later in 1946, after French troops had joined with the communists
to defeat nationalist units and execute their leaders, the marriage of
convenience between Ho and Paris fell apart and the Viet Minh war
began. Ho and his associates now asserted leadership *not* as communists—that fact they obscured and minimized before the people—but
as nationalists leading the Viet Minh. By 1949 the French realized they
could not win a military struggle unless they mobilized Vietnamese to
fight on their behalf. To do so they proposed the Bao Dai solution,
resurrecting as chief of state the former Nguyen Dynasty emperor.
This was but a repetition of an older colonial strategy to rule Vietnam
by means of the traditional mandarin elite. The nationalists, who could
command deep popular followings, were kept at bay and even perse-
cuted at times.

When France grew tired of its colonial efforts in Indochina, another
deal was struck with the communists. This was the bilateral armistice
agreement reached in Geneva in 1954. Ho received the northern half of
the country and Bao Dai the southern. The nationalist plan for a single
Vietnam with a unified army and coalition government, proposed by
Phan Huy Quat, a Dai Viet, and Pope Pham Cong Tac of the Cao Dai
faith, was rejected by Bao Dai on French instructions.

The French-communist agreement of 1954 came apart when
Vietnamese nationalism asserted itself in the headstrong Ngo Dinh
Diem. Diem, who likened his Catholicism to that dour faith of the
Spaniards and not to the habits of French coreligionists, was a mandarin who resented and mistrusted the French. Diem had long-standing
ties with the Dai Viet political movement. Named prime minister in
1954 to win the support of Catholics for the French cause, he soon
turned against Bao Dai. Diem's government, including Phan Huy
Quat, repudiated the Geneva accords as a betrayal of Vietnamese values and refused to accept them. Diem then proceeded to defeat French-
paid private armies, oust Bao Dai as chief of state, and terminate
French influence in South Vietnam.

In 1958, seeing the success of Diem in establishing a viable South
Vietnam, Hanoi began to seek his overthrow. Late in that year orders
were sent south for Hanoi's followers to organize armed units and the
National Liberation Front. Hanoi's cadres then recruited the leadership of the NLF from the rich francophile families of the Mekong Delta

landlords and intelligentsia class, people whom Diem distrusted and would not employ. Early armed units of the NLF came from hill tribes, Hoa Hao, and Cao Dai soldiers formerely in French pay and not trusted by Diem either. The NLF sought neither communism nor union with North Vietnam but the end of Diem and other American-supported regimes. Again, nationalism was used as a cover for communist ambitions. A communist party was not created for South Vietnam until 1962 when the Ho Chi Minh Trail from North Vietnam through Laos into the South was secured. Hanoi now had less need to rely on its Southern supporters. President Kennedy had previously decided to seek a coalition government in Laos rather than fight the communists there. This gave the communists control of the hills. Diem told this author's father, then the United States ambassador in Bangkok, that American policy was condemning South Vietnam to war on adverse terms. On that point, Diem happened to have been correct.

But the NLF could never command significant support within South Vietnam. As the war went on, munitions, cadres and then divisions had to come from North Vietnam. Hanoi could only fight on with support from Moscow and Peking. A losing guerrilla war was transformed into a conventional war of cross-border invasion as American troops withdrew under President Nixon's program of Vietnamization. By 1972 the NLF had all but disappeared from South Vietnam's villages. Upon Hanoi's final victory in 1975, the city of Saigon with a population of nearly three million people could boast no more than five thousand followers of the revolution. No wonder Soviet tanks were necessary to defeat Thieu's army. The ordinary people were under arms on his side. Today nationalist guerrilla resistance continues in Vietnam as the communist regime succumbs to dry rot and the boat people flee.

All this leaves unexplained why the Vietnamese never freely accepted communist claims for a monopoly of political leadership. The answer lies in their sense of ethnic identity as Vietnamese. Being Vietnamese carries with it a discrete set of values and cosmological orientations which feel "right" for the individual who seeks to be a group member.

First is a perception of dependency on prior generations. This arises from a modified Buddhist notion of karma. Vietnamese believe that every individual's fate and fortune depend on the good or bad deeds of forebears, especially mothers. Good mothers produce happy and successful offspring. Thus the self-image of each Vietnamese has a corner for repaying obligations to one's parents. Of course, if a parent was bad or a ne'er-do-well (as Ho Chi Minh's father apparently was), the child need have no such sense of personal responsibility. That is one reason why Vietnamese evaluate others in terms of their family background. Someone from a good family is more likely to be modest, successful, and a trustworthy person. Consequently, Vietnamese resent communist social egalitarianism and denunciation of older relatives to the party as occurred in North Vietnam's land reform program of 1953 to 1956, a program the excesses of which brought forth a tearfully apologetic Ho Chi Minh who placed responsibility for the repression on underlings.

Second, the Vietnamese ethic of personal obligation, *phuc duc*, validates private property. The felicity of wealth is to be enjoyed if it comes from heaven. Property inherited from ancestors has an especially soothing quality to it. Vietnamese thus reject the expropriation of all property by the state and the placing of severe limitations on personal wealth. Communism has no appeal to the average Vietnamese. The communists propose to break the bonds of honor to the past. Thus the boat people include poor farmers and fishermen seeking to escape a system they find claustrophobic.

It is the Vietnamese penchant for private acquisition which has produced a vast engine of corruption in communist Vietnam. With state control of the economy, the state itself is now intensely exploited as private rice fields and small shops once were. Corruption is more legitimate in communist Vietnam than it was under Thieu because to the people the regime has less of a claim on their loyalties as Vietnamese. By denying them their heritage, the state exposes itself to their hostility.

Third, the notion of *phuc duc* justifies a psychology of rampant individualism among Vietnamese. They do not like to be regimented and coerced. In this regard the flight of the boat people is telling. Never have Vietnamese fled their homeland; the pull of the family has always been too strong. But never before have the communists ruled strictly according to their tenets. Prior to 1975 a patina of nationalism enabled Hanoi's leadership to call for sacrifices for the fatherland, but no more; people now do not want the regime to succeed.

Fourth, the communists have resorted to murder in order to get their way. That is the ultimate in personal immorality for Vietnamese who believe in *phuc duc*. Good fortune, *phuc*, comes only to those with virtue, *duc*. *Duc* consists of suppression of ego drives and ego striving. The self must accept the flow of events without the ego consciousness feeling resentful or even stirring itself. When this state of mind is reached, *duc* is attained. Overt selfishness to get whatever does not naturally come one's way causes one to lose *duc*. The communists, with a record of deceit and murder, have no *duc*. They therefore cannot bring *phuc* to the country. Wise persons would be well advised to avoid their rule.

Fifth, the Vietnamese ethic commands a politics of charisma, not of bureaucratic rigidity. The imperial system which the Chinese evolved under the Han Dynasty (221 B.C.E.-6 C.E.) and perfected under the Sung (960 C.E.-1210 C.E.) with help from the conformist neo-Confucian orthodoxy effectively did not reach Vietnam *until* the nineteenth century. The Vietnamese remained more Taoist and Buddhist, valuing individualism over social conformity. Even in the nineteenth century, the sinicized Nguyen Dynasty did not have roots within the villages. When the dynasty could not rally people against the French, many of its elite mandarins had reason to cooperate with the new overlords to make the colonial protectorate work and so to preserve the positions and property they had already acquired under Nguyen patronage.

Vietnamese prefer to follow individuals with *uy tin*, a personal quality of charisma. They do not like formal political parties or regimented participation. Normal Vietnamese politics are fluid and unpredictable. To outsiders events appear chaotic, though the fast moving developments follow a few simple rules from the perspective of insiders. Before they gained power, the communists used the Vietnamese system to sully the charismatic appeal of their opponents; nationalist leaders who could not be besmirched were killed (Truong Tu Anh, Huynh Phu So, Nguyen van Bong).

The gambit was always to keep the nationalists from coalescing around a single person who then could mobilize political energies against the communists. Thus a coalition government as an alternative to Thieu was constantly pushed by Hanoi—not to give South Vietnam its own government but to prevent Thieu from attracting a wider following. For his part, Thieu reacted fiercely against proponents of coalition, damning himself in American eyes, but playing out the politics of *uy tin*.

Once in power, the communists removed individuals with potential *uy tin* from public life. After victory the NLF was abolished and no coalition was offered to the non-communists. Thousands are still kept in prisons and labor camps a decade after Hanoi's victory. Vietnamese do not like that kind of forced leadership.

Thus the Vietnamese ethic offered many reasons for the Vietnamese people to resist communist rule. There was a genuine clash of wills between the communists and the nationalists although the terms of struggle were hidden from American commentators, blinded as they were by French misperceptions. As long as the communists sought an absolute dominion over people with different values, war was inevitable.

The Boat People

The preceding discussion should have previewed the argument that Vietnamese nationalism has provoked a flight of people from Vietnam to seek new lives in the United States. This is the second way in which perceptions of ethnicity have co-mingled the fates of Vietnamese and Americans. If the communists would rule Vietnam according to international human rights standards, the tenets of Vietnamese nationalism would be respected and people would not flee. Their ethnicity brings them to our shores.

From what they know of American laws and mores, many Vietnamese have concluded that ours is a land where they can live according to the rules of *phuc duc* more than they can in a Vietnam ruled by the communists. There is a basic harmony between the individualism and the desire for private property ownership characteristic of the Vietnamese, and the norms of Americanism. This leads one to predict a very rapid adjustment by the Vietnamese to American society. Between July-August 1975 and July-August 1977, one survey showed an increase in the employment rate of Vietnamese men from 68.2 percent to 95.1 percent.[59] Those households earning less than two hundred dollars a month decreased from 42.1 percent of the sample to 3.2 percent over the same period.[60] Montero concluded that the Vietnamese he surveyed had found financial and emotional security in this country.[61]

During the war years, ordinary Vietnamese got along well with Americans in marked contrast to their previous experience with the French. The French had mixed primarily with the elite and had earned resentment from the masses. As time went by, the elite class was ever more shaped in the French image. There was an affinity between the neo-Confucian heritage of mandarin formalism and the Cartesian condescension of the French. Accordingly, the French-trained elite of Saigon later resented American patronage of the parvenus who gained power after 1963 through military channels and open electioneering. For the people, it was different; they did not mind the American ways as much. Given its neo-Confucian orientation, the Vietnamese elite had long been cut off from full sympathy with the ethnic identity of the villages, and so was more predisposed to adopt Western patterns—either French colonial or communist. Communist leadership, it should now come as no surprise, came from the mandarin class.

The Sideshow of Cambodia

Ethnicity appeared more overtly in the more recent tragedy of Cambodia. Traditional fears of Vietnamese expansion at their expense, and memories of the once magnificent kingdom centered at Angkor, emboldened the Cambodian leadership to reject Prince Sihanouk in 1970 after he had allowed North Vietnam to become too free in its use of Cambodian land for prosecution of the war in South Vietnam. Pol Pot later charged in his Black Book that as of 1970, Hanoi was so much on the defensive inside South Vietnam that only the sanctuaries and supply lines in Cambodia kept the communist war effort viable.

Upon overthrowing Sihanouk, the Cambodians demanded an immediate withdrawal of Vietnamese communists from their country. Hanoi responded by turning its forces against Lon Nol's weak and poorly equipped forces in April 1970. This set the stage for President Nixon's decision to send American troops into the border sanctuaries. B-52 bombings of the sanctuaries had been public knowledge for the previous year.

At the time, Pol Pot's faction of the Cambodian communist movement was very weak. Lon Nol's failure to adopt a pacification and rural development program conceded the villages to the insurgents. This was suicide. Slowly the guerrilla noose around Phnom Penh and other cities grew tighter. In 1975 the badly led non-communist effort collapsed. Pol Pot came to power, commenced his genocide, and turned against Vietnam.

Ethnic ambitions were important to Pol Pot. He had established his own communist party in 1960 to break away from Vietnamese communist domination. The Black Book document recounts how the Hanoi leaders then slighted and compromised Pol Pot's version of Cambodian communism, preferring to treat with Sihanouk for use of Cambodian territory. Upon attaining power, Pol Pot depopulated the cities.

All persons living in the cities as of the date of the communist victory in April 1975 were sent to remote areas without food, medicines or housing.[62] Thousands died. Subsequently the survivors among these people were killed because they were considered to be the "new population," a suspect class of people. Those who had lived in a corrupt society—the capitalist society of the cities—were defective, spoiled beyond redemption. The city was bad for in the city was money. Pol Pot's Cambodia printed no currency. There would be no property; only allocations by the cadres. Those from the cities were to be eliminated so that Cambodia could become a brotherhood of the virtuous. Only the pure from the rural areas could be relied upon to rebuild the vigor of the Khmer nation. As one cadre said to a man who escaped: "If you live we gain nothing; if you die we lose nothing. So, why not kill you?" One slogan was, "What is rotten must be removed." A puritan morality was then imposed on the people.

Vacating the cities also crippled Hanoi's ability to use Vietnamese residents in Cambodia as levers against Pol Pot's policies. Most Vietnamese lived in the cities. After Vietnamese coup attempts against him, Pol Pot purged his followers of all pro-Hanoi elements in 1977 and drew closer to Peking.

Khmer Rouge economics rested on a national conception of wealth. Khieu Samphân, one of Pol Pot's closest associates, wrote in his doctoral thesis that the Cambodian economy should accumulate capital internally and not rely on the foreign sector.[63] To increase agricultural productivity, inefficient small holdings should be replaced with larger production units. Non-bureaucratic leadership would stimulate popular energies for the productive effort. There is a taste of fascist national socialism in Khieu Samphân's prescriptions. The Khmer race would be revitalized through a purification which sees total state control of private property.

Perhaps inspired by his personal dream of a rejuvenated Khmer people, Pol Pot defied Vietnamese demands. For his pains, the Vietnamese invaded Cambodia in 1979 and replaced his government with one more to their liking led by Heng Samrin. As neither the Khmer Rouge nor other Cambodians will acquiesce in Vietnamese overlordship, a guerrilla war will continue for the foreseeable future. Ethnic nationalism, once again, has produced reasons for conflict.

NOTES

[1] Karl von Clausewitz, cited in Anatol Rappaport, ed., *On War* (Baltimore: Penguin Books, 1968), p. 101.

[2] Ibid.

[3] Ibid., p. 119.

[4] Thomas Hobbes, *Leviathan*, Chap. XIII.

[5] John Locke, *An Essay Concerning the True Original Extent and End of Civil Government*, Sec. 21.

[6] Ibid., Sec. 181.

[7] Ibid., Sec. 24.

[8] Ibid., Sec. 101.

[9] Ibid.

[10]Ibid., Sec. 221, 222.

[11]Clifford Geertz, *The Interpretation of Cultures* (New York: Basic Books, 1973); Peter Berger and Thomas Luckman, *The Social Construction of Reality: A Treatise in the Sociology of Knowledge* (Garden City, N.Y.: Doubleday, 1966).

[12]Harold Isaacs, "Basic Group Identity: The Idols of the Tribe," in Nathan Glazer and Daniel P. Moynihan, eds. *Ethnicity: Theory and Experience* (Cambridge, Mass.: Harvard University Press, 1975), p. 29.

[13]Erik Erikson, "The Problems of Ego Identity," *Journal of the American Psychoanalytic Association*, 4:1 (January 1956): 56-121.

[14]Ibid.

[15]H. S. Sullivan, *The Interpersonal Theory of Psychiatry* (New York: W. W. Norton, 1953), p. 165.

[16]Robert Bellah, *The Broken Covenant: American Civil Religion in Time of Trial* (New York: Seabury Press, 1975).

[17]Walter Lippmann, *U. S. War Aims* (Boston: Little, Brown & Co., 1944), p. 209.

[18]Ernest Lee Tuveson, *Redeemer Nation* (Chicago: University of Chicago Press, 1968), p. viii. See also, Sacvan Bercovitch, *The Puritan Origins of the American Self* (New Haven: Yale University Press, 1975).

[19]Tuveson, op. cit., p. 91.

[20]Ibid., p. 102.

[21]Ibid., p. 105.

[22]Quoted in Robert Jewett, *The Captain America Complex*. (Philadelphia: Westminster Press, 1973), p. 9.

[23]Henry Steele Commager, ed., *Documents of American History*, 8th Ed. (New York: Appleton-Century Crofts, 1968), p. 393.

[24]Frederick Merk, *Manifest Destiny and Mission in American History* (New York: Alfred A. Knopf, 1963), p. ix.

[25]Ibid., p. 261.

[26]Jewett, op. cit., p. 9.

[27]Ibid.

[28]Wesley Fishel, ed., *Vietnam: Anatomy of a Conflict* (Hayward, Cal.: Peacock Publishers, 1968), p. 144.

[29]John Foster Dulles, "Morals and Power," in David L. Larson, ed., *The Puritan Ethic in United States Foreign Policy* (Princeton, N.J.: Van Nostrand, 1966), pp. 143-144.

[30]U.S. Department of Defense, *The Pentagon Papers*, Vol. I (Boston: Beacon Press, 1971-1972), p. 615.

[31]Ibid., Vol. II, p. 801.

[32]Ibid., p. 803.

[33]Ibid., p. 804.

[34]Ibid., Vol. III, p. 730.

[35]Ibid., p. 743.

[36]Ibid., Vol. IV, p. 633.

[37]Ibid.

[38]Sandy Vogelgesang, *The Long Dark Night of the Soul: The American Intellectual Left and the Vietnam War* (New York: Harper & Row, 1974), p. 169.

[39]Ibid., pp. 177-178.

[40]James Billington, *Fire in the Minds of Men* (New York: Basic Books, 1980).

[41]Vogelgesang, op. cit., p. 178.

[42]Ibid., p. 79.

[43]Ibid., p. 102.

[44]Ibid.

[45]Ibid., p. 73.

[46]Howard Zinn, *Vietnam: The Logic of Withdrawal* (Boston: Beacon Press, 1967), p. 101.

[47]Ibid., p. 5.

[48]Committee of Concerned Asian Scholars, *The Indochina Story* (New York: Bantam Books, 1970), p. 296.

[49]Ibid., p. 299.

[50]Ibid.

[51]Theodore White, *The Making of the President 1972* (New York: Bantam Books, 1973), pp. 130-131.

[52]Ibid., p. 453.

[53]Arthur Schlesinger, *Robert Kennedy and His Times* (New York: Ballantine Books, 1978), p. 832.

[54]Ibid., p. 885.

[55]Ibid., p. 906.

[56]See Stephen Young, "The Land, Property and Elite Prerogatives Under Vietnam's Le Dynasty," *Journal of Asian History*, 10:1 (1976); "Unpopular Socialism in United Vietnam," *ORBIS*, 21:2 (Summer 1977); "Vietnamese Marxism: Transition in Elite Ideology," *Asian Survey*, XIX:8 (August 1979); "Communism and Nationalism in Vietnam," *Problems of Communism*, XXX:2 (March-April 1981).

[57]John T. McAlister and Paul Mus, *The Vietnamese and Their Revolution* (New York: Harper & Row, 1970), p. 116.

[58]Le Duan, *This Nation and Socialism Are One* (New York: Vanguard Books, 1976).

[59]David Montero, *Vietnamese Americans* (Boulder, Col.: Westview Press, 1979), p. 67.

[60]Ibid.

[61]Ibid., p. 68.

[62]See Francois Ponchaud, *Year Zero* (New York: Holt, Rinehart & Winston, 1978).

[63]Khieu Samphân, tr. Laura Sommers, *Cambodia's Economy and Industrial Development*, Cornell Data Paper No. 113 (Ithaca, N.Y.: Cornell University Southeastern Asia Program, 1979).

ETHNICITY AND FOREIGN POLICY: THE QUESTION OF MULTIPLE LOYALTIES

Lawrence H. Fuchs

Meyer and Walter Jaffe Professor of American Civilization and Politics
Brandeis University

War, Loyalty and Nationality

At the beginning of the American revolution, most Americans probably also thought of themselves as Englishmen. As the first "hyphen-
ates," the loyalties of these Anglo Americans were severely tested.
Once the war began, it was necessary to choose sides and many Americans remained loyal to England. In New York, the colonists actually
furnished more soldiers to King George III than to George Washington. Even in New England, the Tory loyalists were numerous. Washington was so disappointed at the rate of reenlistment there that he
wrote:

> Such a dearth of public spirit, and want of virtue, and stock-job-
> bing, a fertility in all the low arts to obtain advantages of one
> kind or another, I never saw before and pray God I may never be
> witness to again . . . could I have foreseen what I have, and am
> likely to experience, no consideration upon Earth should have in-
> duced me to accept this command.[1]

Of the ethnic groups in the colonies, only the extremely small Jewish
population showed an overwhelmingly pronounced loyalty for the revolutionary cause. The English, Germans, Dutch, Irish and Scotch
could be found in ample number on both sides. As Morison and Commager put it, "all peoples then represented in America played an honorable part on the patriot's side; and an equally honorable part on the
loyalist's side."[2]

Although the rebels won their war for independence, American nationality was shaped by its English inheritance more than by any other
factor in United States history. Its Constitution, law, language and
literature—and even to a great extent its major sectarian religions—

have their origins in the original mother country, something which has sustained the Anglo-American alliance ever since the conclusion of the War of 1812. Loyalty to the *writ of habeas corpus* and Shakespeare is the stuff of common ethnic identity no matter how often the citizens of Concord, Massachusetts, on each Patriot's Day ritualistically reenact the battle whose shots were heard around the world.

But a common ethnic identity is not the equivalent of a shared political loyalty as the U.S. Army recognized early in the Revolutionary War when only native-born Americans were enlisted, although the difficulties in recruitment mentioned above subsequently led to a more open policy. Many looked upon the idea that the foreign born could serve in the American army with suspicion at first. An 1825 regulation actually specified that no foreigner could be enlisted without special permission; it was changed, however, in 1843 (just in time for the Mexican War) to read that all free white male persons who were citizens could serve as long as they spoke and understood the English language. Actually, blacks fought in all American wars, and by 1857 no further mention of citizenship was made in the regulations although "a competent knowledge of the English language" was required.[3]

The Civil War was the first to test the proposition that large numbers of immigrants and their children would risk their lives in a war to defend the United States. Immigrants responded rapidly to the call for volunteers and served in the Union army far out of proportion to their numbers in the population as a whole, providing nearly one-fourth of its soldiers.[4] Large numbers of Irish immigrants, however, already unsympathetic to the cause of abolition, resented the Draft Law of March 3, 1863, which favored the well-to-do who could purchase an exemption for $3,000. In New York City in July 1863, they protested by burning the draft headquarters, destroying a black home for orphans, and raiding homes and beating and hanging several blacks, in the midst of a riot which resulted in twelve hundred deaths.[5]

The Irish, who were the largest group of foreign born in the United States (the Germans were second), also contributed strongly to the Union cause. Among the great heroes of the war were the members of General Thomas Meagher's Irish brigade, two-thirds of whom were killed in the Battle of Fredericksburg. Other units were known as the Hibernian Guard, the Hibernian Target Company and the Irish Dragoons. The Germans contributed the German Rangers, the German Turners and the German Heavy Artillery. Other units chose names which marked their ethnic identity such as the British Volunteers, the Cameron Swiss Rifles, the Highlanders, the Polish Legion and the Scandinavian Regiment.[6]

The Civil War tested the loyalty of American immigrant groups to their adopted land, but it did not test them in a situation of conflict of loyalty to foreign nations as had the Revolution and as would World War I. By the outbreak of World War I more than 12 percent of the population was foreign-born, and all of the major immigrant-ethnic groups had a strong stake in the outcome of the conflict. The Poles, Czechs, Serbs, Croats, Slovenians and Slovaks all saw in the war an opportunity for the national liberation of their peoples. Irish Americans also agitated for independence for a united Ireland. But the major ethnic conflict was between Americans of English and German backgrounds. Those of English origin tended to sympathize with the British. The Germans, who made up almost one-tenth of the population of the United States (including second- and third-generation German Americans), and who were especially concentrated in the Midwest, identified with the German cause. "We do not want to Germanize America," the Milwaukee *Germania-Herold* asserted. "We want to Americanize it and therefore we have to de-Briticize it."[7]

No immigrant-ethnic group was as intensely affected by American involvement in World War I as the Germans. A relatively prosperous group, they published over six hundred newspapers in the German language in 1914 and sponsored hundreds of fraternal and cultural clubs designed to preserve German traditions in America. National organizations such as the German-American National Alliance and the German Roman Catholic Central Verein lobbied in a dozen states for German language instruction in the public schools and throughout the country against prohibition and women's suffrage. Although many other Americans saw World War I as the inevitable outcome of Prussian military ambition, many German Americans believed that Germany was defending European civilization against the barbaric influences of the East. Arguing that England was primarily motivated by jealousy of the German empire's economic progress, they saw the United States as having no vital interest in the outcome of an essentially European conflict.

German loyalty was constantly called into question by pro-English participants in the debate over American involvement in the war. Attacks on the "disloyalty" of German Americans escalated between 1914 and 1917 when German-American organizations raised hundreds of thousands of dollars to send to Berlin to help wounded German soliders and other war victims, and when German Americans lobbied energetically to prevent the sale of munitions to the allies and block financial aid to England and France. To some of the Americanists, the virtually unconditional support by the German Americans for Germany's actions—the United States was not yet in the war—along with the tremendous efforts of German Americans to preserve German culture in the United States, made their loyalty as Americans clearly suspect.

The Americanists understandably did not make a distinction between cultural and political loyalties. Many presumed that the love of German Americans for Goethe and Wagner was the equivalent of political loyalty to the fatherland, in opposition not just to England but also to the United States. That the Germans tried to preserve German culture in the United States was clear. Typical of many speeches made by German-American leaders was one by the president of the German-American National Alliance who, in an address to an audience of ten thousand in Milwaukee, asserted:

> We will not allow our two thousand year culture to be trodden down in this land . . . be strong, and German. Remember you German pioneers, that we are giving to this people the best the earth affords, the benefits of German *Kultur*.[8]

Such rallies often opened and closed with the boisterous singing of "Die Wacht Am Rhein" ("The Watch On The Rhine") and "Deutschland Über Alles" ("Germany First"). That the speakers addressed their audiences in German would have aroused resentment in others; that the audiences enthusiastically sang "German First" in front of the red, white and black bunting of imperial Germany and portraits of the German and Austro-Hungarian monarchs offered proof to the suspicious that the German Americans could not be counted on should the United States enter the war.

With United States participation in the war on the side of the Allies, President Wilson and former president Theodore Roosevelt stepped up their campaign against hyphenated Americans. The Germans, of course, were the principal target, although the Irish came in for criticism from both men, too. The German-American Alliance became the object of congressional investigation and quickly disbanded. Other clubs dissolved or changed their activities in order to survive. Strong demands were made for the elimination of the German language press. One proponent of suppression, himself of German birth, argued that only by eradicating all elements of German culture could one have a loyal citizenry. It was a position that would be taken by some Japanese Americans in World War II. For him, language was a key issue, a sign of a willingness to be loyal. "Let Germans come to this country," he said "but when they come, let them be cut off from German influence, from a German press, from a German club . . . if they are forced to speak English . . . they will become different citizens."[9]

Never before or since have Americans felt so strongly that the love of a foregin language or a culture was a sign of political disloyalty. The Espionage Act was amended in 1918 to require foreign language newspapers to file complete translations of all related war news with the Post Office unless granted an exemption, a measure intended in part to eliminate newspapers that operated on small budgets. Many communities banned the teaching of the German language in the public schools and several states even outlawed German language instruction in private schools, an action that was not overturned until 1923 when the Supreme Court upheld the right of private schools to include foreign language instruction in the curricula. In Nebraska, South Dakota and Iowa, actions were taken to limit the use of German over the telephone or in private conversation. Iowa's governor actually issued a proclamation which, among other things, forbade conversation in trains and other public places except in the English language, and which specifically forbade the conduct of religious services in foreign languages.[10] The State Council of Defense in South Dakota insisted that only "in cases of extreme emergency, such as death, severe illness, or fire, or police calls, were people permitted to speak in German."[11]

Harassment of Germans and denigration of German culture were a commonplace. In some Midwestern towns, German Americans were made to kneel down before and kiss the American flag. In Chicago and Boston, patriotic groups encouraged people to spy on their German neighbors for signs of disloyal conduct. In South Dakota, the Hutterites, religious pacifists who were German-speaking and who had come to this country four generations earlier, were deprived of their tax-exempt status as a religious organization, forced to sell property to pay for back taxes, and required to contribute money to the Liberty Loan Committee and the Red Cross.

By the end of World War I, German culture in the United States had been greatly weakened. Before the war, German was the most widely taught foreign language in American schools; at the war's end, the teaching of German had virtually ceased even in communities with large German populations. To this day, German is not widely taught in comparison with French or Spanish.

The Espionage and Sedition Acts (1917 and 1918) may have helped to inhibit disloyal actions. The Espionage Act imposed a fine of $10,000 and a twenty year prison sentence on anyone who interfered with the draft or attempted to encourage disloyalty; the Sedition Act extended the penalty to anyone who would obstruct the sale of United States war bonds, practice insubordination, discourage recruiting, or utter or publish any disloyal or abusive language about the United States government, the Constitution, or the army or navy. But it was not legislation nor coercion which made German-American newspapers and associations quickly declare their loyalty to the United States once it entered the war, or brought about the end of opposition to conscription and liberty bond campaigns.[12] All historians of the period agree that German Americans were overwhelmingly committed to the defense of the American nation in addition to wanting to preserve German culture.

It was only natural that prior to the war, German Americans would think that the interests of Germany were harmoniously congruent with those of the United States. The United States had never fought a war with Germany, as it had with England. Germans had been influential in building American universities, and introducing Christmas, beer and kindergartens to the United States. They had themselves been acculturated to American economic and political life. Even so, it was understandable that English-speaking Americans—however mistakenly—believed that there was a strong link between the loyalty to culture and political loyalty, an assumption which German Americans did little to dispel prior to the American entry in the war.

The belief of many Americans that agitation in behalf of the foreign policy interests of one's ancestral land implied disloyalty to the United States became widespread once again with respect to Japanese Americans in the days prior to and even during World War II. In some ways, the Japanese were even more suspect than the Germans had been. After all, 176,000 German or German-American soldiers had fought in the Union army in the Civil War.[13] German-born Carl Schurz had served as a Civil War general and subsequently as secretary of the interior. Perhaps even more importantly, the Germans, in addition to following familiar religions, were mostly Protestant, light-skinned and blond.

The Japanese were among the newer immigrants to the United States, having arrived mostly after 1890. For the most part Asian immigrants were not wanted as 100 percent or even 50 percent Americans. Ineligible for citizenship under the Naturalization Law, several states passed laws to penalize aliens in that status. Alien land laws in California in 1913 and 1920 were intended to restrict the amount of land which Japanese aliens could acquire, although many of the immigrants worked around the limitation by registering deeds under the names of their children who were citizens by birth. Undoubtedly, economic envy and greed motivated some hostility toward the Japanese on the West Coast who were becoming increasingly successful in small business and farming. Racist feelings were undoubtedly important in spurring anti-Japanese policies. The attorney general of California in 1914 acknowledged that racism was, at least in part, responsible for

restrictive licensing fees, land laws, and measures limiting the employment of Japanese:

> The fundamental basis of all legislation has been, and is, race un-
> desirability. It seeks to limit [the Japanese presence] by curtailing
> the privileges which they may enjoy here, for they will not come
> in large numbers and long abide with us if they may not acquire
> land. And it seeks to limit the numbers that will come by limiting
> the opportunities for activity here when they arrive.[14]

Primarily because of restrictive legislation, the number of Japanese
and Japanese Americans on the mainland on the eve of World War II
was not quite 130,000. Even in California, the state with the largest
number of Japanese Issei (immigrants) and Nisei (first generation born
in the United States), they constituted less than 1 percent of the population. Only in the territory of Hawaii, where 158,000 Japanese made
up 37 percent of the population, were most people aware of the presence of the Japanese. There, the question of the loyalty of the Japanese
to the United States had been raised many times in the twenties and
thirties. The idea of their being loyal struck some as being preposter-
ous. The influential Walter Dillingham put it this way to a congressional committee in 1920:

> Supposing, for the sake of an example, that the Japanese on one of
> our mandated islands in the Pacific should develop the island by
> bringing in a great number of American citizens and finally they
> had a situation where 110,000 red-blooded American citizens
> were on the island where there were 18,000 pure-blooded Japa-
> nese. How would I feel having a college classmate visit me, to
> usher him from the boat to the house, kick off sandals and toss a
> kimono and say "This is my home. My wife and I came here from
> America 15 years ago and we have made our home here and have
> entered into the spirit of the life. I want you to meet my boy." In
> comes a fine, upstanding boy, 15 years of age, I say "He is going
> to the University of Japan. He reads, writes and speaks Japanese
> better than he does English and if we ever have a rumpus with
> Uncle Sam that boy is going to be true-blue; he is going to fight for
> the Empire."
>
> Now just imagine pointing with pride to your son and saying
> that, and you realize what you are asking of the Japanese in Ha-
> waii.[15]

It was self-evident to Dillingham and others like him that the Japanese could not be Americanized. Their language, religion and customs
were too foreign. Many of them actually sent their children back to
Japan to study. The Kibei were, in fact, in some ways more Japanese
than their immigrant parents. And some of the Kibei and other Nisei
continued to retain their Japanese citizenship even though the Japanese Nationality Law of December 1924 made it possible for Ameri-

cans of Japanese ancestry to relinquish it. The cultural customs of the Issei and the Kibei made it difficult for the Nisei to win acceptance, especially in a time of growing tensions between the United States and Japanese governments. And those growing tensions reinforced the view that linguistic and cultural separatism was a sign of disloyalty. Hostility toward the Japanese, including those born in the United States, increased with the advent of the Sino-Japanese War, and a signal of potential disloyalty was given when the Japanese of Hilo on the large island of Hawaii gave two visiting battleships from Japan a warm reception in October 1939.[16] Once again it was difficult for most Americans to distinguish between the affection and cultural affinity which prompted Japanese Americans to support Japan's foreign policy in the Far East from the question of primary political allegiance which, as the Japanese Americans soon showed, belonged to the United States.

Some of the opposition to the Issei and Nisei had been based on racial as well as cultural and economic grounds. Like the Chinese, they were victimized by the fear of "yellow peril." But with the advent of war, it was the question of loyalty which was paramount in the minds of President Franklin D. Roosevelt and others in the administration who supported his executive order empowering military commanders to remove "dangerous persons" from designated areas and put them into relocation camps. Within five months, more than 110,000 West Coast Japanese, 64 percent of whom were American citizens, had been transported to temporary assembly centers from which they were subsequently moved to permanent camps in barren areas of California, Colorado, Utah, Wyoming and Arkansas, there to remain behind barbed wire for four years until in 1944 the Supreme Court found that the detention of persons whose loyalty was not an issue was unconstitutional. Perhaps some of the Issei and Kibei were disloyal. Perhaps a few would have committed acts of espionage or sabotage, or even treason. In fact, no such thing happened in the islands of Hawaii where 159,000 Japanese aliens and Japanese Americans constituted 37 percent of the population, with the exception of one man on the tiny island of Miihau on December 7, 1941. Islanders were interrogated on the basis of the presumption of danger and not indiscriminately rounded up as on the mainland, and only nine hundred Japanese aliens from Hawaii eventually ended up in mainland evacuation centers.

To what would have been the astonishment of Walter Dillingham and many others, the Japanese Americans in Hawaii and on the mainland appear to have been strongly loyal to the United States in its war against the Axis powers. Many Americans in Hawaii and on the West Coast realized that the Nisei had already demonstrated their loyalty in a variety of ways. On the mainland, they formed the Japanese-Ameri-

can Citizens League in the 1920s and other local organizations whose
"names almost always included the words 'loyalty league' or 'citizen's
league'."[17] In Hawaii, the comparable organization was the American
Citizens of Japanese Ancestry, formed shortly after World War I to
promote Americanism. Because more than half of the children in the
public schools of Hawaii had been of Japanese ancestry since 1920 (Mc-
Kinley High School was called "Tokyo High"), there was no lack of
recruits. As early as 1918, Senator William H. King of Utah pointed
out that the Japanese he talked to "manifested the deepest attachment
to our institutions and to our form of government."[18]

By Pearl Harbor, those youngsters were ready to distinguish between love for their parents, ancestors and Japanese customs on the
one hand, and loyalty to American political ideals and institutions on
the other. After first being turned away as army volunteers—a prominent politician asserted "a Jap is a Jap even after a thousand years and
can't become Americanized"[19]—they were finally permitted to form
the 442nd Regimental Combat Team (all volunteer) and, along with
Nisei from the mainland, the 100th Battalion. When the call went out
for twenty-five hundred volunteers for the 442nd, five times that
number, over one-third of all the males of Japanese ancestry in the territory of military age, responded. The two units, consisting of thirty-
three thousand men, became the most decorated in American military
history, suffering more than nine thousand casualties and six hundred
dead. The War Department cited the 442nd ten times for outstanding
accomplishments. Their slogan, "go for broke," reflected the determination of men anxious to vindicate their own and their families'
loyalty.

On the home front, Japanese Americans volunteered in extraordi-
narily high proportions to be air raid wardens and workers in medical
units. Leaders went from house to house to urge their friends and
neighbors not to take part in rituals and ceremonies that would be perceived as signs of disloyalty. Men searched old closets and cellars for
Japanese emblems, swords and family heirlooms which they turned
over voluntarily to the army authorities. Grandfathers and grand-
mothers wept but obeyed when the children warned them not to speak
Japanese. As in World War I with the Germans, American loyalty was
deemed to be incompatible with Japanese culture, and twenty-two
Japanese language schools were abandoned and fourteen cultural and
occupational associations and eight Buddhist and Shinto shrines and
temples were dissolved.[20]

Unlike the German Americans, the Japanese Americans were able to
revivify cultural ties after World War II for many reasons. The very
demonstration of Japanese-American political allegiance during the

war undermined the heretofore accepted idea that old country cultural ties were incompatible with political assimilation. More importantly, perhaps, the United States entered an era in which cultural pluralism, instead of being disparaged, was celebrated as central to the American way of life. Tourism and international business, particularly in Hawaii, reinforced the value of other-country ties and foreign language resources. Immigration itself was no longer seen as a major threat to political unity. Indeed, history had already shown how far that threat had been exaggerated in two world wars.

Political disloyalty to the United States has never been predominantly a result of immigrant-ethnic old country ties. While the first Alien and Sedition Acts in 1798 were aimed against foreign nationals, most of the small number of prosecutions against those deemed to be disloyal to President John Adams and the United States (they were seen as inseparable by the administration) were against native-born Americans of no particular ethnic distinction. Opposition to American wars has been common enough, but not a property of other-nation loyalties. One thinks of Abraham Lincoln disputing the invasion of Mexico—Lincoln supported appropriations to support the war but always maintained that it had been started on spurious grounds. Similarly, internal opposition to the Spanish-American War and the Vietnamese War had nothing to do with nationality.

/There remains the question of whether opposition to war is itself clear evidence of disloyalty/Certainly those who opposed the Revolution thought of themselves as loyal to the only nation they knew, England, and the one that had already bestowed on Americans the blessings of liberty if not independent nationhood. The opponents of the War of 1812 and the Mexican War, the copperheads in the Civil War, the anti-imperialists of the Spanish-American War and the hundreds of thousands who burned draft cards, marched in demonstrations and refused to pay taxes in opposition to the Vietnamese War, did so in the name of American patriotism. But one thing is clear—opposition to war, especially after it has begun, has not come primarily from immigrant-ethnic groups with strong other-nation loyalties/

Immigrants and their children have tended to enlist in the armed services during war for two main reasons:/the desire to assert loyalty and the desire to enhance opportunity. Probably for both reasons, Mexican Americans contributed more than their share of fighting personnel in the Vietnamese War and World War II. In the Great War, 350,000 immigrants served in the U.S. armed forces with seventeen medal-of-honor winners among them. Serving out of proportion to their numbers, it is not surprising that members of recent immigrant-ethnic groups have contributed more than their share of casualties and

heroes. Of 3,216 Congressional Medals of Honor conferred in the century between the Civil War and Vietnam, more than one-sixth went to
foreign-born personnel from thirty-two different nations, a percentage
beyond that of the foreign born in the population as a whole.[21] Americans have become accustomed to having heroes with foreign sounding
names, and probably were not surprised when Sergeant Jimmy Lopez,
one of the Americans taken as hostage by the Iranian revolutionary
students in 1980, confounded his captors by writing on the wall of the
room where he was imprisoned, *"viva el rojo blanco e azul"* (long live the
red, white and blue).[22]

Foreign Policy, Loyalty and Nationality

The presence of large immigrant-ethnic groups in the United States
also has been a cause for concern because of their impact on American
foreign policy. The issue is seen not so much as one of loyalty in war
time but of special interest pressure groups, blinded by their cultural
and emotional ties to other nations, pushing the United States toward
actions against its own best interest. Such an argument was most recently made by Senator Charles McC. Mathias, Jr.[23] The activities of
American ethnic groups in behalf of foreign causes are numerous.
Greeks in the United States oppose arms for Turkey, our NATO ally;
Haitians in this country support the claims of illegal Haitian immigrants for asylum; Jews promote the cause of Israel; Lithuanian Americans seek independence for Lithuania; Poles lobby in support of Solidarity; and Mexican Americans and Italian Americans tend to support
liberal immigration policies. Mathias sees *some* of these activities specifically as going against what he deems to be the American national
interest and, like others before him, wonders what can be done to mute
them without violating our Constitution and traditions of freedom of
speech.

More than thirty years ago, historian Thomas Bailey also com-
plained about the impact of immigrant-ethnic groups on foreign policy.
"It is not unusual," he wrote, "for the Washington government . . . to
make decisions that are more conducive to the interests of foreigners
than Americans."[24] Bailey, who deplored the influence of immigrant-
ethnic groups in promoting isolationism before World War II, thereby
inhibiting the capacity of the United States to ready itself for war
against Hitler, wrote that such influence would lessen in the future.[25]
But sixteen years later, the political scientist Louis L. Gerson, who has
written the only full-length book treatment of the subject, continued
to despair about the harmful influence of other-nation loyalties on

American foreign policy. Despite immigration restriction in the 1920s and the decline of immigration in the 1930s and 1940s, ethnicity was not dead. Indeed, it had already begun an extraordinary revival for a variety of reasons, new refugee and immigrant flows; the development of black consciousness and pride; the search of third-generation Americans for their roots; government policies which stimulated ethnic group claims; the celebration of ethnic pluralism as distinctively American; and the continuing involvement of the United States in world affairs. The persistent power of ethnicity led to the development of nationality divisions in both major political parties, something which the author of the forward to Gerson's book attributed to "the curse of ethnicity in American politics . . ."[26]

The trouble with that formulation seems obvious. Those examples of immigrant-ethnic pressure politics in foreign policy which one thinks are against the American national interest are clearly a curse. Those with which one agrees as serving the national interest are not. But such a formulation begs a larger question. Is there a national interest to be served? Presumably it lies in the safety and well-being of the American people as a whole. To lose to Hitler would have jeopardized the safety and well-being of all but a few. That case seems clear. Most others are ambiguous.

Was it a curse that Poles, Czechs, Lithuanians, Latvians, Ukranians and others living in the United States supported the nationalist aspirations of their countrymen? Is it a curse that recent immigrants from Ghana and Nigeria are working to strengthen economic ties with Accra and Lagos or that Mexican Americans now lobby for liberal immigration policies as did Italians and Jews in the early 1960s?

It is not self-evident that any of these lobbying activities are harmful to the United States, but one can acknowledge that there may be some danger when any passionate pressure group lobbies for interests it believes are paramount as if they were in the interest of all. That is as true for the oil and munitions lobbies as it is for Greek, Polish or Jewish Americans.

It is precisely because Senator Mathias did not agree with the lobbying activities of these three ethnic groups on certain occasions that he wrote his article deploring ethnic politics in foreign affairs. Acknowledging that factional politics generally are dangerous, as James Madison warned in Federalist Paper No. 10, Senator Mathias pointed specifically to George Washington's warning against attachments to particular foreign nations which facilitate "the illusion of an imaginary common interest . . ."[27] It is not ethnicity which troubles Mathias but "original ethnic interest groups, which sometimes press causes that derogate from the national interest."[28] The newer ethnic groups particularly, he writes, have retained and strengthened their ethnic identity while becoming Americans in other respects, unlike the Western Europeans who, he mistakenly writes, "became submerged in the larger American culture . . . "[29] It is the newer groups with their "little Italys," "little Polands," "Jewish ghettos" and "Chinatowns" who began "the dubious political tradition . . . of political appeals to separatism and parochialism, to the frequent neglect of the common aims and interests of all Americans."[30]

That portion of his article is flawed historically. The Whiskey Rebellion which caused Washington to ride out to western Pennsylvania to stop an insurrection against American loyalty was sometimes called the "Scotch-Irish Rebellion." German and Scandinavian immigrants established rural ethnic enclaves in which the languages of the old country were used not only in religious services but also as the language of instruction in schools for two or three generations. The descendants of the English themselves established their own sociological enclaves in the late nineteenth century—hotels, resorts and entire communities—to which others were not welcome.

Senator Mathias made the mistake of comparing the contemporary lobbying activities of Irish Americans with those of Greek Americans, as if both groups were in the same stage of acculturation in the United States. He praised the restraint of leading contemporary Irish-American politicians for warning against the violent activities of the illegal Irish Republican Army in contrast to the zealousness of Greek Americans in advancing Greek foreign policy interests. In the nineteenth century, however, the restraint was less evident as Irish Americans were recruited and openly drilled by the Fenians for armed attacks against Canada.

Senator Mathias presents three case studies as representative of the dangers of ethnic group pressures on foreign policy. The first of these is a resolution adopted unanimously by the Congress in July 1959 calling for a "Captive Nations Week." The resolution demanded freedom and full independence for the peoples of Eastern Europe, an accomplishment which Mathias points out was no closer to attainment in 1981 than it was in 1954 when the captive nations' ethnic groups in the United States formed a unified lobby.[31] The main effect of lobbying activities on behalf of captive nations, Mathias argues, was to obstruct President Johnson's policy of building bridges to Eastern Europe through expanded trade, a result which in his view was inimical to the national interest.[32]

The second case concerns the Greek-sponsored coup in Cyprus in 1974 and the subsequent military intervention, which led to the formation of the new Greek-American lobby that successfully stimulated the congressional decision for an arms embargo against Turkey in February of 1975. Greek Americans, aided by Armenians, applied heavy pressure to maintain the embargo, resulting, according to Senator Mathias, in the closing by the Turks of twenty-six American bases and listening posts in Turkish territory.

/The third case is the most troubling of all to Mathias. It has to do with the influence of the Jewish lobby on congressional decisions concerning the Middle East/ The Greeks, after all, number only three million in the United States. There are, however, six million Jewish Americans who are well organized and located in urban areas. What is known as the Israeli lobby, particularly as manifested through the American-Israeli Public Affairs Committee, was influential in effecting another congressional decision with which Mathias disagreed, the Jackson-Vanik Amendment of 1974 which linked the privilege of non-discriminatory trade for the Soviet Union with freedom of emigration for Jews. It was a decision, says Mathias, which may not only have failed in its own terms, but placed "a lasting strain on the detente of the early 1970s . . . " To support his brief, Senator Mathias quotes former secretary of state Henry Kissinger who said in June 1975 that "no country could allow its domestic regulations to be dictated as we are pushing the Soviets to do . . . I think it was a serious mistake that the Jewish community got hung up on it."[33]

• Senator Mathias' position is clear. He was against the Captive Nations Resolution, the arms embargo for Turkey and the Jackson-Vanik Amendment, none of which would have passed, he believes, without the lobbying of immigrant-ethnic groups. Hence, such lobbying presents a special danger to the well-being of the United States. But it is not self-evident that those measures were against the safety and well-being of a majority of Americans. To the extent that one believes that American security derives at least in part from a consistent application of human rights in foreign affairs, all three measures make sense. As Mathias himself acknowledges, "ethnic advocacy represents neither a lack of patriotism nor a desire to place foreign interests ahead of American interests; more often it represents a sincere belief that the two coincide."[34]

Moreover, one is impressed at least as much by the weaknesses and failures of immigrant-ethnic lobby groups as by their effectiveness and success even in the three cases discussed. Despite the Captive Nations Resolution, few Americans of any ethnic background called for American intervention during the Hungarian Revolution in 1956. Actually, although Captive Nations Week is still proclaimed in the third week of every July, Eastern European ethnic pressures, as Mathias admits, have been directed away from the violent overthrow of communist re-

gimes toward the expansion of trade and economic activities of mutual
benefit to the peoples of Eastern Europe and the United States.

As for the Greeks and the Turks, the arms embargo was lifted by the
Congress in the summer of 1978—not because the Turkish lobby coun-
tered the Greek lobby—but because geopolitical considerations prevailed. The bases were just too important to our overall strategic opposition to the Soviet Union. And the Jewish lobby, alleged to be
virtually invincible, could not prevent the Eisenhower administration
from compelling Israel's withdrawal from the Sinai after the 1956 War
(Is it clear that was in the American national interest?); nor could it
prevent approval of a sale in the spring of 1978 of sixty F-15 fighter
planes to Saudi Arabia. The Saudis, not content to rely upon the National Association of Arab Americans which claimed to represent two
million Americans of Arab origin and oil and other Middle Eastern lobbies, employed professional lobbyists of their own, including a public
relations firm engaged for the sole purpose of securing the F-15s. Nor
could the Israelis prevent Mathias and a majority of the Senate from
passage of yet another military aid measure for Saudi Arbia in 1981,
this time providing sophisticated support equipment for the use of the
F-15s (something the previous administration had pledged would
never be done) along with the famous AWACs, although it is far from
clear that the AWACs sale was in the American national interest.

Senator Mathias is quick to state that there are many good aspects
to ethnic pressure politics. Some good causes are championed that
otherwise might be neglected, and "despite frequently exaggerated
claims and arguments, neither Greek nor Jewish lobbies would command the support they do in Congress and with the American people if
their case did not have substantial merit."[35] What, then, is the problem? The problem is that evidently Greek Americans and Jewish
Americans have presented him with "fractious controversy and bitter
recrimination"[36] for his votes on the Turkish arms embargo and military aid to Saudi Arabia. To his constituents in Maryland, who elected
him overwhelmingly in 1980, he seems to be saying, "I am trying my
best to see things whole and not from the point of view of any particular group. Please respect my desire to serve the national interest. It is
just as strong as yours. Perhaps it is stronger because you are so impas-
sioned. In any case, treat me with civility."[37]

The call for civility—Senator Mathias' word—is similar to the one
issued by Gerson. After detailed descriptions of the impact of ethnic
group advocacy on foreign policy in recent times, the one concrete recommendation he made was for the abandonment of the nationality divisions in both major parties. But Gerson also recommended that there
should be "a gentlemen's agreement between parties not to go beyond

propriety or certain limits and to abstain from making promises which cannot and will not be fulfilled."[38] Of course, civility and propriety are always good for the democratic system, and it is not just the ethnic lobbies that ought to be admonished to observe them, but it is not easy to prescribe limits to free speech which consist solely of advocacy. One cannot outlaw "bitter recrimination" by voters toward their representatives.

Such advocacy obviously is not necessarily in the national interest, although there may be a happy compatibility between the two by chance. Senator Mathias was pleased with the interference of leading Irish-American politicians against the IRA but not with that of leading Greek-Americans politicians against Turkey, although the civility quotient of both groups may have been equal. Gerson asks for restraint by politicians, but there are few who, given the chance, would not mobilize ethnic political pressure on behalf of foreign policy causes in which the politicians believe. Woodrow Wilson is the classic case of someone who deplored ethnic influence on foreign policy when a particular ethnic influence bothered him, and acted to stimulate it when it accorded with his view of what was right. Apparently not recognizing that he himself had ethnic sensibilities and ties which colored his view of Britain's cause in World War I, he tilted toward England in 1915 and began to attack the "hyphenated" German and Irish Americans. It was the Germans who advised him to re-read Washington's farewell address warning against foreign entanglements. During the next year, he sent a telegram to the Committee on Resolutions at the Democractic National Convention attacking hyphenism in the foreign policy debate. The convention itself adopted a resolution condemning political action which "improperly" affected negotiations with foreign powers.[39] But Wilson himself stimulated Polish-American political pressure on foreign issues because it suited him. Despite the strongly negative opinions of Eastern Europeans he had expressed in his 1902 book *A History of the American People*, his sympathy with the cause of national liberation in Eastern Europe merged nicely with his political ambitions. For this, the President of the Polish-American Democratic League praised him for having "solidified the great Polish-American vote."[40]

None of this is to say that there is no special problem with respect to ethnic pressure politics on foreign affairs. The special interest politics of domestic lobbies might weaken the nation or even bankrupt it, but with its people alive and their liberties intact, the nation could presumably right itself./The troublesome quality about ethnic pressure politics in the field of foreign policy, as I wrote in an article on minority groups and foreign policy twenty-four years ago, is that it might lead the nation to war with devastating consequences or keep the nation from taking actions to protect itself against foreign powers.[41]/Presumably the latter was the case in the late 1930s when German, Italian and Japanese Americans agitated against American preparedness as well as involvement to stop the aggressions of Germany and Japan.

The question raised is a classic one:/Should a free society tolerate freedom of speech even at the possible expense of freedom?/ The answers are never neat or simple. All groups which advance propaganda on behalf of a foreign principal can be made to register as they have ever since the passage of the Foreign Agents Registration Act of 1938, but American ethnic groups are not included in the provisions of that Act and could not be under our Constitution. The Alien Registration Act of 1940 and the Subversive Activities Control Act of 1950 put certain limitations on speech, but they are not directed against ethnic group advocacy on behalf of other nations.

Our Constitution is clear. It protects speech, assembly and petition. It cannot guarantee civility or propriety. It certainly cannot assure that every argument advanced by ethnic pressure groups or others in behalf of this cause or that is in the national interest. Nor can it or the state guarantee that in times of crisis the loyalty of members of immigrant-ethnic groups to the United States will transcend any other loyalty.

As was pointed out earlier, immigrant-ethnic group disloyalty has not been a problem in American history in times of crisis, even when the United States was at war with countries which claimed the loyalties of large numbers of Americans. And, despite the hand wringing of Gerson and Mathias, it is not at all clear that immigrant-ethnic pressure politics in foreign policy have undermined or unbalanced the national interests of the United States, despite the isolationist proclivities of several ethnic groups prior to World War II. For one thing, immigrant-ethnic groups strengthen relationships for the United States with other countries through cultural and economic ties. The thesis has yet to be written on the extent to which the American economy has benefited through trade and investment between the United States and nations with substantial immigrant-ethnic ties in this country. Nor has any scholar explored the extent to which immigrant-ethnic groups in the United States have assisted in the implementation of national foreign policy goals. For example, the Camp David peacemaking process owes something to a series of meetings between representatives of the education ministries of Egypt and Isreal held at Harvard University in the late 1970s at the instigation of Israeli Americans. Italian Americans conducted a massive letter writing campaign in the fifties against communist party candidates in Italy, urging their relatives to vote for anti-communists. The movements for national liberation sponsored and supported by immigrant-ethnic communities in the United States have generally strengthened, not weakened, this country's role in world affairs. The existence of Czechoslovakia and Poland as sovereign nations may cause tension between the United States and the Soviet Union, but no one would argue that their existence is not in the interest of the United States; and the national liberation of Israel after two thousand years resulted in the United States having a strong, permanent ally in an area of strategic importance.

E Pluribus Unim: Acculturation, Loyalty and Ethnic Diversity

Other-nation loyalties have not been a serious problem for the United States in times of war or other crisis because of the power of acculturation in this country. Immigrants and especially their children and grandchildren are loyal to the United States because they believe in the principles for which it stands, "one nation, indivisible, with liberty for all," despite its many failures to live up to those principles. Loyalty to the United States has not been insured by Sedition Acts but because there has been enough liberty and opportunity to transform the children of immigrants into strong patriots. They feel they can make better lives—freer and more prosperous—in this country than elsewhere. It is for the same reason that the United States remains a near and distant magnet for emigration from all over the world.

Loyalty is not hard to command from most of the immigrants who remain in the United States, especially from their children. Those immigrants who wish to return to their countries of origin and are able to do so often make that choice. Perhaps as many as 25 percent of the Lithuanians, 40 percent of the Poles and 60 percent of the Hungarians and Rumanians returned to their homelands. In some years, there were more Italian emigrants that immigrants. And between 1899 and 1924, 86 percent of the Turks returned to Turkey.[42] Large numbers of Mexicans and French-Canadians behave as sojourners going back and forth, never giving up their fundamental loyalty to the countries of their birth. Some immigrants, even those who became citizens, identify with the countries of their ancestors by arranging for their bodies to be returned for burial. But the majority choose freely to become Americans in some way or another. And their children, educated and generally socialized in an American environment, often become fiercely attached to things American, sometimes even explicit rejecting the traditions of their ancestors. Many factors speed their Americanization: public schools; a continental economy; opportunities to meet persons from

other backgrounds; participation in the armed services and in war itself; and a civic culture which makes no demand for conformity to a
particular religion and which, indeed, permits a plurality of loyalties.

The United States probably has gone further than any other country in defining national loyalty strictly in political terms since its people no longer believe that American identity is a matter of race, religion, color or nationality. It probably has gone further, too, in allowing
Americans to express their loyalties to other nations without making
their American loyalties suspect. It has done this not just by permit-
ting advocacy of foreign policy issues—guaranteed by the First
Amendment—by ethnic pressure groups, but also through a Supreme
Court decision in 1967 which found it unconstitutional for the Congress to impose loss of citizenship on naturalized Americans who have
lived in foreign countries for a long period of time and participated in
their elections.

In *Afroyim v. Rusk*, the plaintiff, Afroyim, had lived in Israel for ten
years where he had voted in an Israeli election. Reentry to the United
States as a citizen was denied under a provision of the Nationality Act
of 1952 which stipulates that a naturalized United States citizen shall
lose his citizenship if he votes in a foreign political election.[43] A majority of five on the Court declared that the Fourteenth Amendment con-
firms American citizenship as a right which Congress has no authority
to alter. In a stunning reversal of previous law, the Court insisted that
every citizen—including naturalized citizens—had the right to retain
citizenship unless he or she voluntarily relinquished it because:

> Citizenship in this Nation is a part of a cooperative affair. Its citi-
> zenry is the country and the country is its citizenry. The very
> nature of our free government makes it completely incongruous
> to have a rule of law under which a group of citizens temporarily
> in office can deprive another group of citizens of their citizenship.
> We hold that the Fourteenth Amendment was designed to, and
> does, protect every citizen of this Nation against a congressional,
> forceable destruction of his citizenship, whatever creed, color or
> race. Our holding does no more than to give this citizen that
> which is his own, a constitutional right to remain a citizen in a
> free country unless he voluntarily relinquishes that citizen-
> ship."[44]

Many would argue, as did the dissenters in *Afroyim*, that a decision
freely taken to vote in a foreign election or serve in the armed forces of
another nation is a voluntary act, and that loss of American citizenship
under a law passed by the Congress does not constitute the forceable or
even unreasonable taking of citizenship from such a person. Whether
one agrees with the majority or the minority, it is now clear that the
loss of citizenship can be imposed for activities specified in law only

when an American citizen intends by engaging in them to relinquish his or her citizenship. Dual or even multiple loyalties do not constitute disloyalty to the United States as far as the Constitution is concerned.[45]

Paradoxically, the tolerance of multiple loyalties probably advanced American unity, as others have argued.[46] Loyalty to democracy is grounded in consent, and the protection of First and Fourteenth Amendment freedoms helps to make new Americans fiercely loyal to the Constitution they swear to uphold. The protection of speech, religion and assembly binds newcomers and their children to the American idea of liberty as many of them have recorded in autobiographies, essays, letters and other documents.[47]

The objective should be to reinforce those ties that bind all Americans to each other, not to discourage their love of ancestral cultures. In addition to steadfast adherence to First and Fourteenth Amendment rights and protections, public policy can strengthen loyalty to the United States in four basic ways: (1) by endorsement of economic policies which promote individual opportunity and success; (2) by consistent enforcement of laws against discrimination based on ethnicity, color or religion; (3) by strong programs of English language training to promote competency among newcomers and a sense of community among all Americans; and (4) by programs which promote civic competency and encourage naturalization and participation in the American political process on many grounds, not just ethnicity.

This last point is particularly important. Ethnic political mobilization in the United States has not, for the most part, been a source of divisiveness until recent years. American ethnic politics has not been syndicalist. It has not been based on proportional representation or fixed slots or "set asides" or anything else that would tend to perpetuate separate political entities within the policy. On the whole, ethnic associational life has had many purposes, one of which has *not* been to organize and support ethnic political parties.

The American political system says to members of immigrant-ethnic groups that they will be free to maintain linguistic, religious and cultural activities on their own. They may even engage in pressure politics for causes which interest their particular group. But they will not find it profitable to organize as a political party for three main reasons: first, they will be perceived as threatening to the central individualistic values of the culture; second, their base will not be broad enough since all of them are numerical minorities; and third, geographic and economic mobility within each group leads to a diversity of political views based on changes which accompany such mobility. Given their internal diversity, their narrow base and the strong resistance to any group ideology, ethnic political parties do not surface in the United States. Ethnically-based factions are a commonplace at the local level, but ethnic groups can never have enough strength at the national level—where foreign policy matters—to challenge the broader coalitions that constitute our two major parties.

By participating in those parties, members of immigrant-ethnic groups are obliged to compromise their factional points of view. They are propelled invariably toward stronger national loyalty by a political system which promotes the values of individualism in economic and political life while tolerating and sometimes celebrating cultural diversity in social life.

The development of strong feelings of national loyalty toward the United States does not inhibit ethnic groups from promoting the foreign policy interests of ancestral homelands. When the survival of one's homeland is at stake (the feeling of Jews about Israel), or when the liberation of one's people is at issue (what many Armenians feel about other Armenians in the Soviet Union and Turkey), advocacy will become passionate. Only those who do not feel that the freedom or survival of their ancestral people and culture is at stake are likely to get high marks for civility.

There is one other thing which government policy can do to minimize the prospect of disloyalty in times of crisis and/or the divisive impacts of pressure politics in foreign policy. Immigration policy can prevent any one or two nations from dominating immigration flows (as now occurs) through the application of equal per-country ceilings on immigration from all nations regardless of the demand for visas. If the United States had a world ceiling on immigration with no per-country ceilings, immigrants would be admitted on a first-come, first-served basis within overall limits and according to preferences. Thus, if the first preference was the reunification of immediate relatives (spouses, parents and minor children of American citizens and resident aliens), others would have to wait their turn until the world limit for that preference had been exhausted for any given year. Such a policy makes sense if one believes that the unification of families and/or other immigration objectives should be facilitated without regard to the objective of national diversity, but does not make much sense if one gives a higher priority to promoting more ethnic diversity through immigration.

During most of American history there were no limits set by nationality, except for Asia and Africa in a manifestation of the racism of the time. As a result, between 1830 and 1890 there was never a decade in which German nationals did not constitute at least one-fourth of the immigrants who came to the United States. Similarly, in the two decades between 1840 and 1860, four out of every ten immigrants to this country were Irish. It is entirely possible that if German immigration had been double what it was in the nineteenth century, German Americans would have constituted 20 percent of the population instead of 10 percent in 1914. While it is not clear that the interests of the United States would have been better or less well served by a stronger policy of neutrality in the First World War, one has to recognize that such a large immigrant-ethnic group mobilized for political action on behalf of a foreign nation might conceivably present a serious problem for American unity.

Given the multiplicity of ethnic groups in this country and the acculturation powers of the American political system and economic marketplace, the maintenance of immigrant-ethnic group loyalties has not presented a serious problem either for American loyalty or for the formulation and implementation of national foreign policies. For a variety of reasons, immigrant-ethnic cultural loyalties and even ethnic political mobilization itself, at least in this country, appear to have been at least as much a source of national strength as of internal division.

NOTES

[1] Samuel Eliot Morison and Henry Steele Commager, *The Growth of the American Republic*, Vol. I (London: Oxford University Pres, 1942), pp. 202-203.

[2] Ibid., p. 205.

[3] Peter C. Marzio, ed., *A Nation of Nations* (New York: Harper and Row, 1976), p. 18.

[4] Ibid., p. 327.

[5] James McCague, *The Second Rebellion: The Story of the New York City Draft Riots of 1863* (New York: Dial Press, 1968).

[6] Marzio, op. cit., p. 327.

[7] Louis L. Gerson, *The Hyphenate in Recent American Politics and Diplomacy* (Lawrence, Kan.: University of Kansas Press, 1964), quoted on p. 65.

[8] Gustavus Ohlinger, *Their True and Faithful Allegiance* (New York: MacMillan Co., 1916), pp. 69-70.

[9] Charles F. Hartman, *The Necessity of Prohibiting German Newspapers, From A Different Point of View*, pamphlet (n.p., 1918).

[10] W. L. Harding, cited in Moses Rischin, ed., *Immigration and the American Tradition* (Indianapolis, Ind.: Bobbs-Merrill, 1976), pp. 206-208.

[11]Joseph M. Hanson, *South Dakota in the World War, 1917-1919* (Pierre, S.D.: South Dakota State Historical Society, 1940), pp.60-61.

[12]Kathleen Neils Conzen, "Germans," in Stephan Thernstrom, ed., *Harvard Encyclopedia of American Ethnic Groups* (Cambridge, Mass.: Harvard University Press, 1980), p. 422.

[13]Ibid., p. 421.

[14]Quoted in Harry H. L. Kitano, "Japanese," in the *Harvard Encyclopedia of American Ethnic Groups*, op. cit., p. 563.

[15]Cited in Lawrence H. Fuchs, *Hawaii Pono* (New York: Harcourt, Brace and World, 1961), p. 133.

[16]Ibid., p. 137.

[17]Kitano, op. cit., p. 565.

[18]Fuchs, *Hawaii Pono*, op. cit., p. 132.

[18]Ibid., p. 303.

[20]Ibid., p. 304. The evidence of the overwhelming loyalty of the Nisei is clear despite these repressive measures. In all, only two Japanese Americans in Hawaii resisted the draft.

[21]Marzio, op. cit., p. 327.

[22]Lawrence H. Fuchs, *U.S. Immigration Policy and the National Interest*, Staff Report of the Select Commission on Immigration and Refugee Policy (Washington, D.C.: 1981), p. 157. See in particular Chapter 4, "First Principles of Immigration Reform: E Pluribus Unim, More Than a Motto."

[23]Charles McC. Mathias, Jr., "Ethnic Groups and Foreign Policy," *Foreign Affairs*, 59:5 (Summer 1981).

[24]Thomas A. Bailey, *The Man in the Streets: The Impact of American Public Opinion on Foreign Policy* (New York: Peter Smith, 1948), pp. 15-18.

[25]Ibid.

[26]G. Lowell Field in the forward to Gerson, op. cit., p. xxvi.

[27]Mathias, op, cit., p. 976.

[28]Ibid., p. 977.

[29]Ibid., p. 979.

[30]Ibid., p. 980.

[31]Ibid., p. 985.

[32]Ibid., p. 986.

[33]Ibid., p. 996.

[34]Ibid., p. 997.

[35]Ibid., p. 990.

[36]Ibid., p. 997.

[37]Ibid.

[38]Gerson, op. cit., p. 259.

[39]Ibid., p. 65.

[40]Ibid., quoted on p. 69.

[41]Lawrence H. Fuchs, "Minority Groups and Foreign Policy,"*Political Science Quarterly*, LXXIV (June 1959).

[42]Mona Harrington, "Loyalties: Dual and Divided," in the *Harvard Encyclopedia of American Ethnic Groups*, op. cit., p. 676.

[43]*Afroyim v. Rusk*, 387 U.S. 253. (1966).

[44]*Afroyim*, 387 U.S. 253, 268.

[45]There is one fundamental ambiguity in American law with respect to dual loyalty. Under our present Naturalization Law, Section 337, 8 USC 1448 (a)(2), anyone wishing to become a naturalized citizen must take not only an oath of allegiance but also an oath "to renounce and abjure absolutely and entirely all allegiance and fidelity to any foreign prince, potentate, or sovereignty of whom or which the petitioner was before a subject or citizen." That was not an issue in the *Afroyim* case since the petitioner was of Polish birth.

[46]Morton Grodzins, *The Loyal and the Disloyal* (Chicago: University of Chicago Press, 1956), and John H. Schaar, *Loyalty in America* (Berkeley, Cal.: University of California Press, 1957).

[47]Almost every group has produced a filiopietistic literature which emphasizes American patriotism. One example is Joseph A. Wytrwal, *Poles in American History and Tradition* (Detroit: Endurance Press, 1969). Among the better known autobiographies are (Jewish) Mary Anton, *The Promised Land* (Boston: Houghton Mifflin, 1912); (Italian) Edward Corsi, *In the Shadow of Liberty: Chronicle of Ellis Island* (New York: Arno Press, 1969); and (Danish) Jacob Riis, *The Making of an American* (New York: MacMillan, 1970).

HYSTERIA IN WARTIME: DOMESTIC PRESSURES ON ETHNICS AND ALIENS

Frank P. Zeidler

Mayor of Milwaukee (1948-60) and Socialist Party
Candidate for President (1976)

The wartime hysteria that has been directed against ethnics and aliens in the United States can be viewed as one aspect of a recurring social phenomenon which surfaces from time to time in this nation's history and, in fact, in other nations around the world. Social pressures manifesting themselves in expressions of hysterical conduct have been exerted on people in this land from its early settlement. For example, Roger Williams was driven out of the Massachusetts colony fifteen years after the landing of the Pilgrims.

A chronicle of violence in the United States must necessarily include many actions of any hysterical nature as well as violence perpetrated after deliberate calculation. These two types of social conduct, violence and hysteria, appear occasionally in the same events. Violence in connection with social hysteria has occurred in disputes over politics, religion, race and sports, as well as in wartime.

Ethnics and aliens may experience this high level hostility even when there is no war, particularly during a time of tension between the United States and some other nation. Domestic pressure exerted against Iranians during the hostage crisis is a good example. It must also be noted that aliens or naturalized citizens on occasion reverse the process by exercising pressure of their own, including violent hysterical actions, against others based on issues and disputes brought with them as part of their emotional baggage from their homelands. This chapter will be concerned only with hysteria in wartime and the resulting domestic pressures on ethnics and aliens.

Hysteria is defined as "conduct or an outbreak of conduct exhibiting unmanageable fear or emotional excess in individuals and groups."[1] The record shows that in many cases the groups and mobs engaging in conduct exhibiting unmanageable fear or emotional excess have been motivated by propaganda and policies deliberately adopted by governments or groups influential in government.

In the history of the United States there have been two primary occasions when major outbreaks of wartime hysteria were directed against ethnics and aliens.[2] One such occasion was during the First World War. Nationwide repressive actions were aimed at ethnics from the Central Powers and to a lesser degree against Irish Americans. The other occasion was, of course, during the Second World War, when a hysterical national reaction to the bombing of Pearl Harbor resulted in the internment of American citizens of Japanese descent in concentration camps. It was the first action of this kind in the history of the nation and has until recently been largely ignored, but as precedent it bodes ill for the future. In both events the excessive public actions were associated with government policy, less formally in World War I, and very formally and deliberately in the Second World War.

Public abuse during the First World War was focused on the people from the Central Powers—Germans, Austrians, Jewish people and others who spoke German or who had a Germanic cultural background (the term "Germanic" encompasses more than the German nation). As the war progressed, pressure was also applied to those of Mexican and Russian descent. The charge of disloyalty was usually the basis for acts against such people.

The experience of people of German stock or culture was well summarized by Dean Wittke. He wrote:

Unfortunately, the war precipitated an hysterical effort to eradicate everything of German origin from American civilization. The anti-German campaign was directed by extremists, but many Americans approved the patriotic drive against "Teutonism" and the "Hun." German books, music, church services, newspapers, singing societies, German in the schools, and many other features of American life that could somehow be traced to a German origin came under the ban. The wedding marches of Mendelssohn and Wagner were removed from marriage ceremonies; German books were burned; Bismarck herring disappeared from restaurant menus, and "sauerkraut" was renamed "liberty cabbage." Family names were changed to hide a German ancestry, street names were Americanized, singing societies cancelled rehearsals, German-language newspapers were boycotted by readers and advertisers, German books were removed from library shelves, and instruction in the German language ceased in the schools.[3]

One might add to the above list the fact that there was at least one lynching, that of a young German baker in Collinsville, Illinois, on April 4, 1918.[4]

The hysteria against things German that manifested itself in the war period of 1917-18 was not the result of a spontaneous burst of sentiment developing out of thin air. Rather it was the culmination of a long series of events related to the interactions of people with a Germanic cultural background and those with a British background in the United States. The entry of people from Germany into the United States was by no means frictionless. Although it might be said that Germans were assimilated as much as any group into the Anglo-Irish culture, the process was never complete; nor was the identification of Germans as fully American ever complete. In Wisconsin, for example, from 1852 to 1855, the activities of the American Party, the "Know-Nothings," which were directed against Catholics and immigrants, produced a strain between Germans and native-born Americans. In Milwaukee, Germans then formed the "Sag Nicht"—"Say Nothing Organization"—to counter the Know-Nothings.[5] These native-born Americans were fearful of "foreignism." They believed that immigrants would work for less, would not be Protestant, would not support temperance, and would oppose slavery.[6]

In fairness we must acknowledge that the slow acceptance of immigrants from Germany into a complete pattern of assimilation was not wholly the result of native-born attitudes. Apart from political rivalry, there was also to be found among German immigrants the idea that Germans should remain essentially German even though they were free to mingle and intermarry with non-Germans. There was a proposal also that there should be a distinct German state, and Wisconsin with its many German settlers was considered a possibility.[7] Furthermore, where there were a substantial number of German immigrants in one community as in Milwaukee, and where they functioned as a political factor to be reckoned with, they became identified as a distinct group of people, a unified entity. Kathleen Neils Conzen has written about Germans, "Their common language, their common background in the eyes of the natives, were enough to bring them together despite differences of province, dialect, religion, and class brought from their still divided homeland."[8]

This generalized identification of German people in America and the areas in which they lived continued well past the World War I period. Only now is Milwaukee beginning to lose its identity as a German city with other ethnic stocks beginning to be perceived as either culturally or numerically dominant. Nevertheless, at the time of the First World War, German communities, both rural and urban, were fairly easily identified around the nation.

Public opinion about the actions and developing power of the German Empire after 1871 was in part the basis of attitudes toward German culture in the United States. The victory of Germany over France in 1871 and the growing power of the German nation became a matter of concern in world diplomacy. The expansionist policy of Germany in the Samoan Islands almost led to a naval engagement with American and British ships joining forces against the Germans in 1889. As a result, the United States feared that Germany would take over the Philippines when Spain withdrew. These probably were minor annoyances. The aggressive nature of Wilhelm II, the German emperor after 1888, and his efforts to force Germany into a world power were obnoxious and threatening to other powers. Alliances were formed between otherwise unfriendly states. For the United States, England was no longer the enemy.

In 1898 the German government under the influence of Admiral von Tirpitz decided to inaugurate a high seas fleet as a challenge to Great Britain; this action led to an arms race that portended a major war. The image of Germany as a militaristic nation, a "Prussianized" nation, evolved in the United States. This concept of a Germany bent on war gave a tremendous advantage to the British propagandists when war actually broke out. Professor H. C. Peterson notes that at the outbreak of hostilities there already was a pro-British attitude among leading Americans. He writes:

> The immediate task of British propagandists was to make an ordinary political power struggle appear to be a fight between the forces of good and evil . . . In developing the idea that this new war was a holy war the British were very fortunate. The struggle between wearly old England and boisterous new Germany readily adapted itself to the stereotype of virtue versus iniquity. The new expanding German power aroused all the usual opposition to change. The British government, on its part, had the customary support of the great majority who believe that that which is is sacrosanct. In addition, throughout the war years and the prewar years, the Germans were constantly doing things which angered the entire world, and these the propagandists exploited to the full.[9]

Peterson advances the argument that other nations were opposing a Germany which could not expand and that therefore became explosive, loud and truculent. He also argues that Germany's statesmen, not accustomed to great power, played their parts badly so that heavy-handedness and a lack of restraint seemed apparent. Thus at the outset of the war in Europe in 1914 there was a disposition on the part of Americans to be friendly to the aspirations of Great Britain and the British side, and hostile to the Germans.[10] Peterson also notes that it was the objective of British propaganda agents to have Americans identify their interests with the British interests. In this they were aided by the German submarine campaign and the contention that if the Germans prevailed, they would seek to penetrate South America and thus violate the Monroe Doctrine.[11]

In the struggle for the control of American public opinion, the British were the victors through superior organization, superior application of psychological techniques, and because of certain actions taken by the German government. Principally offensive to Americans were the invasion of Belgium, a neutral nation; the sinking of the passenger ship *Lusitania* on May 7, 1915; acts of sabotage; and the Zimmermann note. This last was a message which Alfred Zimmermann, the German foreign secretary, sent to the German minister in Mexico advising him of unrestricted submarine warfare. The note said there was likely to be an outbreak of war with the United States and that Mexico should join and attempt to reconquer Texas, New Mexico and Arizona. This information was released on January 16, 1916, by British sources.[12] About the sinking of the *Lusitania*, the *Nation* said, "The torpedo that sank the *Lusitania* also sank Germany in the opinion of mankind." American outrage demanding entry into the war was roused.[13]

These events occurred against a background of propaganda which, according to some historians, was largely under British control.[14] One very effective form of propaganda was the attribution to German soldiers of individual cases of atrocities and ferocious behavior which stigmatized Germans as barbarians. The stories included accounts of gang rape, bayonetting children, cutting off breasts, and boiling down bodies of dead soldiers for fat to make soap. Some tales were, of course, fictitious, and others were accounts of actual occurrences deliberately misrepresented.[15]

Along with the ineffectiveness of German propaganda, the sabotage engaged in by Germans in order to stop American supplies from reaching the Allies also damaged their cause. The Black Tom Island explosion of munitions docks on July 30, 1916, resulting in a great loss of life, crippled the efforts of German Americans as well as the non-German advocates of United States neutrality. Similarly, the attempt on July 2, 1915, by a man of German extraction to assassinate J. P. Morgan, who was considered primarily responsible for the traffic in munitions to the Allies, turned public sentiment against the Germans.[16]

The effect of the war for control of American public opinion through propaganda was to cause everything German in the United States to be "regarded as part of an organized propaganda of the German government to make the United States an appendage of the Kaiser's empire. Hyphen hunting became a popular pastime among American superpatriots . . . "[17] The daily excitement of the war news from Europe tended to polarize the American population between friends of the Central Powers, particularly friends of Germany, and people who were of British heritage. The dispute over the causes of war and the righteousness of each side was waged at every intellectual and social level.

The issue grew to be one of loyalty. The pressure on the German community and German-speaking people became immense. Some defended the German culture, others became extreme German nationalists, and still others became superpatriots.[18]

It was widely thought that in this struggle for the mind of America, the president and those around him were committed to the Allied cause by virtue of their ethnic backgrounds. A strong belief existed that President Wilson, even though he at first sought to keep the United States neutral, had been converted to the idea of intervention by the spring of 1916.[19] Supporters of the Allies had started a successful "preparedness" movement which was designed to prepare Americans to enter the war on the side of the Allies. Literature and motion pictures were used to stir up opposition against Germany. President Wilson joined this movement in January 1916 with a series of speeches.[20] Thus the psychological groundwork for war hysteria was laid by the time war was actually declared. Even before the declaration of war the animus toward things German had become so great that any opposition to joining the conflict, including that of non-Germans, brought about bitter condemnation. Hence Theodore Roosevelt could suggest that Senator Robert M. LaFollette, Sr., not of German extraction but an opponent of the war, was a "Hun within our gates."[21]

The unrestricted German submarine warfare aimed at American shipping, and its resultant success, precipitated President Wilson into calling for a declaration of war on April 2, 1917. The Congress voted its support on April 4. At this stage the notion of "loyalty" took hold of the public mind and continued to run rampant not only throughout the war but afterwards, expressing itself first against German Americans and people with a German cultural background, and then against all kinds of people.

The "loyalty" forces included a large number of organizations, among which were the American Defense Society, the National Security League, the Liberty League and the All-Allied Anti-German League. Most ubiquitous of all was the American Protective League that was sponsored by the Department of Justice and which caused as much mischief as any. This last group had a membership in 1918 of 250,000; its major function was to report the names of disloyal people.[22] The forces pressing for war included jingoists like Theodore Roosevelt, nationalists, and those who found it necessary to cover the war loans made to the Allies.[23]

A brief look at situations exemplifying the impact of loyalty movements around the country is useful here since it gives a more vivid picture of the hysteria of the times. A captain in the U.S. Army, D. A. Henkes, whose father had been born in Germany, tried to resign his commission. He was court-martialed, convicted, and sentenced to twenty-five years in Leavenworth.[24] A minister in North Dakota who preached against the war and refused to buy Liberty Bonds was sentenced to three years in prison, although later his case was reversed.[25] Theodore Roosevelt and the councils of defense backed the abolition of German from the schools. It was described as a "barbarous tongue." The language was forbidden in Montana schools, and in Iowa it was forbidden for public use.[26]

In Milwaukee, at the time a city with a majority population of German extraction, the Wisconsin Loyalty Legion held a meeting on March 22, 1918, to urge a boycott of the German press. The organization also opposed the teaching of German, engaged in coercing individuals to purchase Liberty Bonds, and perpetrated annoyances such as threatening the patrons of German drama. The *Milwaukee Journal* waged and won a campaign to remove compulsory foreign language teaching from the schools. Thus there was no German taught in the elementary schools after 1918.[27]

Book burnings took place in Montana and Oklahoma, and German books were thrown into a ditch in Indiana. A person considered pro-German had his barn and grain elevator painted yellow and later was beaten. A person of German birth was thrown into a bin of dough where he nearly suffocated. In Illinois a physician with a German name was dunked in a canal and forced to kiss the flag. Other people were lashed, tarred and feathered.[28] A professor in Ashland, Wisconsin, was kidnapped, tarred and feathered.[29] Beatings were common. In Wisconsin, the press reported that mobs were riding roughshod over the law to punish alleged disloyalty.[30] The *Milwaukee Leader*, a daily publication edited by Victor L. Berger, an Austrian by birth and a socialist and opponent of the war by conviction, lost its mailing privileges. Its officers were not permitted to receive business letters or other selected newspapers in the mails.[31] Demands for demonstrated loyalty were not limited to German Americans. Because of his opposition to the war, Senator LaFollette of Wisconsin was the subject of censorious resolutions from the Wisconsin Council of Defense.[32]

In the wake of this vilification and hostility, some German Americans sought forms of protection. In Milwaukee, it was reported that 250 people Americanized their names in the first four months of the war. The Deutscher Club became The Wisconsin Club, the Germania Bank became the Commercial Bank, and the Germania Building became the Brumder Building. Germans generally tried to Anglicize their culture.[33] As an example of newspaper editorial conduct generally, the *Milwaukee Journal* strongly supported the attack on German culture in Milwaukee, a stand for which it was awarded a Pulitzer medal.[34]

The great pressure on persons with a German cultural background effectively silenced them and obtained the support of a good many of them for the war effort. Many thousands of German Americans served in the armed forces. Nevertheless, the 32nd or "Red Arrow" Division, composed of National Guard troops from Wisconsin and Michigan, was suspect because of the large number of men of German extraction in the ranks.

The terrifying demand for loyalty was not pressed solely against Americans of German extraction. It was exercised against anyone who opposed the war, though German Americans were automatically assumed to be disloyal. It was also exercised against anyone who was not sympathetic with the war or who urged neutrality. These included Puerto Ricans, Mexicans, Russians, Austrians and Scandinavians, as well as many native-born persons.[35] Although Irish leaders were opposed to the war, the record does not show clearly that they were subjected to much of the same mob hysteria that other ethnic groups experienced, or why they escaped the pressure.

Perhaps not surprisingly, the record of that period discloses that the work of educators was an effective force in generating hysterical conduct. All over the nation some teachers busily promoted war preparedness and the cause of war when war came. Wisconsin did not escape from this type of influence. Professor James M. Elroy of the National Security, a group promoting entrance into the war on the side of the Allies, called the University of Wisconsin "a bunch of damned traitors" with "souls of Prussians." The University, however, did issue a series of pamphlets known as the University of Wisconsin War Pamphlets in support of the war.[36]

The success of pro-war propaganda, coupled with threats of violence and violence itself, was sufficient to silence almost all opponents of war once the war began. Wittke wrote of the results, "To many a German-American, it seemed as though the shining cultural monument of the Forty-Eighters had been destroyed forever."[37] After the war, it still seemed necessary to Americans of German extraction to write of the patriotism of German Americans and to point out the existence of American war heroes of German extraction, including General John Pershing and combat fliers Joseph Wehner, Frank Luke and Edward V. Rickenbacker.[38]

As the war dragged on and the voices of persons of German extraction speaking against the war either were muted or raised in support of the war, the public hysteria found new objects of their hatred and derision, among whom were pacifists, socialists and members of the International Workers of the World. This chapter will not touch on their experiences except to say that a particular fury lashed out at those socialists who also had a German cultural background. Socialists were not against the war primarily because they descended from any particular ethnic stock, but because they conceived the war to have come from the "commercial and financial rivalry and the intrigues of the capitalist interests in the different countries." They conceived the war to be directed against the German people and conducted in the interests of the ruling classes who gained in wealth and power.[39]

The Milwaukee socialist editor, Victor L. Berger, came under indictment for editorials written in his paper which were alleged to be in violation of the Espionage Act of June 1917. The act forbade interference with the draft and attempts to encourage disloyalty. Berger was indicted on February 2, 1918, and not brought to trial until late that year. In the meantime he was elected to the Congress. He was found guilty with four other socialists in February 1919 and sentenced to twenty years in prison. On November 10, 1919, the House of Representatives refused to seat him. The matter again went to the electorate of his district in December 1920, and Berger was again elected. In January 1920 he was again refused his seat. He was reelected in November 1922 and this time the House allowed him to take his seat. The hysteria had somewhat abated toward Germans and socialists by that time.[40]

Although the hostility lessened toward German Americans after the war, and was not as virulent toward socialists, it began with renewed force on a new target as a result of the Bolshevik Revolution of October 1917. Here was an unknown, more lasting and sinister political specter for anyone who felt a need to identify and attack the ideological enemies of the nation. About the mind of the American people at the time, one writer has expressed this judgment:

> In spite of the nation's desire for a rapid return to peace, it was obvious the American public of 1919 was still thinking with the mind of a people at war. Many prosecutions, already begun on the basis of the acts mentioned above (Espionage and Sedition Acts), were just coming before the courts and served to remind the nation of the existence of disloyalty. Returning soldiers, evidencing intense love of country, added to the excitement by howling for the immediate and summary punishment of all such nonconformity. To the 1919 public the German was still a barbarian capable of committing any atrocity, while those who had sympathized with him or who had even slightly opposed the war were equally depraved. Indeed, anyone who spoke with an accent or carried a foreign name, German or otherwise, remained particularly suspect as American superpatriots continued to see spies lurking behind every bush and tree. Still in existence were the National Security League, the American Defense Society, and other such patriotic organizations which in order to live now

sought to create new menaces. In short, insofar as the 1919 social mood was concerned the nation was still at war.[41]

There followed the era of the raids of Attorney General A. Mitchell Palmer, and the beginning of a long series of events in which aliens and citizens of such ethnic extraction as might make one presume they were friendly to the Bolshevik Revolution were under legal and illegal attack from patriotic groups. The important stance of anti-communism which is now manifested in the current version of the Cold War had begun.

It is important to note that the phenomenon of social hostility against German Americans as such did not appear again during the Hitler era or the Second World War. If Milwaukee is any case in point, enough Germans were opposed to the Hitler movement in the United States that the efforts of the Hitler government to rally German Americans to its support were relatively ineffectual. The threat of another world war, however, produced a hysteria of a new type, relatively limited, but much more ominous in its long range implications than the frenzy of patriotic loyalty which had resulted in so many types of repressive action during World War I. This time Japanese Americans were the victims. This time the United States did something it had never done before. It put American citizens into concentration camps.

The experience of the Japanese Americans during World War II has been the subject of extensive scholarly reporting and analysis. Since that experience is the subject of the following chapter in this volume, this chapter will refer to it only briefly in order to point out some common elements and major differences with earlier examples of wartime hysteria.

Among the common elements must be included the latent feeling of ethnic or racial differences on the part of native-born Americans toward an ethnic minority. In the case of the Japanese they were a very tiny minority and a very concentrated one, they were not Caucasian, and compared to people of German stock, they were not here very long.[42] In 1940 there were about 127,000 Japanese in the United States. Of these more than one-third were in Los Angeles County, and another third were concentrated in six other counties. They made up less than one-tenth of one percent of the population.[43]

The Japanese in California were subject to popular hostility almost from their first arrival, a hostility which was part of a general hostility toward Asians. Morton Grodzins, in his work *Americans Betrayed*, has cited numerous causes and sources of hostility to the Japanese. These included agricultural and business competition; racism; fear that the Japanese would outbreed Caucasians; and animosity from American labor organizations.[44]

The existence of powerful political pressure groups against the Japanese Americans influenced the politics of state and local governments which were later translated into national policy.[45] In addition, there was the long-range, evil effect of the idea of the "yellow peril" that was promulgated by, among others, publisher William Randolph Hearst. This was the idea that a conquering people would come out of Asia and overrun the West Coast.[46] The suspicion that Japan constituted this threat was reinforced by its defeat of China off the Yalu River in 1894 and of Russia in 1904-1905. The impetus to the detention in camps of American-born Japanese, the Nisei, and their immigrant parents, the Issei, however, was the attack on Pearl Harbor on December 7, 1941, and the later allegation by Secretary of the Navy Frank Knox that the devastating losses were the result of "effective fifth column work in Hawaii." These two events were sufficient to stir up the deep-seated racial hostility toward Japanese Americans which culminated in a drive to remove them from their residences in California and place them in concentration camps well inland. Unlike the German and Italian Americans at that time, all Japanese Americans were held to be disloyal.[47]

A combination of junior military officers and local politicians and racists in California had sufficient political strength to procure from President Franklin D. Roosevelt his Executive Order 9066, dated February 19, 1942. Under this order the secretary of war was authorized to establish military areas in the United States from which any or all persons could be excluded. On February 20, 1942, the secretary authorized the commander of the Western Defense District to carry out an evacuation, and by March 2, 1942, Lieutenant General John L. De Witt began ordering Japanese Americans, including citizens, to be evacuated to concentration areas.

⹗Like the German Americans in the First World War, the Japanese Americans experienced violence, beatings and death. They suffered through great physical and emotional harassment. They endured loss of property and status, and the indignities of camp life. They were traumatized by the experience and by the tensions that developed among themselves over how to respond to the events. Even after the camps were finally closed, they encountered hostility as they sought to return to their former residences and home areas.[48]

The elements of experience common to German and Japanese Americans included a long-time animus and cultural clash, language differences, violence exercised against individuals, suppression of cultural attributes, and a slowly dying hostility after the war.⹗The big difference was that German Americans were too numerous to put into concentration camps at the time of World War I. Also, German Americans were not seen as people generally successful in business who were getting all the land, nor as people who were outbreeding others in the United States.

The wartime hysteria evidenced against the German Americans in the First World War and the Japanese Americans in the Second are but specific examples of a social phenomenon that occurs not only with ethnics as targets, but against all kinds of people on all kinds of issues in the United States. It is not unreasonable, therefore, to expect that hysterical outbreaks will occur again against others. One has only to note how the hysteria originally directed against German Americans in the World War I shifted subtly to a hysteria against socialists. It reached its peak in the jailing of Eugene V. Debs, the most prominent socialist leader of the time, for opposing the war. Subsequently, it diverted its attack toward immigrants from Russia who were suspected of being sympathetic to the Bolshevik Revolution and continued to vent its fury against members of the International Workers of the World.

Similarly, the hysteria against the Japanese Americans did not die quickly after the war. The treatment of Japanese Americans led to something far worse than that which resulted from the German-American experience. The Japanese-American experience led to the "Emergency Detention Act of 1950," which allowed the detention of persons about whom there were "reasonable grounds to believe that they will commit or conspire to commit espionage or sabotage."[49] A precedent has been established for future concentration camps for those American citizens who dare dissent from the policies of a headstrong national authority.

Conditions leading to the appearance of the social hysteria which engendered persecution and the use of concentration camps against ethnics, aliens and dissenters are again present. The elements of racism, economic competition, nationalism and superpatriotism, fear of challenge to culture, fear of a native stock being outbred by a minority, fear of a military defeat and, above all, fear of a challenge to one's way of life by an alien and hostile philosophy, all exist in the United States today. Coupled with frustration over a seeming lack of progress in the solution of domestic and foreign difficulties, these conditions can easily produce a new wave of hysterical reactions against individuals or groups.

During the hostage crisis there were incidents in the United States approximating hysterical reaction against Iranian students. The stalling by the government of Iran in releasing the hostages after interminable negotiations and shifts in Iranian demands produced a sense of frustration and helplessness within the American populace.[50] The election of Ronald Reagan as president has been attributed to the feeling of

American impotence in world politics, and the incumbent president and senators had to bear the brunt of the public reaction.

Among the current political conditions which might have ethnic ramifications in case of a war are those prevailing in Central and South American affairs. It is conceivable that a state of war could lead to persecution of or reaction against some or all persons in the United States who have family origins in Central and South America.[51] Hysteria which is latent in domestic racial politics could again openly be expressed in conflicts between whites and blacks as a result of record-breaking unemployment and economic pressures. Specific incidents of racial hatred as evidenced by the Liberty City riots in Miami are exemplary of what lies beneath the surface of the body politic. It is anyone's guess how these racial groups would react toward each other in the case of a major war with a foreign power. If there were to be a war between a small country like a Caribbean nation and the United States, it is possible that dissidents of several racial and ethnic groups might oppose such an action, and any resulting governmental backlash might then be considered an action of ethnic prejudice. Shades of this occurrence could be perceived in the invasion of Grenada.

A most ominous condition affecting the future is the long-time animus that has existed between the Soviet Union and the United States. It is a distrust based on opposing ideologies, different cultures and, to a certain extent, varying perceptions of ethnicity. This hostility has prepared the basis for hysterical public reactions in the event of the threat of war. Such reactions might result in new concentration camps to be populated with any groups or individuals thought to be friendly to the Soviet Union. Yet, in spite of the actions of the past, the prospect that this animus might manifest itself against ethnic groups does not seem at the time to be probable.[52]

There may be a residual hostility left among German Americans, Japanese Americans and their sympathizers for some of the degradation they or their ancestors experienced in the course of United States history.[53] In the case of the German Americans, however, the advent and actions of the Nazi movement in Germany seemed to have given credence to the earlier fear that if Germany had won the Second World War, it would have sought to conquer the world. Further, their racial practices were such as to support the idea that the Allied propaganda of 1917-1918 was not propaganda as much as a correct appraisal of the German state's motivation.

Some circumstances continue to convince German Americans that there remain problems with their acceptance in American life. One such circumstance is the frequent portrayal of Nazis as the villains in television drama, and another is the adoption of some of the Nazi trappings by native-born white racists. Also, like many others, German Americans have not come to a conclusive understanding of how people of their ethnic stock could have caused the Holocaust.

Currently there are problems for the American labor movement because United States corporate enterprises are unable to compete with Japanese corporations in some fields. Jobless Americans are bitter over Japanese success, but it does not seem likely that American corporate and labor unhappiness with the Japanese will adversely affect Japanese Americans, especially since the war sacrifices of Japanese-American military units are celebrated in literature. Nevertheless, one cannot be sure given labor's earlier attitudes toward Asian Americans. The recent killing of a young man in Detroit mistakenly believed to be Japanese American, although a single incident, cannot be ignored.

There are warning signs to predict the rise of social hysteria against almost any ethnic group if the evidence of United States history can be said to offer clues for the future. The endangered group must be a minority of the population, its culture must be considered threatening to the culture of the majority, and the minority group must be thought capable of outbreeding the majority. There also must be a threat of war or an existing war which gives rise to the thought that the ethnic group, by virtue of its blood or cultural ties, is predisposed to being disloyal.

Can future wartime hysteria against ethnics and aliens be averted and reduced? The answer could be affirmative if certain conditions obtain. Voluntary groups and governments must work to abate cultural and ethnic hostility existing in peacetime in an effort to bring about cultural understanding. Admittedly this is difficult since it has been shown that political leaders both in the case of the German- and Japanese-American experiences found it to their advantage to set groups against each other. It is also necessary for the judicial process not to lose its sense of justice, and for the local police and sheriffs not to lose control in their jurisdictions nor of themselves. It is also essential for individuals not of the same ethnic stock as those suffering pressure to organize and assist them in preventing and in obtaining relief from injustice. Likewise, it is vital that an overzealous bureaucracy be checked to prevent the information system from transmitting propagandistic falsehoods. Finally, the role of political leaders such as presidents and governors is crucial. Their excesses can be checked best by an opposing major political party, but if that opposition is not present, then minor parties must act as the conscience of the nation.

NOTES

[1] *Webster's Third New International Dictionary of the English Language* (Springfield, Mass.: G. & C. Merriam Co., 1976).

[2] There were pressures on aliens in the United States during the Korean War and during the Vietnam War. Also, there were attempts at control of Germans and Italians suspected of disloyalty during World War II. These situations, however, were caused by the deliberate actions of the government and did not occur as the result of widespread public sentiment. One deliberate policy at the time of World War II was preventing the immigration of Jews to the United States despite the official awareness of the persecution Jews endured. Indeed, if the extent of their persecution and that of others had been common knowledge, there might well have been a great public outcry resulting in a hysterical drive for vengeance.

[3] Carl Wittke, *The Germans in America* (New York: New York Teachers College Press, 1967), p. 23.

[4] H. C. Peterson and Gilbert Fite, *Opponents of War, 1917-1918* (Madison, Wis.: University of Wisconsin Press, 1973), p. 202.

[5] Bayrd Still, *Milwaukee, The History of a City* (Madison, Wis.: The State Historical Society of Wisconsin, 1948), p. 128. See also James Buck, *Milwaukee Under the Charter*, Vol. IV (Milwaukee: Swain & Tate, Printers, 1886), p. 49. Buck tells of a letter written by a group of leading Germans demanding to know of the Democratic and Republican (Whig) nominees for State Assembly where they stood on the Know-Nothings and Catholics. Buck implies that this was a trick used by Democratic candidate James B. Cross to discredit the Republican candidate, William A. Prentiss, as a Know-Nothing. Prentiss, while asserting that he neither had been a Know-Nothing nor anti-Catholic, told the writers to take their votes elsewhere. The episode did not make for good feelings for Germans.

[6] Richard Hofstadter, William Miller and Daniel Aaron, *The United States, History of a Republic*, 2nd Ed. (Englewood Cliffs, N.J.: Prentice Hall, 1967), p. 397.

[7] Fred L. Holmes, *Wisconsin: Stability, Progress, Beauty* (Chicago: Lewis Publishing, 1946), p. 340.

[8] Kathleen Neils Conzen, *Immigrant Milwaukee, 1836-1860* (Cambridge, Mass.: Harvard University Press, 1976), p. 226.

[9] H. C. Peterson, *Propaganda for War: The Campaign Against American Neutrality, 1914-1917* (Norman, Okla.: University of Oklahoma Press, 1939), pp. 33-34.

[10] Ibid.

[11] Ibid., pp. 35-36.

[12] Ibid., p. 313.

[13] Hofstadter, et. al., op. cit., p. 672.

[14] See Peterson, op. cit. Also, see Charles Hunter Hamlin, *Propaganda and Myth in the Time of War. Comprising: The War Myth in United States History and Educators Present Arms* (New York: Garland Publishing, 1973), p. 88.

[15]Peterson, op. cit., pp. 53-60.

[16]Ibid., pp. 148-150.

[17]Carl Wittke, *We Who Built America* (Cleveland: The Press of Western Reserve University, 1939), p. 259.

[18]See Phyllis Keller, *States of Belonging: German-American Intellectuals and the First World War* (Cambridge, Mass.: Harvard University Press, 1979). The lives of Hugo Muensterberg, George Sylvester Viereck and Herman Hagedorn, and their responses to World War I, are examined. The work relies heavily on what the author perceives to have been the psychic needs of her subjects, but the work also contains many references to the ideological conflicts among British, German and German-American opinion formers.

[19]Hamlin, op. cit., p. 88.

[20]Peterson, op. cit., p. 203.

[21]Ibid., p. 316.

[22]Peterson and Fite, op. cit., p. 19.

[23]See Peterson and Fite, op. cit., pp. 17-18, for a discussion of the motivation of people in the loyalty movement.

[24]Ibid., p. 83.

[25]Ibid., p. 85.

[26]Ibid., pp. 195-196.

[27]Still, op. cit., pp. 460-462.

[28]Peterson and Fite, op. cit., pp. 196-199.

[29]Ibid., p. 105.

[30]Ibid., p. 199.

[31]Ibid., pp. 47-48.

[32]Ibid., p. 70.

[33]Still, op. cit., p. 461.

[34]Ibid., p. 457.

[35]See Peterson and Fite, op. cit., Chapter VIII, pp. 881 et. seq.

[36]Hamlin, op. cit. Hamlin gives an extensive account of how war hysteria in the schools and colleges led to a great hatred of all things German.

[37]Wittke, *We Who Built America*, op. cit., p. 260.

[38]Joseph Wandel, *The German Dimension of American History* (Chicago: Nelson-Hall, 1979), pp. 188-189.

[39]Peterson and Fite, op. cit., p. 8. The quotation is from the April 7, 1917, platform of the Socialist Party of the United States.

[40]Ibid., pp. 165-166. John M. Work, American-born editor of the *Milwaukee Leader*, told this writer that Berger was indicted for editorials which he, Work, wrote. Work was never charged with anything.

[41]Robert K. Murray, *Red Scarce: A Study in National Hysteria, 1919-1920* (Minneapolis: University of Minnesota Press, 1955). pp. 14-15.

[42]See Richard B. Morris, ed., *Encyclopedia of American History* (New York: Harper & Brother, 1953). According to this source, about twenty-six thousand Japanese entered the United States between 1891 and 1900. Another 130,000 had entered by 1910, and by the time of the exclusion laws, about 300,000 had arrived.

[43]Roger Daniels, *Concentration Camp, U.S.A.* (New York: Holt, Rinehart and Winston, 1972), pp. 1-5.

[44]Morton Grodzins, *Americans Betrayed—Politics and the Japanese Evacuation* (Chicago: University of Chicago Press, 1949), Chapter 2, "The Activity of Pressure Groups."

[45]Ibid. See Chapter 3, "Pacific Coast Congressional Delegations," and Chapter 4, "State and Local Political Leaders."

[46]Daniels, op. cit., pp. 29-31.

[47]Michi Weglyn, *Years of Infamy: The Untold Story of America's Concentration Camps* (New York: William Morrow & Co., 1976), p. 68.

[48]Camp experiences are described in detail in Dillon Myers, *Uprooted Americans: The Japanese Americans and the War Relocation Authority During World War II* (Tucson, Ariz.: University of Arizona Press, 1971), as well as in Daniels, op. cit., and Weglyn, op. cit.

[49]See the comments in Daniels, op. cit., p. 143.

[50]"Iranians Wear Out Their U. S. Welcome," *U.S. News and World Report* (November 19, 1979); "Turnabout Is Foul Play," *Newsweek* (August 18, 1980); "We're Going to Kick Your Butts," *Time* (November 18, 1979).

[51]"For Cubans: Hospitality and Hostility," *U. S. News and World Report* (May 19, 1980).

[52]The Soviet Union in World War II uprooted Volga Germans in the fear that they would be disloyal.

[53]The author recently received a mimeographed newsletter, "The Christian Way" (January-March 1982), in which the editor, an Ohioan who had neither a German nor a Japanese name, speaking of the events at Pearl Harbor, charged that, "To promote war and resulting prosperity, Roosevelt had to promote hatred of the German and Japanese people." Old animuses die slowly.

A RECONSIDERATION OF THE UNITED STATES MILITARY'S ROLE IN THE VIOLATION OF JAPANESE-AMERICAN CITIZENSHIP RIGHTS[1]

Lane Ryo Hirabayashi

Asian American Studies Department
San Francisco State University

James A. Hirabayashi

Anthropology Department
San Francisco State University

Introduction[2]

On February 19, 1942, two months after the outbreak of war between the United States and Japan, President Franklin D. Roosevelt signed Executive Order 9066. As a result, over 120,000 people of Japanese ancestry were evacuated from their homes and imprisoned in camps in the interior of the United States. Intrinsically and historically significant, this case has resulted in research and debate over a wide range of policy issues since seventy thousand of those affected were United States citizens.[3] Still further discussion and analysis are necessary in order to draw out the implications of this historical incident for understanding the experiences of racial/ethnic minorities in America.[4]

Authors of previous studies about the incarceration of Japanese Americans during the Second World War have diligently searched for the true perpetrator(s) of this event. One frequent explanation is to blame the United States military for conceiving, advocating and implementing the evacuation decision. This chapter will consider this hypothesis in some detail, outline the evolution of the decision, and evaluate different explanations of the policy. It will also formulate an alternative interpretation, and present some general ideas about the conditions and processes which can lead to military control over civilians in a democracy.

Critical Review of the Literature

In the many books and articles written about the wartime evacuation and imprisonment, there have been numerous attempts to identify the particular causes of the violation of Japanese-American citizenship rights. It is impossible to assess all of this material here. We shall, however, review some of the key explanations which have been advanced.

While most authors mention the role of the American military, at least four authors specifically blame military officials. McWilliams's early study is quite direct: "It was General DeWitt who made the decision in favor of mass evacuation, and who, along with the West Coast Congressional delegation, had recommended it."[5] It can be emphasized that "military necessity" was the first official explanation for the evacuation.[6] In retrospect, the rationale of military necessity was motivated by a deep fear of sabotage and espionage by Japanese Americans on the mainland. Underlying this rationale was the assumption that Japanese in the United States, whether citizens or not, were ultimately loyal to the Japanese government. On both levels the disloyalty of the Japanese Americans was assumed; guilt was a matter of race. Unlike those of Italian and German ancestry in the United States, no allowances were made for possible individual differences of loyalty among Japanese Americans. Since many scholars, including McWilliams, have competently discredited the rationale of military necessity, this theme will not be considered further.[7]

Historians Conn and Daniels also focus on the military, but their access to military records, including the transcripts of meetings and even telephone conversations between the key actors, gives their analysis a depth and substance not found in previous accounts. The research of both these scholars demonstrates the influence of the Provost Marshall General's office in formulating and advocating the evacuation decision. Both Conn and Daniels, though, place the ultimate blame upon Roosevelt as the commander-in-chief. In their view it was Roosevelt who gave final approval and signed E. O. 9066, thereby authorizing questionable policy actions against United States citizens.[8]

Weglyn is yet another author who focuses on the military. Her analysis differs in that she is able to show that the American government had no less than a hemispheric strategy for the evacuation and detention of Japanese in the United States, in Latin America, and even in Europe.[9] Weglyn argues that overseas Japanese were to be held primarily as "barter" and "reprisal" reserves in case the United States needed to trade "prisoners of war" or wanted to insure the humane treatment of American soldiers who were held as prisoners. Weglyn also cites declassified documents which conclusively prove that United States officials were contemplating the arrest and confinement of overseas Japanese in concentration camps, even before the attack on Pearl Harbor.[10] In this regard, Weglyn's findings are novel and suggestive.

What are we to make of these theories of military responsibility? There is no doubt that the military was heavily involved in the decision to evacuate and intern the Japanese Americans. Certainly, a share of the blame rests on the key military actors: General John L. DeWitt, General Allen W. Gullion and Major Karl R. Bendetsen of the Provost Marshall General's office; and President Roosevelt as the commander-in-chief. It is now clear, though, that there were a number of policy alternatives being argued within the military, at different times and at different levels in the chain of command.

At this point it is helpful to go back and review the events that led up to the evacuation decision.

The Development of the Decision to Evacuate the Japanese Americans.[11]

Apart from a long history of "anti-Oriental" prejudice and discrimination, it is clear that the groundwork for the evacuation of the Japanese Americans was laid *before* the United States entered World War II.[12] A number of studies based on declassified documents reveal that United States intelligence paid considerable attention to the Japanese immigrants and their activities in the pre-war years.[13]

In June 1941, the Alien Registration Act was passed. The following month the Justice Department was assigned control over enemy aliens, predominantly German, Italian and Japanese immigrants. Within the Justice Department, the Federal Bureau of Investigation was specifically charged with this task. As part of its duties, the FBI began to compile lists of suspect aliens in conjunction with officials in the military and naval intelligence. We now know that as early as August 1941, Army Intelligence had asked the judge advocate general if it would be possible to arrest and detain civilians who were also American citizens if the need arose.[14] On the other hand, a full month before the outbreak of war, both President Roosevelt and Secretary of War Henry Stimson received reports by a special representative of the State Department, Curtis B. Munson. Munson testified to "a remarkable, even extraordinary, degree of loyalty" among the Japanese Americans. Immediately after the attack on Pearl Harbor, suspect aliens were arrested and detained. Roosevelt issued presidential proclamations focusing on the control of German, Italian and Japanese aliens. The proclamations were gradually enforced by the Justice Department over the next two months.

Meanwhile, on December 10, the Ninth Corps Area staff formulated a plan for the immediate evacuation of the Japanese on the West Coast to the interior of the country. Although this plan, which came from the headquarters of the Western Defense Command of General John L. DeWitt, was not implemented, it was forwarded to the office of Provost Marshall General Gullion. On December 19, the newly formed Western Theater of Operations, under the leadership of General DeWitt, formally advocated the internment of all enemy aliens. Echoing DeWitt's recommendations, Provost Marshall General Gullion suggested only two days later that control over enemy aliens be given to the War Department. By December 26, a week later, DeWitt had modified his position. Now he believed that the FBI and the Justice Department could handle the alien situation and went on record to this effect. Evidence shows that at the end of December neither the chief of staff, General George C. Marshall, nor General DeWitt believed that there was an immediate danger of invasion.[16] DeWitt, however, continually pressured the Justice Department to allow more control over aliens.

In early January 1942, two important developments took place. One was that representatives from the Justice Department and the Provost Marshall General's office were sent to work with DeWitt in San Francisco. Gullion also arranged for DeWitt to communicate directly with his office, avoiding the standard link through general headquarters. Second, Major Bendetsen, who acted as chief of the aliens division for the Provost Marshall's office and as a representative for the War Department, made two significant recommendations to DeWitt: (1) that a new registration of aliens be undertaken; and (2) that a pass system be developed for aliens. Not many days before, Bendetsen had also recommended that the War Department would be the most effective supervisor of alien affairs.[17] Only two days later, the West Coast military and naval commanders submitted their recommendation that the Japanese Americans be evacuated. By mid-January, public and private sentiment in favor of evacuation was also escalating.[18]

Claiming that a raid on the mainland would be accompanied by sabotage, DeWitt made an initial recommendation for the exclusion of all aliens from the state of California. Exclusion, in DeWitt's formulation, involved creating two types of zones: category "A" zones which were off limits to aliens; and category "B" zones which were to be limited to those with passes. Despite the fact that no concrete evidence confirmed DeWitt's claim of military necessity, Secretary of War Stimson accepted DeWitt's proposals.[19] At the end of January, Stimson passed the recommendations along to Attorney General Francis Biddle, asking that the plans for restricted zones be implemented.

On January 25, 1942, the Roberts Report, which was the study on the attack at Pearl Harbor compiled by the U. S. Senate, was issued. The report claimed (erroneously) that there was evidence of Japanese sabotage on the islands, both before and after the attack. A few days later DeWitt met separately with California governor Culbert L. Olson and California attorney general Earl Warren. Both believed that Japanese Americans should be removed from the state. By the end of January, DeWitt began to waver. He now stated that evacuation was the only sure answer to the threat of Japanese-American sabotage.

On January 30, there was an informal meeting of the California congressional delegation. Here, legislative pressure in support of evacuation began to take shape. Major Bendetsen was present and suggested that, if the Justice Department could not handle matters, the War Department could and would take over the supervision of aliens if given the proper authority. The delegation's recommendations—favoring military control over aliens and the evacuation of Japanese Americans from the coast—were signed and sent to the secretary of war.

Until February 1942, the civilian heads of the War Department, Stimson and Assistant Secretary John J. McCloy, favored a policy of barring aliens from a limited number of restricted areas. When they learned, then, of DeWitt's supposed support of a mass evacuation policy, McCloy phoned DeWitt and explicitly told him not to take a position on this matter. DeWitt denied he had made any commitment to an evacuation plan, although verbally, in fact, he had.[20] The Provost Marshall General's office was already formulating an evacuation strategy, acting perhaps on the assumption that key officials like DeWitt were in agreement. DeWitt chose to back down.

During the beginning of February 1942, the policy position of the Justice Department became explicit. DeWitt, the Provost Marshall General's office and the War Department put increasing pressure on the Justice Department to further restrict the Japanese. The Justice Department, however, grew increasingly concerned because it did not have the manpower to oversee a mass evacuation. Attorney General Biddle was also adamant that the Justice Department would not interfere with the rights of American citizens, even if they were of Japanese descent. In effect, Biddle had decided that if larger numbers of aliens or American citizens became subject to mass evacuation, the Justice Department would have to bow out.

In reaction, Bendetsen issued a memo on behalf of the Provost Marshall General's office which was essentially a plan for mass evacuation, including exclusion, evacuation and resettlement. A summary of this memo was presented by Gullion to both DeWitt and McCloy. During the second week of February, Stimson and McCloy began to support fully the idea and necessity of mass evacuation.[21]

By February 11, there was sufficient agreement between the Provost Marshall General's office and the War Department (i.e., Stimson and McCloy) to go directly to the president. In response to a memo from the War Department requesting instructions on how to deal with the Japanese question, Roosevelt gave the military his permission to do what they thought was necessary. Thus Roosevelt agreed: (1) that it was necessary and legal to evacuate the Japanese Americans—citizens and non-citizens alike; and (2) that he would issue an executive order (which was to be Executive Order 9066) giving the War Department direct power over citizens and civilians.

Through the entire debate and decision-making process there was one key argument justifying the removal of aliens—the rationale of "military necessity." In this formulation, it was assumed that *all* persons of Japanese descent were suspect (if not guilty), and no allowances were to be made for individual variations. This last point is especially glaring when one considers the case of the Japanese in Hawaii. In a setting of actual combat, martial law was quickly established on the islands. The commander of Hawaii, General Delos C. Emmons, considered and argued successfully against a policy of mass evacuation.[22] Resorting only to limited restrictions, military security was insured and more extreme policy alternatives were avoided.

Even after President Roosevelt had signed Executive Order 9066, there was still debate over what actual procedure should be implemented. This debate reflects that, even at this stage, not all the parties agreed on the scope of the evacuation. For example, although the General Staff argued that a full scale evacuation was neither necessary nor practical, when a program of "voluntary migration" seemed to be failing, Gullion and Bendetsen pushed for total evacuation. McCloy and Stimson finally went along with this plan.[23] In the end, under the authority of the United States government, McCloy took firm control over the implementation of E.O. 9066 (although the program he put into effect was basically that of Bendetsen).

On March 2, 1942, General DeWitt issued the order for the evacuation of all persons of Japanese descent from all security areas. Thus, under the rationale of military necessity, almost 80 percent of the Japanese Americans living in the United States were evacuated and incarcerated.[24]

The evacuation proceeded in two stages. First, Japanese Americans living within security areas were removed by the Army to temporary assembly centers. This stage was completed by late March of 1942. A second stage involved removal to more permanent concentration camps and was completed by November 3, 1942.[25] There were ten concentration camps in all, each surrounded by barbed wire and manned by armed soldiers.[26] Most camps were located in desolate areas in the interior of the United States. The conditions of these makeshift institutions were inadequate and often harmful to the inhabitants, contrary to the claims of spokepersons for the government and the planners and administrators involved.[27]

In summary, then, an examination of the events and statements prior to the signing of E.O. 9066 indicates that several policy positions were articulated: DeWitt, the "man on the ground," vacillated, but for the most part he favored the evacuation of *all* enemy aliens from the West Coast; Gullion and his staff at the Provost Marshall General's office were solidly and consistently in favor of the total evacuation and internment of Japanese Americans; Stimson and, for a while, McCloy, as the civilian chiefs of the armed forces, were in favor of limited removal of aliens from vital and sensitive areas; and the General Staff, made up of professional soldiers, was against the idea of a mass evacuation of Japanese Americans, and even considered opposing this policy alternative.[28]

As we have seen, Gullion and his staff prevailed. Enlisting the support of DeWitt and then McCloy, the plan which had been outlined by Bendetsen was taken directly to the president himself. Once approval was obtained, the Provost Marshall General and his allies used the presidential sanction to overwhelm any opposition.[29] Thus, it would be misleading to suggest that there was one unified military position on the "Japanese question." Our contention that there were several positions, with one ascendant, is supported by the atmosphere of ambiguity found at all stages of the decisionmaking and even the implementation process.

Other Theories

Beyond these initial points, what insights can we gain from other theories of responsibility?

While most authors mention the role of the United States military, some go on to specify other key "actors." One type of explanation focuses on the influence of pressure groups, including civic, patriotic, special interest and political associations. Two early studies of the legal bases for the evacuation take this approach,[30] but the major analysis along these lines is presented by Grodzins.[31] Briefly, Grodzins argues that the decision to evacuate the Japanese Americans was the result of the clamoring of a wide range of pressure groups on the West Coast. Grozdins presents extensive documentation indicating that pressure groups were largely motivated by the twin interests of racism and economic greed. As Grodzins states, "The war provided the unique situation whereby patriotism (i.e., a desire to protect the West Coast from the enemy) could become parallel with economic, racial, and political considerations."[32] These pressure groups were then able to influence local and national officials, who responded by developing and implementing the evacuation decision. While the general thrust of his argument is undeniable, Grodzins' analysis leads him to believe that there was no initial military interest in mass evacuation, and that only later was interest stimulated as a result of popular outcry.[33] As we have seen, this claim cannot be maintained in light of the evidence cited.

A second type of explanation was developed by tenBroek and his colleagues, Barnhart and Matson.[34] Explicitly challenging Grodzins' explanation, they deny that pressure groups or politicians played any systematic, influential role in the decision. As an alternative they propose a complex, historical model geared to explain " . . . the responsibility for this flagrant breach of the nation's constitutional and moral ideals."[35] According to tenBroek, the people of the nation (and the West Coast in particular), the military (with General DeWitt and the Western Defense Command singled out), President Franklin D. Roosevelt and the Supreme Court of the United States must all bear the final responsibility.[36] This is a model where many agents share the blame. In documenting this thesis, tenBroek and his coauthors add important information and perspectives to the historical context of the decision.

Analysis

The studies considered so far have searched for single or multiple causes of the incarceration of the Japanese Americans. Examination of most of these studies reveals various shortcomings in conceptualization and in analysis.

Some scholars have focused on the role of certain actors, in specific sectors of the society, as being of primary importance in the transgressions against Japanese-American civil rights. Difficulties arise in considering any of these, including the military, as omnipotent or monolithic in thought or in action. When a framework of multiple causation is used as the explanatory model, additional difficulties arise in identifying and assigning rank-order importance to the many relevant variables or "actors" involved. Or, alternatively, we are presented with a chronological series of events, but are given no general understanding of how events are related to general principles or to a larger historical context. A fundamental source of the problem lies in the implicit and/or explicit use of biased models of race relations, which leads to subtle empirical and conceptual distortions. Specifically, many scholars have carried out their research and analysis within an assimilationist framework.

The assimilation model was originally developed by the sociologist Robert Park. He formulated a "race relations cycle" which postulated successive stages—including contact, competition, accommodation and assimilation—that each ethnic group undergoes in its adjustment to the dominant society.[37] This model was based primarily on an analysis of the patterns of adaptation of various European ethnic groups in America.[38] We note that an assimilation model assumes that there are no inherent barriers which will prevent the eventual attainment of full and equal participation by a minority group in the dominant society. Concomitantly, if the cycle of race relations is interrupted or blocked, then the model implies that a search must be made for the cause of obstruction.

As a result, there is a marked tendency to view the evacuation as an anomaly which interrupted the progress of Japanese Americans through the race relations cycle. Thus researchers focused their attention on finding the key "author" of the evacuation decision, or the precise area of breakdown in the traditional structure of American government, with its intricate system of checks and balances. We shall argue that such analyses are misleading.

One final explanation which should be mentioned is Miyamoto's recent multi-causal analysis that breaks the causes down into three categories: collective dispositions, situational factors, and collective interactions.[39] Miyamoto sees all of these causes as combining to produce the evacuation decision.

Although Miyamoto's analysis is global and well-balanced, two critical points should be raised. One is that the research of Conn and Daniels indicates levels and subtleties in the War Department's participation in the formation of policy that Miyamoto's presentation omits. Second, we believe that there is a deeper, underlying dynamic that generated causes in each of the three categories Miyamoto identifies—that is, the dynamic of racism.

If we now reconsider and apply these different contributions to the question of the role of the military in the violation of Japanese-American civil rights, it is apparent that the formation of military opinion and policy at all levels cannot be seen separately from developments in other public and private sectors of the larger society.

One brief, but very important, example will suffice. General DeWitt gave erroneous information in justifying his suspicions of the occurrence of, and potential for, Japanese-American sabotage.[40] Local and national press and politicians picked up this information, expanded on it, and fed it to the public. The resulting clamor and hysteria then became a point of reference as the military and other public officials debated policy alternatives.[41]

In summary, *there was no consistent military position, and, furthermore, the contributions of the military toward the evacuation decision cannot be separated from the larger context.* Granted, DeWitt's panic, racism and lack of judgment fanned the flames of hysteria, and the Provost Marshall General and his staff very skillfully manipulated key actors and the situation toward the ends they desired. Nonetheless, as ten-Broek concludes, the nation demanded evacuation, President Roosevelt empowered the Provost Marshall General's plan, the Congress ratified it, McCloy and DeWitt implemented it, and the courts of the nation confirmed that the whole proceedings were legal. Given this concordance, the critical question is not so much what were the relative degrees of responsibility, but how a public policy—which we contend was unconstitutional and discriminatory—gained such wide and uncritical support in a country whose wartime efforts were justified on the moral principles of freedom and democracy.

An Alternative Perspective

In the preceding section we examined various explanations of the evacuation decision and evaluated their strengths and weaknesses. We have seen that explanations which blame the military have a certain validity, but underestimate the internal differences which actually existed. An examination of other types of explanations shows that it is impossible to view the military—or any other public or private sector—as the sole agent of the evacuation decision.

We propose that a racist ideology lay at the base of collective sentiment and action that resulted in the public policy of mass evacuation and incarceration.[42] By racism we mean:

> . . . a principle of social domination by which a group seen as inferior or different in alleged biological charactertistics is exploited, controlled, and oppressed socially and psychically by a superordinate group.[43]

The roots of racism in the United States go back to the founding fathers of the republic. To quote historian Ronald T. Takaki:

> The rational part of the self, Republican leaders insisted, must be in command. Identifying whites with rationality or mind, they associated peoples of color with the body. Thus mind was raised to authority over the other parts of the self, and whites were raised above blacks and Indians.[44]

It is not surprising that the white immigrants came with a colonial mentality, for they arrived during the early period of European world-wide colonial expansion. Their relationship with the Indians was characterized by what can only be called a "precursor" to the policy of manifest destiny. This allowed the colonists to appropriate freely the land from "savage" Indians. Initial formulation of colonial relations with the American Indians and blacks was then successively applied to Chinese, Japanese, Filipino, East Indians, Chicanos, Latinos and, more recently, to post-World War II Asian immigrants and refugees.[45]

Briefly examining the specific case considered here, it was as if "racism" was on the docks to greet the initial wave of Japanese immigrants as they came down the gangplanks. The Japanese inherited the legacy of anti-Chinese sentiment and behavior that had festered since the middle of the nineteenth century.[46] This was merely the beginning, however. Racism directed toward the Japanese emanated from many quarters during the first decade of the twentieth century. Politicians, scholars, labor unions and local and national political and civic organizations were all involved in agitation against the Japanese. Exclusion leagues were formed to ban Japanese immigration, Japanese children were thrown out of the San Francisco public schools in 1906, and rumors of the inevitability of war with Japan abounded.[47]

In the years that followed, a flurry of anti-Japanese bills were introduced in the legislature, restricting immigration, property ownership, and even relationships with women (in the form of anti-"miscegenation" laws and the banning of "picture-bride" marriages), and otherwise discriminating against the Japanese.[48] Anti-Japanese racism manifested itself informally and formally among individuals, groups and institutions, and became symbolized in the phrase, "yellow peril." Private and public sentiment finally culminated in the passage of the Immigration Act of 1924 which stopped Japanese migration—and, in fact, all migration from the Asian countries—entirely. This brief synopsis of the early history of race relations in the United States gives us sufficient evidence of a pervasive and underlying attitude of racism against the Japanese.[49]

Considering this background, is there evidence to support the hypothesis that racist beliefs were held by persons in public and private positions of power during World War II? TenBroek and his colleagues carried out extensive research on the general state of mind of the population on the West Coast and found:

> . . . a deeply rooted and broadly diffused attitude of suspicion and distrust towards all persons of Japanese descent, which demonstrated scant regard for distinctions of birth or citizenship,

for "minute constitutional rights," for the record of political loyalty or the facts of social assimilation.[50]

A number of authors have also commented on the role of the press.
Daniels states:

> Day after day, throughout December, January, February, and
> March, almost the entire Pacific Coast press . . . spewed forth
> racial venom against all Japanese. The term Jap, of course, was
> standard usage. Japanese, alien and native-born, were also
> "Nips," "yellow men," "Mad dogs," and "yellow vermin," to
> name only a few of the choicer epithets.[51]

TenBroek and his colleagues identify the *San Diego Union* as one of the
first major journals to call for evacuation as it did on January 20,
1942.[52] Continuing to raise questions about the loyalty of Japanese in
the United States, writers of the *Union* argued: "We are confronted on
both sides by enemies who have devoted their entire careers to development of treachery, deceit, and sabotage."[53] Not many months later
similar arguments were made by nationally-known columnists like
Westbrook Pegler and Walter Lippmann.[54]

Civic organizations, and even official political organizations, were
often militant in their anti-Japanese stance. Many of these groups, including the American Legion, the Native Sons, the Farm Bureau and
the Joint Immigration Committee, had long histories of anti-Japanese
activities. In the *Grizzly Bear*, the official journal of the Native Sons
and Daughters of the Golden West, an editorial listed the "errors"
leading up to the attack on Pearl Harbor, including: giving citizenship
to alien offspring; allowing "Japs" to colonize in strategic locations; the
lax enforcement of the Alien Land Laws; and so on.[55]

Members of agricultural associations, such as the Vegetable Association of Central California, were even more direct:

> We're charged with wanting to get rid of the Japs for selfish rea-
> sons. We might as well be honest. We do. It's a question of
> whether the white man lives on the Pacific Coast or the brown
> men. They came into this valley to work and they stayed to take
> over.[56]

Local politicians played their part. The governor of California
claimed that Japanese residents of the state had directly aided the Japanese military.[57] The mayor of Los Angeles echoed these charges and
argued that the Japanese in America were unassimilable because they
had been denied property rights and immigration rights, and because
of physical and philosophical differences. His conclusion was that
" . . . all of these contributing factors set the Japanese apart as a race,
regardless of how many generations have been born in America."[58]

In retrospect, the statements of some United States congressmen seem incredible. Some public officials, like Representative John Rankin of Mississippi, made little attempt to disguise their true sentiments. Rankin was in favor of catching:

> . . . every Japanese in America, Alaska, and Hawaii now and putting them in concentration camps and shipping them back to Asia as soon as possible . . . This is a race war, as far as the Pacific side of this conflict is concerned . . . The white man's civilization has come into conflict with Japanese barbarism . . . One of them must be destroyed.[59]

Although the Supreme Court cases testing the constitutionality of the evacuation and the internment orders are quite complex, then Supreme Court Justice Frank Murphy believed very strongly:

> [that] this forced exclusion was the result in good measure of [the] erroneous assumption of racial guilt rather than bona fide military necessity is evidenced by the Commanding General's Final Report on the evacuation from the Pacific Coast area.[60]

Murphy also commented in an earlier case in which he gave a reluctant concurring statement: "Today is the first time, so far as I am aware, that we have sustained a substantial restriction of the personal liberty of citizens of the United States based upon the accident of race or ancestry."[61]

As is well known, military officials who played an important role in policymaking made openly racist remarks. General DeWitt's view was that: "A Jap's a Jap. They are a dangerous element, whether loyal or not."[62] Colonel Karl Bendetsen's stand on who was eligible for incarceration was: "I am determined that if they have one drop of Japanese blood in them, they must go to camp."[63] Indeed, the full and even the mixed-blood children in the orphanages of Los Angeles were evacuated and sent to Manzanar.

As for President Roosevelt, the commander-in-chief, Daniels reports that there were two reasons why he agreed to sign over power to the military: " . . . in the first place, it was expedient; in the second place, Roosevelt himself harbored deeply felt anti-Japanese prejudices."[64]

As the evidence cited above shows, "The range of those attacking the Japanese was truly remarkable . . . Also as damaging to the future of the Japanese was the silence of the standard liberal organizations."[65] Furthermore, this same evidence suggests that racist beliefs became systematic and explicit during the war. Although racism can be manifest or latent, depending upon a given historical period with its particular circumstances, when it does become explicit it can dominate the consciousness of the entire society. Racism then becomes an ideology, providing "individuals and groups with a frame of reference that includes assumptions, projected ideals, and expected patterns of behavior and processes."[66]

In summary, the wartime events coalesced established beliefs and antagonism into an overt, systematic racist ideology which justified discriminatory actions against persons of Japanese descent. Although not causal *per se*, the shared racist ideology played a central role as a common ideological theme that allowed a variety of "actors" and groups to act in concert with each other.[67] Although each participant—whether individual or collective—may have been animated by a different set of motives, a common racist ideology allowed enough cooperation to result in the violation of the constitutional, civil and human rights of the over 120,000 persons of Japanese descent who were imprisoned without regard for due process of law.

This interpretation allows one to give each participant or group its due share of blame, since "actors" at both the local and the national levels were fully involved even though their motives and impact may have differed. It also helps to bring out a critical point: The decision was not an isolated event or an anomaly. It was fully consistent with beliefs and practices that date back to the founding of this country and which permeate the history of racial/ethnic minorities in the United States.[68]

It should be emphasized, however, that racism is not always overt, nor is it invariably manifested in discriminatory public policies. In the conclusion which follows, we will specify the conditions under which racism is likely to be put into practice as formal policy.

Conclusion

We have adopted a model of analysis which rests on an assumption of an ideology of racism. This model can provide a comprehensive explanation for the manifestation of behavior against racial/ethnic minorities, particularly during times of crisis. This leads to the consideration of two basic interrelated themes in our analysis. The first is an assessment of the military as the principal causal agent involved in the incarceration of the Japanese Americans. The second theme considers the issue of process, i.e., the implementation of racism into public policy.

As was mentioned earlier, studies of the incarceration of the Japanese Americans have heretofore searched for the "author(s)" of this event. One consistently used explanation is to blame the United States military for conceiving, advocating and implementing the evacuation decision. Our examination of the historical record, however, reveals that the military was hardly a unified, monolithic entity but, in fact, was internally divided on this question.

It is our thesis that the wartime violations of civil rights and civil liberties were not merely the result of actions by specific, identifiable agents. Nor did they constitute a particularistic, anomalous or isolated episode in the history of the United States. In terms of the ethnic experience discussed above, racist beliefs were historically an integral part of social relations between members of the dominant society and Japanese Americans. The outbreak of war with Japan created a situation where "war-politics"[69] and hysteria held sway. The result was that the racist, anti-Japanese prejudices soon became overt and were manifested by many in the public and private sectors of society.

In this setting a group of military and governmental officials was able to manipulate the situation to their ends. Their plans succeeded largely because a shared racist ideology unified a wide range of organizations and individuals into common cause and action. A model based on an ideology of racism results in a more comprehensive analysis compared to previous explanations which seek to fix specific blame or which see the event as an anomaly. Our analysis clearly shows that while certain military leaders played a key role, the military by itself did not "make" the evacuation decision. Ultimately, blame rests on the United States government as a whole, since its officials failed to uphold their vows to protect the constitutional rights of American citizens.

This case, furthermore, is illustrative of the role and power of the military in a democracy and the processes by which the military can gain unusual powers, since the wartime decisions empowered the military to act in an unprecedented fashion and to an unprecedented extent. The case of Japanese American evacuation shows that military evaluations and decisions are not always susceptible to an intelligent, objective review or appraisal in a crisis situation. As is now known, the rationale of military necessity did not rest upon concrete evidence. In fact, important decisions were made on the basis of information that was erroneous in spite of the fact that evidence to counter unfounded claims and charges was available at the time that the evacuation decision was made.

Theoretically in our democratic system, any decision made by one branch of the government or its officials is subject to the review of the others. Because of a shared set of racist assumptions and beliefs, most of the civilian leaders of the War Department and in the other branches of the United States government did not actively press for a thorough review of the situation of presumed "military necessity."[70] In not doing so, civilian leaders relinquished their ultimate responsibility and authority to protect the Constitution and the rights of United States citizens. Certain military leaders were able to gain and exercise direct control over citizens and civilians, which is specifically forbidden under the Constitution except in cases where martial law has been declared. This case, therefore, set a dangerous precedent.[71]

In principle, the military is always to be controlled by civilian review in our system. As both Rostow and Dembitz emphasize, this stems from a deep and fundamental distrust of military motives and logic.[72] This systemic check over the judgment and powers of the military assumes that civilian control is, in and of itself, enough to curb military excesses. However, since civilian authorities were operating on the same biases as the military officials, the military cannot be solely blamed for the wartime policy decisions.

According to Louis Smith in his examination of military power in American democracy, the creation of a "garrison state" does not occur simply because of the willful usurpation of power on the part of the military, nor even individual military leaders.[74] Smith argues that military control which develops in the context of a democratic government is actually a matter of successive steps of adaptation for defense purposes which has the full support of the public at all stages.[75] We concur with this analysis, and believe that it offers a powerful insight into how militaristic values come to hold sway in a democratic political system.

The general principles underlying the Japanese-American evacuation and internment can now be formulated. As Smith points out, a crisis which results in "war-politics" creates a climate for the development of a garrison state, as well as for militaristic values. A state of war has also historically resulted in public hysteria which has been expressed by verbal and physical attacks upon scapegoats.[76] Thus, American's inability to distinguish between the *cultural* and the *political* loyalties (see chapter in this volume by Lawrence Fuchs) of ethnic minorities seems to be highlighted in a state of war, and these two qualitatively distinct commitments may flow together in the eyes of the public.[77]

Finally, the case of the Japanese Americans indicates that when a group (1) is identifiable physically, (2) has suffered from a history of racial stereotypes and actions, and (3) is targeted as a scapegoat or a suspected enemy in a national crisis, racist and discriminatory sentiments can be formalized, legalized and implemented as public policy.[78]

The centrality of the military's role in the implementation of racist public policy in a crisis situation is enhanced for two reasons. First, with the development of a garrison state, military rationales and measures become very appealing as the response to crisis. Second—and this is key—*policy measures which are developed under the rationale of "military necessity" are able to sidestep the time-consuming and encumbering process of democratic review.* Dembitz observes:

> It may be inferred that the deposit of the authority in the hands of the military was not because the proposal to exclude was one which originated in military minds, nor because the military were peculiarly competent to determine the proper manner of executing it. One reason rather clearly seems to have been that *it was thought such deposit would insure the constitutionality of the exclusion.*[73]

This expediency, however, bears grave implications for the very system it is formulated to preserve. In this sense, it is ironic to note that although the World War II policy was made and carried out in order to "protect" democracy, as long as the evacuation and incarceration of Japanese Americans remains unchallenged and unrectified, no one's constitutional rights are safe should a condition of national crisis or war arise again.

As evidence of the long-term implications of the wartime evacuation, it is frightening to note the statements of John J. McCloy and retired Col. Karl R. Bendetsen before the Presidential Commission on the Wartime Relocation and Internment of Civilians, 1981. Clearly, neither man has changed his mind about the necessity or the morality of the internment.[79] Not content with stating that he would do it over again if given the chance, McCloy has even identified *other* potential enemies within the United States. In his 1981 statement, McCloy testified that:

> Within 90 miles of our shores [there are] . . . roughly a hundred thousand people, thoroughly trained, thoroughly equipped, well-trained in modern warfare, that are being set up to serve as proxies of the Soviet Union in the various strategic parts of the world. Suppose there was a raid some ten, twenty, thirty years hence of [Florida], wouldn't you be apt to think about moving them [Cuban Americans] if there was a raid there?[80]

Thus, racist ideology has been present since the founding of the country; it affected World War II decisionmaking, and it remains an active force in the minds of some of the nation's leaders even today.

The Japanese-American case illustrates the fact that an attack on one is a threat to all racial/ethnic minorities. Racism could become overt and institutionalized again with the outbreak of an international event, crisis or war. A concerted effort is still needed to rout out the ideology and practice of racism in the United States for—in and of itself—it threatens the principles and procedures of a truly democratic society.[81]

NOTES

[1] We would like to thank the University of Wisconsin System American Ethnic Studies Coordinating Committee, especially Dr. Winston A. Van Horne and Thomas V. Tonnesen. The gathering they organized—the Third Annual Green Bay Colloquium on Ethnicity and Public Policy held at the University of Wisconsin-Green Bay on May 14-15, 1982—provided us with the opportunity to research this topic.

The comments of our fellow participants at the colloquium were most useful in revising a preliminary draft of this paper. In addition, conversations we had with Dr. William Hohenthal, Professor Yuji Ichioka, Professor Lloyd Inui, Chris Kitchel, Roy Nakano and Dean Toji helped clarify a number of points. We would also like to thank Audrey Yamamoto for typing the final draft of this paper. We alone are responsible for the final product.

[2] Two caveats are in order. One is that our approach in this paper is interpretive, and the analysis is based on previously published materials. Second, as sociocultural anthropologists, we have focused on *general* themes and patterns in the culture and society of the United States. Thus, when we focus on racism—which typified the attitude held by members of the dominant society toward Japanese Americans—we do not mean to deny the efforts of those groups and individuals who fought to defend the rights of their fellow citizens.

[3] Jacobus tenBroek, Edward N. Barnhart, and Floyd W. Matson, *Prejudice, War and the Constitution: Causes and Consequences of the Evacuation of the Japanese Americans in World War II* (Berkeley, Cal.: University of California Press, 1970) and Morton Grodzins, *Americans Betrayed: Politics and the Japanese Evacuation* (Chicago: University of Chicago Press, 1949) both contain extensive discussion of the policy issues involved.

[4] Our use of the term "racial/ethnic minorities" is essentially the same as Blauner's term "third world minorities." Both terms posit that racial/ethnic minorities (i.e., Native Americans, blacks, Latinos and Asians) share a common experience based on colonization and on racial oppression in the United States. See the essay "Colonized and Immigrant Minorities" in Robert Blauner, *Racial Oppression in America* (New York: Harper and Row, 1972), pp. 51-81.

[5] Carey McWilliams, *Prejudice; Japanese-Americans: Symbol of Racial Intolerance* (Boston: Little, Brown & Co., 1944), p. 109.

[6] United States Department of War, *Final Report: Japanese Evacuation from the West Coast, 1942* (Reprinted in New York: Arno Press, 1978).

[7] McWilliams, op. cit., pp. 106-153; tenBroek et. al., op. cit., pp. 261-310; Michi Weglyn, *Years of Infamy: The Untold Story of America's Concentration Camps* (New York: Morrow Press, 1976), pp. 33-53; and Commission on Wartime Relocation and Internment of Civilians, House Report 82-22257, Committee on the Judiciary, *Personal Justice Denied* (Washington, D.C.: Government Printing Office, 1982).

[8] Stetson Conn, "The Decision to Evacuate the Japanese from the Pacific Coast" in Kent R. Greenfield, ed., U.S. Dept. of the Army, Office of Military History, *Command Decisions* (New York: Harcourt, Brace, 1959), pp. 105-109; Roger Daniels, *Concentration Camps USA: Japanese Americans and World War II* (New York: Holt, Rinehart & Winston, 1971), pp. 64-73.

[9] Weglyn, op. cit., pp. 54-66.

[10]Ibid. Our thanks to historian Yuji Ichioka of the Asian American Studies Center, UCLA, for bringing this to our attention.

Unfortunately, no direct link has yet been found between the officials in the State Department who developed this hemispheric strategy and the officials who advocated the policy of mass evacuation of Japanese Americans from the Pacific coast.

In a similar vein, historian Roger Daniels's latest research findings indicate that discussions held *prior* to Pearl Harbor may have been responsible for the "coincidence of policy" between the governments of Canada and the United States. See Roger Daniels, "The Decision to Relocate the North American Japanese: Another Look," *Pacific Historical Review*, 51 (Fall 1982): 71-77. Daniels concludes, " . . . I think it must now be agreed that at least a step towards preplanning had been taken." Ibid., p. 77.

[11]This section is a synthesis focusing on the main events leading up to the evacuation. Our account relies heavily on the following books: Daniels, *Concentration Camps USA*, op. cit., and Roger Daniels, *The Decision to Relocate the Japanese Americans* (New York: Harper & Row, 1975); Conn, op. cit.; Weglyn, op. cit.; tenBroek, et. al., op. cit.; and *Personal Justice Denied*, op. cit. We have reserved footnotes in this section for the documentation of key points.

[12]Weglyn, op. cit., pp. 54-66.

[13]One author cites extensive evidence in this regard. See Bob Kumamoto, "The Search for Spies: American Counterintelligence and the Japanese American Community, 1931-1942," *Amerasia Journal*, 6:2 (1979): 45-75, *passim*.

[14]Daniels, *Concentration Camps USA*, op. cit., p. 39.

[15]Weglyn, op. cit., pp. 33-53. Munson, it might be added, did believe that certain segments of the community, such as the Kibei, were more likely to be suspect.

[16]See Peter H. Irons, "Japanese American Internment and the Legal Profession," a written statement presented to the Commission on Wartime Relocation and Internment of Civilians at Harvard University, December 9, 1981. Irons states that by December 24, 1941, the Chiefs of Staff had concluded that a major invasion by the Japanese was unlikely. This information was passed on to both the secretary and the assistant secretary of war, Henry L. Stimson and John J. McCloy, within a few weeks after Pearl Harbor. Irons, pp. 2-3. As for DeWitt, see Daniels, *The Decision to Relocate the Japanese Americans*, op. cit., p. 24.

[17]Daniels, *Concentration Camps USA*, op. cit., p. 45.

[18]Conn, op. cit., p. 94.

[19]Irons, op. cit., pp. 3, 7 and *passim*; Daniels, *Concentration Camps USA*, op. cit., p. 49.

[20]Daniels, *Concentration Camps USA*, op. cit., p. 57.

[21]Ibid., pp. 64-65; and *Personal Justice Denied*, op. cit., pp. 72-86.

[22]See Daniels's summary of the case of Hawaii in the *The Decision to Relocate the Japanese Americans*, op. cit., pp. 26-28.

[23]DeWitt's "final report" specified that people of Japanese descent were inherently capable of espionage and sabotage. See United States Department of War, *Final Report*, op. cit. For the actual facts about the incidence of sabo-

tage on the islands and on the mainland, see tenBroek et. al., op. cit., pp. 188-189. Not one documented case was ever substantiated.

[24]The cabinet put a civilian in charge of the general evacuation program, but, in fact, this involved only the administration of these permanent camps.

[25]Extensive case studies of the "relocation centers" can be found in Edward H. Spicer, Asael T. Hansen, Katherine Luomala and Marvin K. Opler, *Impounded People: Japanese Americans in the Relocation Centers* (Tucson, Ariz.: University of Arizona Press, 1969); and Dorothy S. Thomas and Richard Nishimoto, *The Spoilage: Japanese-American Evacuation and Resettlement During World War Two* (Berkeley, Cal.: University of California Press, 1969). For an extensive comparative study, see Rita Takahashi Cates, *Comparative Administration and Management of Five War Relocation Authority Camps: America's Incarceration of Persons of Japanese Descent During World War II*, Ph.D. Dissertation (Pittsburgh, Pa.: University of Pittsburgh, 1980).

[26]For firsthand accounts of conditions in the camps, see the statements made by Japanese Americans who testified at the Commission on the Wartime Relocation and Internment of Civilians hearings. *Amerasia Journal* 8 (1981).

[27]McWilliams, op. cit., p. 109.

[28]Daniels, *Concentration Camps USA*, op. cit., pp. 65-67, 71, 81; Daniels, *The Decision to Relocate the Japanese Americans*, op. cit., p. 51.

[29]tenBroek, et. al., op. cit., p. 111.

[30]The two studies are: Nanette Dembitz, "Racial Discrimination and the Military Judgment: The Supreme Court's Korematsu and Endo Decisions," *Columbia Law Review*, 45: 2 (March 1944): 175-239; and Eugene V. Rostow, "The Japanese American Cases: A Disaster," *Yale Law Journal*, 54 (June 1945): 489-533.

[31]Grodzins, op. cit.

[32]Ibid., p. 60.

[33]Ibid., pp. 297-298.

[34]tenBroek, et. al., op. cit.

[35]Ibid., p. 327. TenBroek and his associates' criticisms of Grodzins can be found at pp. 185-208. A reevaluation of Grodzins' findings, in light of the detailed research of Conn and Daniels, suggests that he—rather than tenBroek and associates—was on the right track as far as the role of pressure groups was concerned.

[36]Ibid., pp. 325-334.

[37]Robert E. Park, *Race and Culture* (Glencoe, Ill.: Free Press, 1950).

[38]See the critical evaluation of this model developed by Paul Takagi in "The Myth of 'Assimilation in American Life'," *Amerasia Journal* 2 (1973): 149-158.

[39]S. Frank Miyamota, "The Forced Evacuation of the Japanese Minority During World War II," *The Journal of Social Issues*, 29:2 (Summer 1973): 11-32.

We have considered Miyamoto's analysis separately because it does not suffer from the assimilationist biases that can be identified in much of the literature published in the 1940s and 1950s.

A similar analysis can be found in *Personal Justice Denied*, op. cit. Here the commission's explanation is divided into three levels; the context of the decision, making and justifying the decision, and the conditions which permitted the decision. Ibid., pp. 4-9, 47-92.

We note that while the commission's account is quite global, the analysis of the decision stresses particular elite actors, most notably General DeWitt.

[40]We have already commented on DeWitt's charges of sabotage (Note 16, above). Dr. Peter H. Irons notes that DeWitt's charges of ship-to-shore signaling, by radio or by lights, was explicitly challenged by the chief of the F.C.C.'s Radio Intelligence Division *as early as January 9, 1942*. See the statement of Dr. Irons, op. cit.

[41]This kind of "chain reaction" can be seen in the case of conversations held between DeWitt and Earl Warren, then attorney general of California, and their effect on Warren's subsequent speeches; see Daniels, *The Decision to Relocate the Japanese Americans*, op. cit., pp. 31, 40. Furthermore, Daniels shows that there was a direct link between DeWitt, Warren, and the influential columnist, Walter Lippmann; ibid., p. 49. Lippmann's column, advocating strict treatment of Japanese Americans, was read in the War Department, the Justice Department and the White House; Daniels, *Concentration Camps USA*, op. cit., pp. 68-69.

[42]We realize that this is not a new observation; cf. Harry H. L. Kitano, *Japanese Americans: Evolution of a Subculture* (Englewood Cliffs, N.J.: Prentice-Hall, 1969), pp. 43-44. We give this variable more emphasis than most authors do, however, and focus on *how* racist beliefs can be transformed into public policy in a crisis situation.

[43]Blauner, op. cit., p. 84. This definition is similar to that used in anthropology: e.g., Paul Bohannon, *Social Anthropology* (New York: Holt, Rinehart & Winston, 1963), p. 185; and Pierre L. Van Den Berghe, *Race and Racism: A Comparative Perspective* (New York: John Wiley & Sons, 1957), esp. p. 11. Van Den Berghe goes on to delineate three main factors which combine to form an adequate social explanation for the genesis of Western racism. These include: (1) colonial expansion and capitalist exploitation; (2) social Darwinism; and (3) the need to dehumanize the slaves and the colonized so that the "egalitarian and libertarian ideas of the Enlightment" could not be applied to them. Ibid., pp. 17-18.

[44]Ronald T. Takaki, *Iron Cages: Race and Culture in Nineteenth-Century America* (New York: Alfred A. Knopf, 1979), p. 13.

[45]Ibid. See also: Joe R. Feagin, *Racial and Ethnic Relations* (Englewood Cliffs, N.J.: Prentice-Hall, 1978), pp. 329-362, on Japanese Americans; Juanita Tamayo Lott, "The Migration of a Mentality: The Filipino Community," *Migration Today* 2(1974); Sucheta Mazumdar, "Punjabi Immigration to California in the Context of Capitalist Development," *South Asia Bulletin*, 2:1 (Spring 1982): 19-28; and Mario Barrera, *Race and Class in the Southwest: A Theory of Racial Inequality* (Notre Dame, Ind.: University of Notre Dame Press, 1979). For a recent look at the situation of Vietnamese in the United States, see Kenneth A. Skinner, "Vietnamese in America: Diversity in Adaptation," *California Sociologist*, 3:2 (Summer 1980): 108-109 and *passim*.

[46]See Stanford M. Lyman, *Chinese Americans* (New York: Random House, 1974), pp. 54-85. Clearly, however, racism against Japanese Americans

is a complex phenomenon which has both ideological *and* economic roots. See Yuji Ichioka, "The 1921 Turlock Incident," in Emma Gee, ed., *Counterpoint: Perspectives on Asian America* (Los Angeles: UCLA Asian America Studies Center, 1976).

[47]Detailed research by McWilliams, op. cit., and by Roger Daniels in *The Politics of Prejudice: The Anti-Japanese Movement in California and the Struggle for Japanese Exclusion* (Berkeley, Cal.: University of California Press, 1962), provides extensive documentation of these developments.

[48]Frank Chuman, *The Bamboo People: The Law and Japanese Americans* (Del Mar, Cal.: Publisher's Inc., 1976).

[49]For documentation, see the studies cited in notes 45 and 46. For additional information, see the chapters by Lawrence H. Fuchs and Frank P. Zeidler in this volume.

[50]tenBroek, et. al., op. cit., p. 96.

[51]Daniels, *Concentration Camps USA*, op. cit., p. 32.

[52]tenBroek, et. al., op. cit., p. 75.

[53]Ibid.

[54]Daniels, *Concentration Camps USA*, op. cit., pp. 68-69.

[55]tenBroek, et. al., op. cit., pp. 79-80.

[56]The Japanese Americans Citizens League, *The Experience of Japanese Americans in the United States: A Teacher Resource Manual* (San Francisco: 1975), p. 32. The original statement appeared in *The Saturday Evening Post* (May 9, 1942).

[57]Daniels, *Concentration Camps USA*, op. cit., p. 60.

[58]Ibid., p. 61.

[59]tenBroek, et. al., op. cit., p. 87.

[60]*Korematsu v. United States*, 323 U.S. 214, 235-236 (1943).

[61]*Hirabayashi v. United States*, 320 U.S. 81, 111 (1943).

[62]Minoru Masuda, "Japanese Americans: Injury and Redress," *Rikka*, 6 (Autumn 1979): 3.

[63]Ibid.

[64]Daniels, *Concentration Camps USA*, op. cit., p. 72; Daniels, *The Decision to Relocate the Japanese Americans*, op. cit., pp. 44-45.

[65]Kitano, op. cit., p. 32.

[66]DeVere Pentony, Robert Smith and Richard Axen, *Unfinished Rebellions* (San Francisco: Jossey-Bass, 1971), pp. 55-56.
We might add that the phrase "ideology of racism" has been utilized by other social scientists. See the definition developed by Tamotsu Shibutani and Kian M. Kwan in their book, *Ethnic Stratification: A Comparative Approach* (New York: MacMillan, 1965), pp. 241-249.
In its strength and pervasiveness, this ideology approached what Antonio Gramsci called "cultural hegemony": ". . . an order in which a certain way of

life and thought is dominant, in which one concept of reality is diffused throughout society in all its institutional and private manifestation, informing with its spirit all taste, morality, customs, religious and political principles, and all social relations, particularly in their intellectual and moral connotation." For this quotation and further commentary about the concept, see Ronald T. Takaki, op. cit., pp. xiv-xv.

Accounts of racism in American society and culture can be found in Alexander Saxton, *The Indispensable Enemy: Labor and the Anti-Chinese Movement in California* (Berkeley, Cal.: University of California Press, 1971); Takaki, op. cit.; Barrera, op. cit.; and David Wellman, ed., *Portraits of White Racism* (Cambridge, Eng.: Cambridge University Press, 1977).

[67]Our focus on a common, unifying ideology should not be taken as a denial of the economic motives surrounding the evacuation decision. It is important to remember, however, that economic and material interests were both varied and, to a greater or lesser extent, disguised. Local pressure groups, local and national politicians, Gen. DeWitt and the Provost Marshall General's office, and the State Department, did not stand to gain the same "benefits" from the evacuation. The ideological rationale thus played an important role; (1) in allowing different sectors of society, with different immediate interests in mind, to cooperate, and (2) in allowing participants to hide motives involving self-interest and economic gain from each other, and from the general public.

[68]In some respects, as a result, the Japanese experience in the United States can be analyzed in terms of the internal colonialism theory of racial inequality. Internal colonialism is a situation where the interests of privileged groups lead them to establish and reinforce a pattern of structural discrimination at all levels of a society, especially in its economic, political and cultural institutions. As sociologist Robert Blauner states:
". . . various processes and practices of exclusion, rejection, and subjection *based on color* are built into the major public institutions . . . with the effect of maintaining special privileges, power, and values for the benefit of the white majority." (Emphasis added.) Blauner, op. cit., p. 84.

Although this model has a number of features which need not concern us here, a fundamental component of internal colonialism is that *there is an ideology of racism at the base of structural discrimination, resulting in a system based upon racial/ethnic inequality.*

[69]For a definition of "war-politics" and a description of its implications, see the introduction to this volume by Winston A. Van Horne and W. Werner Prange.

[70]Note the role of the Supreme Court in this regard. TenBroek and associates state that the Supreme Court's wartime decisions on the evacuation "disclose a judicial unwillingness to interfere with—or even to look upon—the actions of the military taken in time of global war, even to the extent of determining whether those actions are substantially or somehow connected with the prosecution of the war." tenBroek, et. al., op. cit., p. 259. The analysis they present of the role of the Court is a useful summary. Ibid., pp. 211-310.

[71]Rostow, op. cit., p. 491. In effect, should a war or national emergency arise, because of the World War II precedent the United States government has the power to: (1) determine who is a national enemy; (2) violate the constitutional rights of that enemy without due process of law; and (3) remove and detain that enemy—all on the basis of national security and military necessity. This is because, as Rostow points out, the Supreme Court's failure to strike down this abuse "converts a piece of war-time folly into political doctrine, and a permanent part of the law." Ibid.

[72]Ibid., p. 519; Dembitz, op. cit., pp. 238-239.

[73]Dembitz, op. cit., p. 207. (Emphasis added.)

[74]Citing the work of Harold Lasswell, Louis Smith provides an extended definition of the garrison state. "This is a state on a permanent war-footing, with the population in genuine fear of imminent conflict, so unlimited in its nature as to involve the total resources of the nation and so uncertain in its outcome as to necessitate the subordination of every consideration of democracy or welfare to 'military necessity'." Louis Smith, *American Democracy and Military Power: A Study of Civil Control of the Military Power in the United States* (Chicago: University of Chicago Press, 1951), pp. 7-8. Smith also adds, "In the garrison state, the prevalent value system becomes militarism . . ." Ibid.

[75]Cited in tenBroek, et. al., op. cit., p. 222.

[76]See the chapter in this volume by Frank P. Zeidler.

[77]This important distinction is discussed in Fuchs' chapter.

[78]In fact, we believe that it is under precisely such conditions that the violation of the constitutional rights of any group identified on the basis of "race," national origin, religion or even beliefs can be put into practice as a public policy.

[79]Bendetsen's statement is described in the *Los Angeles Times* (November 3, 1981), Part I, p. 20. An account of McCloy's testimony appears in *Rafu Shimpo* (November 18, 1981).

[80]*Rafu Shimpo*, ibid., p. 1.

[81]Those who would be inclined to believe that discrimination against Japanese and Asian Americans has vanished are invited to examine the recent publication, U.S. Commission on Civil Rights, *Success of Asian Americans: Fact or Fiction?* (Washington, D.C.: Clearinghouse Publication #64, Sept. 1980).
After reviewing a variety of empirical evidence, the commission concluded that: " . . . Asian Americans as a group are not the successful minority that the prevailing stereotype suggests. Individual cases of success should not imply that the diverse peoples who make up the Asian-American communities are uniformly successful. Moreover, despite their relatively high educational attainment, Asian Americans earn far less than majority Americans with comparable education and are reported to have been victims of discriminatory employment practices." Ibid., p. 24.
Thus, while racism may be more latent now as compared to the past, structural discrimination based on "race" is still extant.

REPRESENTATION IN THE AMERICAN MILITARY AND ITS IMPLICATIONS FOR PUBLIC POLICY

Alvin J. Schexnider

School of Community and Public Affairs
Virginia Commonwealth University

Both as an intellectual pursuit and as a manpower consideration, the subject of black participation in the American military has occasioned vigorous debate, strident protest, and sustained interest as a matter of public policy. The deep involvement of American blacks in every major military adventure since the Revolutionary War notwithstanding, questions persist regarding the role, quality, numbers and even commitment of black servicemen and women to this day. Although abhorrent, these reservations are real in many quarters. Consequently, while the temptation to do so may be great, one cannot be cavalier about addressing these questions, and especially their implications.

History is replete with accounts of the participation of blacks in the armed services. While the preoccupation with numbers is fairly recent, it can safely be said that participation by blacks in all four of the service branches (Army, Air Force, Navy and Marine Corps) has never been completely *unrestricted* at either the officer or enlisted levels.

From the Revolutionary War to the present, black troops have been recruited as expedience and/or the economy dictated. For example, about five thousand blacks, fighting in both segregated and integrated units, were pressed into service in the War of Independence. Similarly, several thousand blacks participated in the War of 1812. Following the successful conclusion of the war on January 8, 1818, General Andrew Jackson's headquarters issued a general order praising two corps of black volunteers for their "courage and perseverance."[1]

It is acknowledged that blacks were indispensable to the Union's success in the Civil War. Approximately 180,000 blacks enlisted in the Army, and 29,000 more manned Union ships. Thus, "by the middle of 1863," as the secretary of the navy confided to his diary under date of June 6, "all of our increased military strength now comes from Negroes."[2]

One of the earliest indicators of the federal government's posture vis-à-vis black servicemen in a post-war context can be seen in its treatment of them at the end of the War Between the States:

> Following the Civil War, all black units were disbanded excepting the following four: the Twenty-Fourth and Twenty-Fifth Infantry and the Ninth and Tenth Cavalry. Numbering a composite strength of about 12,500, these men were consigned to fighting Indians, cattle thieves, and Mexican revolutionaries. Significantly, they spearheaded the settlement of the West and protected its expansive frontiers. With horses too old for effective combat use, and retrograded field gear, under the constant harassment of white commanders who were generally ashamed to be a part of them, these black cavalrymen proved equal to the tasks they were ordered to accomplish.[3]

The westward journey of the all-black Ninth and Tenth Cavalries in the spring of 1867 commenced over twenty years of continuous service on the Great Plains and in the deserts and mountains of Arizona and New Mexico.[4] Historian William Leckie observed that "one can search the dusty archives in vain for an instance where a detachment, company, battalion, or regiment bolted under fire or failed to do its duty."[5] Black cavalrymen also served with distinction during the Spanish-American War. Lieutenant John J. Pershing of the Tenth Cavalry was convinced that the "storming of San Juan Hill had forged a deeper bond of unity between the victors, white and Negro regiments, showing that they were 'unmindful of race or color' in the dedication as to their common duty as Americans."[6]

In an especially insightful modern analysis of black participation in the military, Charles Moskos notes that it was not until the early twentieth century that American citizens exhibited reservations about black servicemen. Moskos observed:

> In the early twentieth century . . . owing to a general rise in American racial tensions and specific outbreaks of violence between Negro troops and whites, opinion began to turn against the use of Negro soldiers . . . In the interval between the two world wars, the Army not only remained segregated but also adopted a policy of a Negro quota that was to keep the number of Negroes in the Army proportionate to the total population. Never in the pre-World War II period, however, did the number of Negroes approach this quota.[7]

As the foregoing discussion indicates, the *concept* of calibrating the proportion of black participation in the armed services on the basis of black representation in the civilian population has historical antecedents which constituted official policy. As a result of the quota system, by the end of World War I segregated all-black units had been reduced in number to only five officers and five thousand enlisted men. Moreover, the five officers included a father and son, Benjamin F. Davis, Sr. and Jr., with the remaining three black officers serving in the chaplaincy.

At the peak of World War II, close to seven hundred thousand blacks had been inducted into the Army, two-thirds of whom served overseas. For the most part, blacks were led by white officers and served in such non-combat units as the transportation, quartermaster, and engineer corps.

Towards the end of World War II a manpower shortage led the Army to request black volunteers for combat duty. About twenty-five hundred men volunteered for this assignment and several black platoons were placed in white combat units. From the vantage points of both the black soldiers' combat performance and the reactions of white soldiers, this experiment was an unqualified success and was later used as evidence in support of efforts toward a policy of degegregating the armed forces.

Following World War II, mounting pressure from black and liberal groups, along with the realization that black troops were being poorly utilized, led the Army to take another look at its racial policies.[8] In June 1948, President Harry Truman ordered the desegregation of the armed forces and established a committee chaired by Charles Fahy to oversee its implementation. Moskos points out that as a result of the efforts of the Fahy Committee, "The Army abolished the quota system in 1950, and was beginning to integrate some training camps when the conflict in Korea broke out. The Korean War was the *coup de grâce* for desegregation in the Army."[9]

President Truman's desegration order had a clear and noticeable effect on black participation in the armed services. Essentially the armed forces began to be viewed as organizations in which blacks had a fair chance of succeeding. Thus, between 1949 and 1954 the proportion of blacks in the Army increased from 8.6 percent to 11.3 percent.[10] By the end of 1955, 28 percent of the black enlisted men were in the top three non-commissioned officer (NCO) grades compared to 26 percent of the white enlistees.[11] Similarly, the proportion of blacks serving in the Air Force rose from around 5 percent in 1949 to 8.6 percent in 1964. Although the Navy and Marine Corps tended to be more racially restrictive than other service branches during this era, between 1949 and 1964 black participation in the Marines rose from 2 percent to 8.2 percent.[12]

The perception of the armed services as egalitarian, along with the harsh reality of limited opportunity structures in the civilian sector, has had a discernible impact on black participation in the military, particularly since Truman's desegregation order. That is to say, mili-

tary service for far too many blacks has become a viable source of gainful employment and career mobility. Although in recent years the all-
volunteer force has been decried as an employer of last resort, in fact
black servicemen have had a pronounced tendency to reenlist since at
least World War II. By 1965 the black reenlistment rate was twice that
of whites; close to half (47 percent) of all first-term black enlisted men
elected to remain in the armed services for at least a second term. The
expansion of the armed services, prompted in large measure by the Vietnam War, brought into focus serious concerns about the implications
of higher-than-average reenlistment rates among blacks. More precisely, not only was the propensity of blacks to reenlist at higher rates
alarming, but so was the overrepresentation of blacks in the combat
arms of the military. As early as 1966 Moskos pointed out that although "the percentage of Negro enlisted men in the Army increased
only slightly between 1945 and 1962, the likelihood of a Negro serving
in a combat arm [was] almost three times greater in 1962 than it was at
the end of World War II."[13] It was the war in Vietnam that first raised
questions about the implications of a fighting force disproportionately
manned by blacks, but it was the abandonment of conscription and the
advent of the all-volunteer force which focused and reinforced concerns
about "overrepresentation," "racial balance" and "too many" blacks
in the armed forces.

"Representation," a term coined by the Department of Defense,
suggests that the population of the armed services should at least approximate a cross section of the American male population aged eighteen to twenty-four. Although this may seem ideal to defense analysts
in the Pentagon, obtaining an approximate cross section of the population remains an elusive goal, as it was during the draft.

Apprehensions regarding "too many blacks" in the military or a
"representative" armed force must be examined within the context of
sentiment against the all-volunteer force(AVF) which has never been
accepted in certain quarters. Indeed, the convergence of anti-AVF sentiment and calls for representation are wholly comprehensible given
the fact that from the outset, "representation" was seen as antithetical
to the all-volunteer force. The draft, which the Nixon administration
replaced with the all-volunteer force in 1973, was never broadly representative of the American populace in the first place. Generally, draftees were drawn from the lower-middle and working-class segments of
society. This pattern was further reinforced by the tendency of young
men to "volunteer" for service in the Air Force, Navy or Marine Corps
in an effort to avoid conscription. Although manpower shortages during the Vietnam War resulted in the conscription of college graduates,
this was a short-term expedient. Historically, the solid middle and up-

per strata of our society have been able to escape military duty if they desired, thereby reinforcing the perception of the armed forces as working-class in character.[14] Indeed, it was as a direct result of the strident protests of college students and other middle-income citizens that the anti-war protests of the late 1960s and early 1970s led to an abandonment of conscription.

The end of the draft did not ensure that monolithic support of the all-volunteer force would prevail. It is, in fact, difficult to ascertain how much criticism of the AVF is based on concerns regarding overproportionate black participation in it. From 1967 to 1971, when the idea of the all-volunteer force was under active consideration, one of the major objections raised was the fear that it would become disproportionately black. The Gates Commission, whose 1970 report to President Nixon addressed this issue, concluded that this concern was unfounded. Ultimately, the commission proved to be wrong on this subject. Between 1972 (when the draft ended) and 1980, the proportion of blacks in the Army's enlisted levels increased from 15.6 percent to 32.5 percent. Indeed, as Table I indicates, the proportion of blacks in the Army has almost tripled since the peak of the Vietnam War.

TABLE I

PROPORTION OF BLACKS IN THE ARMY, SELECTED YEARS

Fiscal Year	Percentage
1968	11.5
1970	12.1
1972	15.6
1974	19.0
1976	21.3
1978	26.3
1980	32.5

Source: U. S. Department of Defense

While blacks constitute only 11.8 percent of the nation's population, black volunteers comprise 22 percent of all United States military enlisted personnel, and 32 percent of all Army personnel. Conversely, black representation in the officer corps is less than 5 percent. Although most of the concern regarding representation centers upon the enlisted ranks, the underrepresentation of blacks in the officer corps remains a crucial issue also. Since today's senior black officers represent the effects of career decisions made decades ago when segregation prevented them from pursuing civilian job opportunities, the prospects for replenishing their ranks appear dim. Young, educated blacks with marketa-

ble skills are more inclined toward the private sector than a military
career. Focusing exclusively on representation in the enlisted ranks
without addressing the problem of underrepresentation in the officer
corps is both duplicitous and bad policy.

Even though black participation in the armed forces has been expanding steadily since the end of conscription, a provocative essay by
two military sociologists, Morris Janowitz and Charles Moskos, helped
to shape the debate on representation significantly. Their exhortation
to the Pentagon for measures calculated to achive representativeness
was premised on several assumptions:

a) That a national fighting force, if it is to enjoy political and
   democratic legitimacy, must be broadly representative of the
   population it is established to defend;
b) that black overrepresentation will discourage white
   participation;
c) that black overrepresentation may lead to disproportionate
   black casualities in war times; and
d) that an overrepresentative force may be unreliable.[15]

There are several deficiencies in this argument, not the least of which
is the attempt to mask racial quotas as "representativeness." There
has been a general reluctance on the part of Department of Defense
officials to admit that representation is even an issue worth discussion
for fear of being labeled racist. Thus the Defense Manpower Commission, on the basis of a survey of unit commanders across all four service
branches, concluded that "representation" was immaterial to mission
capability or effectiveness.[16] Curiously, however, while commanding
officers contended that representation was not an issue, the Pentagon,
by shifting its recruitment efforts from urban to rural and suburban
areas, reduced the proportion of new black recruits in the Army from
29 percent in 1974 to 17 percent in 1975.[17] By May 1978, however, the
percentage of new black enlistees in the Army had reached 33 percent
with the economy figuring prominently in black enlistment rates. Richard V. L. Cooper, author of a comprehensive study of the all-volunteer
force by the Rand Corporation, concluded that although joblessness
among black youth was a major reason for higher enlistment rates, it
was not the only one. Cooper offered an explanation:

Specifically, the increasing percentage of blacks in the enlisted
ranks can be attributed to three basic factors: 1) a dramatic increase over time for military service; 2) particularly high unemployment rates that plagued the young black population during
the beginning of the all-volunteer force; and 3) a lag in earning
potential for young blacks in the civilian work force.[18]

It is acknowledged that excessively high unemployment rates among black youth impel them toward the military. Consequently, the services have become the employer of last resort for many black youth who cannot find gainful civilian employment. Former Secretary of the Army Clifford Alexander, in response to concerns about representation, underscored the problem of employment:

> A large number of blacks have *enlisted* in recent years, causing alarm in some quarters. That alarm is misdirected. The truly alarming fact is that unemployment among black teenagers is running at 40 percent. The Army offers qualified men and women an opportunity which just does not exist for them in many sectors of corporate America.[19]

This view was also reinforced by M. Kathleen Carpenter, former Deputy Assistant Secretary of Defense for Equal Opportunity, who said, "The economy does not offer the same degree of opportunities for equally qualified minorities. So a lot of minorities look to the military not only to learn skills but to acquire a level of sophistication."[20]

Thus, while the economy and discrimination in the civilian workplace induce black enlistments, they also tend to encourage reenlistments among blacks. Since the mid-1950s, blacks have registered higher reenlistment rates than whites. Although the profile has changed dramatically since 1972 when blacks were twice as likely to reenlist as whites, black enlisted men and women remain clearly more inclined toward a military career path than their white counterparts. Table II indicates that since the advent of the all-volunteer force this trend has become more pronounced.

TABLE II
ARMY REENLISTMENT RATES IN THE ALL-VOLUNTEER FORCE, 1972-1979

Fiscal Year	Percentage Reenlisting	
	Black	White
1972	61.3	42.6
1973	69.8	60.9
1974	80.5	70.4
1975	82.7	70.3
1976	82.0	69.1
1977	80.3	66.3
1978	78.0	63.4
1979	74.9	59.6

Source: U.S. Department of Defense

In view of the historical tendency of blacks to reenlist at rates higher than that of whites, and also in view of a recent decline in the birthrate of American whites, many defense manpower analysts forecast an expansion of black participation in the armed forces in the 1980s. As a consequence, the issue of representation will not soon disappear. Since the policy considerations which attend this issue have yet to be addressed in any systematic fashion calculated to inform official action, it is all the more important to focus on the underlying factors contributing to calls for representation. We turn now to a discussion of these factors.

It seems odd, if not querulous, to link the armed services with concerns about proportional representation of blacks. After all, it was the military which paved the way for racial integration in American society. President Truman's desegregation order antedated the landmark *Brown* decision by six years, and when Southern governors were issuing "states rights" manifestoes in defiance of the Supreme Court, the last all-black Army unit had long since been disbanded. What, then, explains the salience of representation?

Several factors influence a preoccupation with the issue of representation: the economy; changes in the concept of military participation; and the rise of neo-conservatism.

The Economy

As was noted above, the nation's economy has long been a factor influencing both the numbers and quality of military manpower. When the economy has been in a downturn, the services have had less difficulty meeting manpower quotas. Conversely, as the economy has improved, the services have experienced greater difficulty in securing the desired quantity and quality of manpower.[21]

Essentially, persistently higher-than-average unemployment rates have resulted in higher-than-average enlistment and reenlistment rates for blacks. As one analyst has described it:

> In the open marketplace of volunteer recruiting, many more blacks than whites were found to be in the ranks of the unemployed or underemployed, and these men and women were receptive to service opportunities. Second, within the context of continuing fears and suspicion between the races in most segments of U.S. society, the armed forces have been in the forefront of those institutions making progress toward eliminating the remaining vestiges of racial bias. Also contributing to the rise in black enlistments was a major increase in the numbers of blacks eligible for military service, a consequence . . . of the increasing number of black high school graduates.[22]

While a sagging economy has prompted spiraling enlistments, in recent years massive changes in the national economy have tended to exacerbate this problem as increasingly larger numbers of black youth are eliminated from the labor market, perhaps permanently. The transformation of our economy from a goods-producing, manufacturing-based economy to a services-oriented marketplace has wrought dramatic changes in our ways of life. More importantly, it has substantially altered the world of work, and for hundreds of thousands of unskilled and low-skilled blacks, it has diminished the availability of work. Recently, an economist described the following scenario:

> A perfect example of the effects of technology on the job market may be observed in the American automobile industry which in recent years has been laying off hundreds of thousands of workers. It should be clear to those workers who have been laid off and to all of us that in ten years, many of the jobs from which auto workers have been laid off will no longer exist. American automobiles in the future will be assembled primarily by robots as they are in Japan today . . . the only alternative is an ever-growing black segment of the underclass—that group of people who are at the bottom of the socio-economic ladder by any criterion that may be applied and who have little or no chance to move up.[23]

As a result of this type of economic segmentation, many blacks who may join the military as an employer of last resort, so to speak, often end up in low-skill occupations (48.5 percent of personnel in petroleum handling, 41.7 percent of personnel in supply, and 40.2 percent of personnel in wire maintenance) or in the combat arms.[24] While there has been much lamenting of the fact that blacks must risk their lives in the armed forces in order to be gainfully employed, as long as the economy remains weak, it is plausible to assume that blacks will find the armed services to be a reasonable alternative to joblessness. In December 1981 the nation's unemployment rate was 8.9 percent; for black teenagers the unemployment rate nationally was 39.6 percent. These figures provide a stark but realistic backdrop against which to assess the relationship between the economy and black participation in the military.

Changes in the Concept of Military Participation

Although the state of the economy has had a major impact on black enlistments and reenlistments, the perceived overrepresentation of blacks is also a function of a disinclination of white youth to serve in the armed forces. While in previous wars military service was viewed both as a civic duty and a rite of passage, among the residual effects of the anti-Vietnam War protest was and is a noticeable shift in attitudes regarding military service. As the Defense Manpower Commission notes in its final report, "The effect of shifts in the attitudes of young men and women regarding military service is not subject to quantification, but major changes could profoundly alter the prospects for sustaining DOD manpower requirements in the next decade."[25] Indeed, the acknowledgment of this singular fact has led to a renewed discussion of the merits of conscription or some form of compulsory national service. Janowitz and Moskos, for example, have argued that "if compulsory induction were used, many would attempt to avoid military service, which will bring on its own problems. Moreover, we believe that a return to conscription would be conducive to a form of trade unionism among draftees."[26]

Perhaps the most compelling evidence that there has been a shift in the attitudes of American youth toward military service can be seen in their reluctance to register for the draft which was reinstituted by President Carter in 1980. Even though non-registration is a felony punishable by up to five years in prison and a $10,000 fine, during the last quarter of 1981, registration levels declined to 71 percent of the draft eligible in the eighteen to twenty-one age range. Thus, despite the fact that President Reagan early in 1982 extended the grace period for young men to register, by the date of its expiration on the last Sunday of February 1982, *one of every eight young men required to register had failed to do so.* Moreover, "since a draft would take place by lottery, the Selective Service says the draft would be fair only if 98 percent of those required to register did so. Right now, less than 90 percent appear to have registered."[27]

Simply put, any serious talk of a return to conscription is anathema. The reluctance of America's youth to register for the draft underscores the pervasiveness of this sentiment. For the time being at least, the absence of the draft notwithstanding, the services are experiencing few difficulties in meeting their manpower quotas. As a consequence of the economy, during fiscal year 1981, for the first time in five years, each branch of the armed services met or exceeded enlistment recruitment targets. In other words, a sluggish economy is achieving what the draft might not be able to do.

Additionally, the Pentagon has seized this opportunity to introduce higher quality standards for new recruits as well as those seeking reenlistment. In 1980 Congress established qualitative recruitment standards which required that the Army enlist no more than 35 percent non-high school graduates among non-prior service male accessions. Similarly, stricter standards for reenlisting have also been implemented in order to improve the overall quality of military manpower.

The desired effects of these policies are already being manifested. Secretary of Defense Caspar Weinberger noted that significant improvements were achieved in fiscal year 1981 with respect to levels of education of new recruits and reenlistment among first-term and career personnel. Weinberger highlighted the following statistics in his 1982 annual report to Congress on United States defenses:

1. DOD recruited nearly 265,000 high school graduates in fiscal year 1981, up 9 percent from fiscal year 1980;

2. First-term reenlistment in fiscal year 1981 climbed to an all-time high of 43 percent compared to only 39 percent in fiscal year 1980;

3. Reenlistment among career personnel increased from 70 to 86 percent from fiscal year 1980 to fiscal year 1981, registering a gain for the second consecutive year.[28]

Secretary Weinberger warned that unless congressionally-imposed quality controls were relaxed, recruiting targets would be difficult to achieve in fiscal year 1983 and beyond. Moreover, he admonished, an improved economy and a projected decline in the youth population would further exacerbate the problem. In the interim, limited civilian job opportunities have enabled the armed services to be more selective in their recruiting efforts. This has had the noticeable effect of moderating the number of new black inductees. Representation is thus being achieved short of mandated quotas. Put differently, despite the shift in attitudes toward military service, the Pentagon is availing itself of improved manpower recruitment prospects resulting from the state of the economy. Accordingly, negative views toward military service among American youth, abetted by the prevalence of limited civilian job opportunities, are enabling the services to be highly selective.

If more white youth chose to serve in the armed forces, the issue of overrepresentation would likely disappear overnight. The validity of this assertion is underscored by the decision to return to conscription as well as by the various proposals for some type of universal service.[29]

In order to fully appreciate the issue of representation, we must examine it within the context of a growing disinclination toward military service on the part of American youth. The economy has temporarily muted the impact of this disenchantment, but it is an ironic twist for the hundreds of thousands of black youth who, when they too had the opportunity to flee to Canada, elected instead to bear arms in defense of their country.[30]

The Rise of Neo-Conservatism

It is undeniable that genuinely complex issues attend the calls for representation. For example, there can be no gainsaying the fact that a ground combat force that is disproportionately black will subject black troops to excessive casualties during times of war. Similarly, few would quarrel with the notion that a fighting force, ideally, ought to reflect a broad cross section of the American populace. The realization of this goal has been elusive, however, prompting the question whether blacks should be penalized because of the difficulty of reaching the goal of "representation."

Aside from the considerations discussed above, it is imperative that the issue of representation be examined within the context of the rise of neo-conservatism and a retreat from relatively recent liberal commitments. The stridency of calls for representation is to some extent a manifestation of the belief that blacks have come too far too fast. Further, in an era of limited growth, competition over scarce resources assumes a primacy which exacerbates latent racial tensions and escalates fears about policy outcomes that in calmer times might be considered innocuous. As a consequence, "long-standing partnerships between blacks and whites have cracked under the weight of competition between both groups for jobs, housing and efforts to achieve and maintain the good life."[31] Historically, for disproportionately large numbers of blacks, the military has represented a chance to acquire the good life; now, however, for growing numbers of white youth the services also represent a viable employment option. Representation thus assumes the character of a racially inspired policy designed to optimize white participation while moderating the involvement of blacks. Although calls for representation may be tinged with altrustic considerations, efforts to moderate black participation in the military have emerged during an era of noticeable conservatism and a declining commitment to traditional civil rights goals. In the words of one keen observer of neo-conservative theoreticians:

> They express a mood and a fashion rather than a deeply felt political stance. They seem to be sustained by a desire to seize the shifting *Zeitgeist* by its tail, and they batten on the mood of disillusionment that has seized the country after the hopes of the early 1960s. They wish to bring about a counterrevolution of declining expectations."[32]

From a neo-conservative perspective, while integration of the military remains laudable, strategies must be designed to ensure that this goal is not destroyed by allowing disproportionate black participation. This posture presupposes that blacks must be protected from themselves. Additionally, the logic of this approach reinforces the perception that when the level of black involvement in an organization reaches a certain threshold, the organization becomes dysfunctional. An extension of this logic is that a military that is disproportionately black is dysfunctional, or at a minimum, cannot be relied upon to carry out its mission effectively. This is of course wrongheaded. Furthermore, it is a tenuous basis for policy formulation. Nonetheless, in the context of the current conservative mood in the nation, it has a certain pragmatic appeal. As Lewis Coser reminds us, "neo-conservatives pride themselves on their practicality and pragmatism."[33] One hopes that these regressive tendencies will not inflict permanent wounds on the aspirations of black youth. Neo-conservative pragmatism will probably in more critical times succumb to the expedience of manpower requirements. If history provides any clues about future behavior, under such conditions efforts toward representation will be jettisoned posthaste.

Summary

Modern concerns about black participation in the military were first voiced at the height of the Vietnam War when black combat troops sustained, for a while, an excessive number of casualties. More recently, since the end of conscription, Pentagon officials, politicians and a number of defense manpower analysts and scholars have expressed reservations about the so-called overrepresentation of blacks in the armed forces.[34] At present, blacks constitute 22 percent of the total Department of Defense enlisted strength and 5.2 percent of the officers across the services. A different profile emerges in each branch of the military as depicted in Table III.

TABLE III

BLACK REPRESENTATION, ENLISTED AND OFFICER, IN ALL SERVICES, 1981

Branch	Percentage
Army	29.7
Marine Corps	20.4
Air Force	14.3
Navy	10.6

Source: U. S. Department of Defense

Historically, the Army has had larger numbers of blacks than the other services. In both fiscal year 1980 and fiscal year 1981, blacks

made up 33 percent of the Army's total enlisted strength. This figure
has led to a growing concern about the "legitimacy," "effectiveness"
and "quality" of the nation's armed forces. It now appears that in lieu
of viewing numbers alone, proponents of representation have focused
their attention on the *relative quality* of enlisted personnel. As Charles
Moskos has noted, "Since the end of the draft, the proportion of male
entrants with a high school diploma has been 64 percent for blacks
compared with 53 percent for whites.[35] Nevertheless, despite the high
school diploma, blacks continue to be overrepresented in combat, combat support or other low-skill occupations. Analyses of enlisted evaluation reports demonstrate that high school diplomas are good predictors
of soldierly performance. Indeed, in an effort to improve the quality of
military manpower, Congress recently imposed stiffer standards for recruitment and reenlistment. The effects of these policies are already
being felt. Also in the name of quality control, the Pentagon in 1980
authorized a massive national survey of almost twelve thousand youth
in order to assess their performance on the Armed Services Vocational
Aptitude Battery (ASVAB).[36] The results of the survey and their potential use raise a number of crucial questions surrounding the quality
of future manpower accessions.[37]

The issue of the quality of military manpower (partially reflected in
standards imposed by Congress), strategic shifts in recruiting efforts,
as well as the possible uses to which the ASVAB survey results may be
put, do not auger well for continued black participation in the armed
forces at the levels experienced since the end of the draft. Consequently, we can expect a reduction in the proportion of blacks serving
in the armed forces, especially in the Army. This will not be the first
time that changes of this type have occurred. The Army has in the past
shifted recruiting areas from urban to suburban locales in order to be
near middle-class high schools and college campuses.

Further evidence of the thrust toward quality control can be seen in
the Army's program for retaining only the best soldiers. In addition to
the quality control standards imposed by Congress, Army commanders can weed out "marginal performers" or "unsuitables" who
have fewer than six years of service.[38] The Army is, of course, encouraged by reenlistment statistics: in 1981, 66.7 percent of its eligible
personnel reenlisted compared to 15 percent in the late 1970s. Even in
the combat arms (infantry, armor and artillery), reenlistments are up.

Essentially, a full court press is in effect to counterbalance the so-
called overrepresentation of blacks. Although unemployment in the civilian job market aids this effort in a benign fashion, calculated strategies employed by the Pentagon appear to be contributing to a gradual
decline in the proportion of blacks in the armed forces.

It is unfortunate that we continue to be preoccupied with the racial composition of our armed forces. Further, it is regrettable that the racial composition of the military has been defined as a quantity versus quality issue. Policies have been developed and implemented by the Congress and the Pentagon in order to moderate black participation under the guise of quality control. While proponents of representational policy may be pleased with these developments, for many others, this writer included, these policies as well as their probable outcomes constitute more ironies of democracy.

Few would quarrel with the notion that, *ideally*, the military *ought* to be broadly representative of our society. As the foregoing discussion attests, this has proven to be an elusive goal. Our efforts in pursuit of this objective should not, however, result in exclusionary practices which favor one group or class of individuals over another. Recently, it has become apparent that suburban shifts among armed forces recruiters as well as stricter application of reenlistment standards are slowly reducing the proportion of blacks in the armed forces.

The effects of these changes may not be seen for years. Their implications for public policy are enormous, however, and underscore the need to examine the role of the armed forces not only from the vantage points of defense, national security and foreign policy, but from the point of United States domestic policy as well.

NOTES

[1] Benjamin Quarles, *The Negro in the Making of America* (New York: Collier Books, 1964), p. 91.

[2] Benjamin Quarles, *The Negro in the Civil War* (Boston: Little, Brown & Co., 1969), p. xii.

[3] Alvin J. Schexnider, *The Development of Nationalism: Political Socialization Among Blacks in the U.S. Armed Forces*, Ph.D. Dissertation (Evanston, Ill.: Northwestern University, 1980). The daring exploits of these four cavalry units are chronicled in William H. Leckie, *The Buffalo Soldiers* (Norman, Okla.: University of Oklahoma Press, 1967).

[4] Schexnider, *The Development of Nationalism*, op. cit., pp. 2-3.

[5] Leckie, op. cit., p. 259.

[6] Quarles, *The Negro in the Making of America*, op. cit., p. 179.

[7] Charles C. Moskos, Jr., "Racial Integration in the Armed Forces," *American Journal of Sociology*, 72:2 (September 1966): 133-134.

[8] One of the foremost studies of this genre is Samuel A. Stouffer, et. al., *The American Soldier* (Princeton, N.J.: Princeton University Press, 1947).

[9]Moskos, "Racial Integration in the Armed Forces," op. cit., p. 135.

[10]Charles C. Moskos, Jr., *The American Enlisted Man* (New York: Russell Sage Foundation, 1979), p. 214.

[11]Eli Ginzberg, *The Negro Potential* (New York: Columbia University Press, 1956), p. 89.

[12]Moskos, "Racial Integration in the Armed Forces," op. cit., p. 136.

[13]Ibid., p. 138.

[14]Kenneth J. Coffey, *Strategic Implications of the All-Volunteer Force* (Chapel Hill, N.C.: University of North Carolina Press, 1979), esp. Chapter 2.

[15]Morris Janowitz and Charles C. Moskos, Jr., "Racial Composition in the All-Volunteer Force," *Armed Forces and Society*, 1:1 (Fall 1974).

[16]Defense Manpower Commission, U.S. Department of Defense, *Defense Manpower: The Keystone of National Security* (Washington, D.C.: U.S. Government Printing Office, 1976), p. 10.

[17]Alvin J. Schexnider and John S. Butler, "Race and the All-Volunteer System: A Reply to Janowitz and Moskos," *Armed Forces and Society*, 2:3 (Spring 1976): 421-432.

[18]Quoted in Alvin J. Schexnider, "Blacks and the Military," *Focus* (December 1978): 3.

[19]*New York Times* (October 7, 1979).

[20]*Army Times* (November 17, 1980).

[21]Jack D. Foner, *The United States Soldier Between Two Wars* (New York: Humanities Press, 1979).

[22]Coffey, op. cit., p. 66. See also George Davis, "Blacks in the Military: Opportunity or Refuge?" *Black Enterprise*, 10:12 (July 1980): 22-30.

[23]James D. McGhee, "The Black Teenager: An Endangered Species," in National Urban League, *The State of Black America 1982* (New York: National Urban League, 1982), p. 189.

[24]Charles C. Moskos, Jr., "The Enlisted Ranks in the All-Volunteer Army," in John B. Keely, ed., *The All-Volunteer Force and American Society* (Charlottesville, Va.: University Press of Virginia, 1978), p. 44.

[25]Defense Manpower Commission, op. cit., p. 411.

[26]Morris Janowitz and Charles C. Moskos, Jr., "Five Years of the All-Volunteer Force, 1973-1978," *Armed Forces and Society*, 5:2 (February 1979): 171-218.

[27]*Washington Post* (February 28, 1982).

[28]*Army Times* (February 22, 1982).

[29]Charles C. Moskos, Jr., "Making the All-Volunteer Force Work: A National Service Approach," *Foreign Affairs*, 60 (Fall 1981), and Paul N. McCloskey, Jr., "National Youth Service As An Alternative," *Commonsense*, 2:3 (Fall 1979).

[30]As is generally known, the anti-war draft resistance movement of the 1960s was principally composed of "the better educated and upper economic classes." Blacks and other ethnic minorities had minimal involvement in the movement. See Coffey, op. cit., especially Chapter 1.

[31]Quoted in Alvin J. Schexnider, "Symposium: Race and the United States Military," *Armed Forces and Society*, 6:4 (Summer 1980): 609-610.

[32]Lewis A. Coser and Irving Howe, eds., *The New Conservatives: A Critique from the Left* (New York: Quadrangle, 1974), p. 4.

[33]Ibid., p. 8.

[34]Much of the relevant literature has already been cited above. This discussion has also occasioned a fair amount of congressional testimony. See, for example, Senate Armed Services Committee, Subcommittee on Manpower and Personnel, Hearing on the Status of the All-Volunteer Force, June 20, 1978.

[35]Moskos, "Making the All-Volunteer Force Work," op. cit., p. 19.

[36]U.S. Department of Defense, *Profile of American Youth* (Washington, D.C.: U.S. Department of Defense, March 1982).

[37]While the *Profile of American Youth* might have revealed a disparity in black and white test scores, it also revealed the effects of differential educational opportunities in our society. See editorials by William Raspberry and Carl T. Rowan in the *Washington Post*, February 26 and 27, 1982, respectively.

[38]*Richmond News Leader* (April 13, 1982).

AS LONG AS THE GRASS GROWS . . . THE CULTURAL CONFLICTS AND POLITICAL STRATEGIES OF UNITED STATES-INDIAN TREATIES[1]

Donald L. Fixico

Department of History
University of Wisconsin-Milwaukee

> *Brothers: Open your ears to the truth. I speak from my heart, not with my lips. I wish to make you happy. I wish to make peace between you and the United States.* (Rufus Putnam, Indian Agent, 1792)[2]

A study of the negotiations which occurred prior to the signing of each of the 389 treaties between Indian tribes and the United States from 1778 to 1871 reveals the true nature of federal-Indian relations.[3] Examining the negotiations and military strategy illuminates the motives behind treaty making and the one-sidedness of federal-Indian relations in favor of the white man. Crucial misunderstandings on the part of both American officials and Indian leaders, misunderstandings arising from cultural differences, affected each group's interpretation of treaty-making proceedings and the agreements themselves.

Historically, the common element of federal-Indian relations has been land. The way in which Indians and whites viewed land demonstrates the fundamental differences between their cultures. The white man saw the land as soil to be owned and tilled. He cleared fields to make room for his home and to raise crops, essentially changing the face of the earth in the small area he inhabited. The Indian perceived "Mother Earth" as the provider for all living things, the Indian people and the animals, the two-legged and the four-legged. Mother Earth could not be owned. The struggle between the two sides, one wanting to preserve and live in harmony with Mother Earth and the other wanting to cultivate the soil, resulted in wars. Peace treaties were often used to halt the fighting, but cultural differences perpetuated the conflicts until one side emerged as dominant.

During the early stages of federal-Indian relations, each side treated the other as a sovereign people. The Indian nations clearly held an advantage in military strength, causing American officials to negotiate cautiously with the tribes. The United States had no official army in the 1790s and relied on voluntary militia, consisting of untrained settlers, for defense. Naturally the young American government tried as a policy to avoid conflicts, but this proved impossible.

The young republic's weak military status called for a careful strategy in defending its national interests. Recognition as a new sovereign nation became a prime objective of the United States government and treaty making was a means to gain this recognition. United States government agents negotiated treaties with Indian nations asking them to recognize the young republic as a sovereign nation. In return, American officials promised to be the Indian's protector. In addition, the United States sought the tribes as allies in an effort to give itself a monopoly over trade relations with them, effectively hampering the expansionism of foreign powers. If the negotiations failed, as they sometimes did, the officials tried to persuade the tribal nations to remain neutral during conflicts between the United States and the imperial powers, England, France and Spain.

The first United States-Indian treaty, signed in 1778 with the Delawares, exemplified the careful strategy used in gaining the Indians as allies. The United States was aware that the Delawares were threatened by larger tribes; following promises of mutual aid in case of war, the United States was able to persuade the Delawares to promise Americans safe passage through Delaware land, supplies if needed, and warriors to fight against the British who were trying to gain control of the Upper Great Lakes area.[4] By developing alliances the United States would be assured of peace. Smaller, more vulnerable tribes like the Delaware could be negotiated with easily; the larger and more warlike tribes, however, presented a potential threat. Secretary of War Henry Knox suggested to Governor Arthur St. Clair of the Western Territory in 1790 that the Indians on the Wabash River and the west end of Lake Erie could be put in awe of the whites by the construction of military posts. Exhibitions of troops would impress the Indians, thus insuring peace in the area.[5]

Such a plan seemed promising but not practical. The cost of building a sufficient military force was beyond the limitations of the U.S. Treasury. The need for increased military strength and careful strategy in dealing with the neighboring tribes grew as American settlers began trespassing increasingly on Indian lands. Traders and troublemakers encouraged the tribes to attack white settlements. Federal officials were concerned with keeping the Indian nations peaceful. The secretary of war wrote the governor of Georgia on August 31, 1792, that "An Indian war is so adverse to strict economy, and the due order of finances, . . . and any new and considerable source of expense, as it would tend to protect the extinguishment of the public debt and would be particularly unfortunate."[6]

American officials approached Indian leaders in a peaceful but shrewd manner. By utilizing the kinship term "Brother," they attempted to show the Indians that they came as friends. Documents of peace talks are filled with the jargon of kinship terms, hinting that white officials seized opportunities to establish friendly relations by establishing kinship bonds. Not only did they exhibit an affinity with Indian people, but they succeeded in elevating their status during treaty talks. Both Indian and white leaders referred to the president of the United States as "Great Father" and Indian agents as "Elder Brothers."[7] The Indians' acceptance of the kinship misnomers only served to verify the Americans' belief in white supremacy. Federal officials convinced the Indians that the white man and his government held a higher status than the Indian and his government. The historical records of treaty negotiations indicate that American officials addressed the Indian leaders as "Younger Brothers" and as the "Red Children of the Great White Father of the United States." This placed the Indians in a subordinate role, which many surprisingly accepted.

Whether or not the Indians believed that the white man and his culture were superior is questionable, but it is known that Indian leaders tended to show respect towards white officials. This can, in part, be attributed to Indian traditions which stressed treating visitors and guests with the utmost consideration, even if one had reservations about them. It is interesting that Indian officials enhanced their presumed subordinate status by accepting the lower kinship terminology. Many believed the white men were superior. Their steel knives, looking glasses and firesticks were impressive. The Great Father image loomed over the Red Man as his presumed protector and keeper.

No previous study of Indian-white relations attempts to explain the Indians' acceptance of the president of the United States as their Great White Father. Part of this acceptance can be attributed to the Indian cultural concept of "dependency" on the Great Spirit. Virtually all Indian nations believed in the Great Spirit and they felt that the heavenly force supplied all of their needs. They remained religiously devoted to practicing ceremonies to pay homage to the Great Spirit and to give thanks for their earthly possessions. Indian theologies are and were a deep part of Native American life, and the Indians believed they were the children of the Great Spirit. Tribal references to Mother Earth and Father Sun are part of the common, fundamental concepts in Native American philosophies. The Native American people depended upon the unison of these two powers, along with others, to protect them and give them guidance. Eventually, this dependency resulted in the downfall of the Indian nations. With shrewd manipulation, white government officials substituted the Great White Father image of the president of the United States for the Great Spirit.

The federal government thus became the new provider for Indian people. In addition to the promised provisions mentioned above, government officials gave Indians gifts of mirrors, bells and assorted metal utensils like iron pots and steel knives. The introduction of iron and steel goods into Native American cultures altered their non-metal cultures; as the Indians became dependent upon white man's goods in their daily lives, they also became dependent upon the United States government.

Advancing white settlement into the Ohio Valley and the South forced officials to deal continually with Indian nations. Land remained the major cause of controversy. The Indians could not understand why the white man could not simply use the land as they did. The notion of land ownership was inconceivable to them. As settlers began crossing the Ohio River in search of new land, local tribes resisted. The strongest resistance was in the form of military actions from the Northwest tribes under Little Turtle, the Miami chief, and later, Tecumseh, the famous Shawnee leader. Tecumseh once asked, "How can the white man own land?" He knew that a tomahawk or a rifle could be owned, but how anyone could own land was beyond his ken since land was like the air and water, an inseparable part of Mother Earth.

Under the leadership of Brigadier General Josiah Harmar, the United States Army forded the Ohio River and marched into the Northwest Territory to confront the Indian nations. Harmar wrote the secretary of war on November 14, 1790, that he had a total force of 1,453 men consisting of 320 federal troops and 1,133 milita. The American force successfully defeated small Indian parties, plundering their villages and burning their crops. Harmar estimated that his soldiers killed between one and two hundred warriors, burned three hundred loghouses and wigwams, and destroyed twenty thousand bushels of corn.[8]

The military strategy of the United States was to defeat the Indians quickly and to demonstrate to them the superiority of American strength in war. As Secretary of War Knox stated to Major St. Clair, "It will be sound policy to attack the Indians by kindness, after demonstrating to them our power to punish them, on all occasions."[9] United States officials were rapidly growing in confidence and felt they now had the military strength to conquer the Indian nations.

Prejudiced white officials deemed the Indians inferior and thought they could deal with them just as easily off the battlefield. Their strategy included getting the Indians to compete with each other for prestige and recognition during treaty talks. The Indians believed that recognition from one's brethren or enemies was a basis for acknowledging leadership. Leadership among the majority of Native American cultures was achievable and sought after, although certain clan memberships, taboos and hereditary rights restricted the earning of leadership status. Many tribes utilized a dual system; a civil leader during times of peace and a war leader during times of crisis. American officials understood the Indians' desire for leadership and used this desire to play one leader against another until they found one who was agreeable to signing treaties. The Indians' personal desire for prestige helped to weaken their political leadership and undermine their strength. While tribal leaders vied for the attention of American officials, the latter stood ready to play leader against leader and tribe against tribe. Commander St. Clair wrote President Washington that arousing jealousy among the Six Nations of the Iroquois, the Wyandots, and other northwestern tribes increased the possibility of negotiating separate treaties.[10] The officials often designated Indian people as chiefs when it would serve the purposes of the United States. At the Council of Prairie du Chien some years later, the Chippewas had nine principal chiefs and American officials created nearly sixty chiefs in all to gain the necessary signatures for treaties![11]

It is clear the United States took advantage of Indian leaders during treaty talks. Top officials in Washington directed territorial officials on the frontier to increase land holdings. They were not to renegotiate agreements that would give back land to the Indians, but any opportunity to acquire more land via treaty should be pursued.[12] During early negotiations in the late 1700s and early 1800s, treaties were a legal means to obtain land; but as Indian military strength decreased and U.S. military strength increased, the government began placing restrictions upon Indian nations.

Lieutenant Colonel James Wilkinson warned the tribes living on the Wabash River, "The arms of the United States are again exerted against you and your towns are in flames, and your wives and children made captives; again you are cautioned to listen to the voice of reason, to sue for peace, and submit to the protection of the United States, who are willing to become your friends and fathers, but, at the same time, are determined to punish you for every injury you may offer to their children."[13] It is evident that the United States wanted to control the Indians. Their chief concern was no longer developing alliances to protect a young republic, but in dominating a people who represented a barrier to expansion.

The American army suffered two major defeats in the Ohio Valley, yet the United States remained steadfast in its decision to conquer the

Indian nations. American officials continued the campaign against Indians in the Northwest. To compensate for its weakened army, the United States sought to obtain Indian allies in the South to defeat the northwestern tribes. The secretary of war wrote the governor of Virginia in 1792, "It would appear that if, by necessity, the war with the Indians, northwest of the Ohio, must progress, that we could obtain five or six hundred Southern Indians to join our army."[14]

The governor of Georgia addressed the Cherokees, one of the largest Indian nations in the South, with a smooth tongue. "Then Brothers: Let the hatchet be buried, and the big sword shall remain in rust; we will then take each other high by the arm, and fast by the hand; we shall sit under the same tree, the smoke of our pipes shall make one cloud, and we will taste of the same cup."[15] While the Georgia governor courted the Cherokees in hopes of getting them to join ranks with the United States, white settlers were coveting the Cherokees' land in Georgia.

Excerpts from a speech given several years earlier by Corn Tassel, a Cherokee leader, indicate that his people were well aware of the motives of the white man. Corn Tassel noted the white man offered to teach the Cherokees his civilization, but wanted land in return. The wise Cherokee stated, "Indeed, much has been advanced on the want of what you term civilization among the Indians, and many proposals have been made to us to adopt your laws, your religion, your manners and your customs. You say: Why do not the Indians till the ground and live as we do? May we not, with equal propriety, ask, why the white people do not hunt and live as we do?"[16]

Americans felt justified in their superior attitude towards Indians. They considered their civilized ways highly advanced compared to the various modes of Indian life, and they believed their Christianity obliged them to save the Red Man from his so-called heathen ways. The Americans believed that God was on their side and their quest to defeat the Indians of the Ohio Valley was a religious duty. Christianity and civilization would overcome the "savages," who stood in the path of the Americans' Manifest Destiny to cultivate the soil with the seeds of crops as God intended it to be. This feeling of Christian superiority is reflected in William Henry Harrison's communication to William Eustis, the secretary of war, after his troops suffered an ambush by a part of the Shawnee Prophet's warriors. "To their savage fury," said Harrison, "our troops opposed with cool and deliberate valor which is characteristic of the Christian soldier."[17]

The idea of forcing one's beliefs and way of life on another group of people was new to the Indians. They fought wars based on the desire for territorial gains or recognition, or wars arising from blood feuds, but they did not fight to further the cause of their religion. The Indians looked to the Great Spirit for guidance and protection in battle. They prayed for a vision, a sign, a successful outcome. Their way of life, culture and people were in danger. All was at stake. They relied upon their leaders for direction and upon their religious beliefs to survive this crisis.

The combined leadership of the Prophet and Tecumseh unified the Indians of the Northwest. The teachings of the Prophet and the words of Tecumseh had a powerful, magnetic effect on the tribes, whose warriors readily joined the pan-Indian movement. The Indians were led to believe that the white man was evil and coveted their lands, and would corrupt them if they took up his ways. The Dance of the Lakes, a ceremony evolving from the Prophet's religious fervor, entranced the Indians, touching their inner spirits and creating a union of all believers. The supernatural feats of the Prophet and the charismatic talks of Tecumseh convinced the followers that the prophecy would come true—the white man would be destroyed.

War raged throughout the Ohio Valley between Indians and American soldiers. Indian war parties raided settlements and the United States responded by sending William Henry Harrison to lead a large force against the Northwest Indians. Prior to marching against the Indians, Harrison trained his men for combat in the wilderness environment. His army and sharpshooting frontiersmen won decisively at the Battle of Fallen Timbers in 1811. On October 5, 1813, the Battle of the Thames resulted in the Indians' final defeat and the death of Tecumseh. In 1814, the Treaty of Greenville was signed with several tribes, bringing a final peace to the Ohio Valley.[18]

Ironically, during this period some of the weaker tribes sought an alliance with the United States, or at least neutrality, and wanted protection. These groups pleaded innocent to the attacking of white settlements and the American army. Now it was the Indians who wanted alliances, rather than a young United States republic.

The influence of the Prophet and Tecumseh had spread to the South among the Cherokees, Choctaws and other tribes. White settlers encroaching on their domains triggered Indian anger and the tribes retaliated by raiding white settlements unmercifully. Colonel Benjamin Hawkins, agent for Indian Affairs in the South, reported that the Chickasaws had committed one of the most inhumane acts of murder: "Seven families have been murdered near the mouth of the Ohio, and most cruelly mangled, showing all the savage barbarity that could be invented. One woman was cut open, a child taken out and stuck on a stake."[19]

Indian aggressions convinced American officials that they could never be civilized enough to live alongside white Americans. John C. Calhoun, secretary of war, wrote Joseph McMinn, acting agent for the United States, in 1818, "Universal experience proves that a people still in a savage state cannot reside in the immediate neighborhood of a civilized nation, without falling into a state of vice and misery."[20] He advised that the Indians in the South should be moved to the West, so that they could become civilized under the teachings of agents who would supervise them in the white man's way of life. Secretary Calhoun communicated to a Cherokee delegation a year later, "You see that the Great Spirit has made our form of society stronger than yours, and you must submit to adopt ours, if you wish to be happy by pleasing him."[21]

American officials had very little appreciation for Indians and their cultures. To them, Indians were heathens and hardly civilized. Ethnocentrism blinded the white man, and his inability to understand the Indian ways of life fostered disrespect for tribal cultures. The traditional ways of the Indian convinced federal officials that the Red Man could not compete with the white man according to his standards.

Federal officials undertook plans to teach Indians the civilized ways of white America. While American ethnocentrism demeaned Indian cultures, Christian influences encouraged the United States government to reform the Indian race. Government officials believed Indian adults would have difficulty in reforming their ways, but that the Indian youth could be educated to learn the better way of life that white civilization offered.

The promise of educational opportunities was a common provision in many treaties. A report of the commissioner of Indian Affairs in 1831 showed that 1,601 Indian students were enrolled in schools established by missionary groups throughout the country. An excerpt from the commissioner's report reflects the belief that education would inspire Indians to adopt the American way of life. "Many Indian youths, who have therein received the benefits of tuition, have already returned to their respective tribes, carrying with them the rudiments of learning, the elements of morals and the precepts of religion, all apparently calculated to subdue the habits and soften the feelings of their kindred, and to prepare the way for the gradual introduction of civilization and Christianity."[22] To the white man, the growing attendance of Indian children at white schools was evidence that the native cultures of America were slipping away.

The increasing dependency of Indians on Euramerican trade goods was additional evidence of the domination of white American culture over the Indian nations. The most acute sign of the demise of native

America was the Indians' addiction to alcohol. Trading rum and giving cheap whiskey to the Indians was a ploy utilized by government officials and traders which had devastating effects on Indian behavior and broke down the traditional standards of Indian societies. As Native American leaders witnessed the evil impact of white men's vices and culture on their people, their immediate reaction was to drive the whites from their lands. The reality of the Indians' situation grew worse. The evils of white civilization undermined in a short span of years the Indian cultures which had taken centuries to develop. The Indian world was disrupted.

White greed for Indian lands was the catalyst for westward expansion. The course of Manifest Destiny pressured the government to deal with the Indian presence on the frontier. Federal officials utilized propaganda to convince the Indians that their ways of life were soon to be lost. Indian agents who spoke before the Chickasaw council during October 1826 tried to tell the Indians that their situation was hopeless and that removal west of the Mississippi River, away from the white man, was the best solution. The rhetoric of government representatives became standardized, much like this statement: "The tomahawk and scalping knife must be laid aside for the scythe and pruning knive; the bow and arrow, for the plough; the wandering hunter must change his garb and his occupation for one more congenial with the pursuits of civilization."[23]

The military and political strategy used by the United States to deal with the Indian nations was to seize Indian lands for white settlement. This became clear when Congress passed the Indian Removal Bill in 1830. President Andrew Jackson, a staunch advocate of Indian removal, and other removalists asserted that American citizens were already settling on Indian lands and that the Indians could not coexist with white men and needed time to adopt white ways. In a council with the Cherokees, Commissioners Duncan G. Campbell and James Meriwether told the Indians that the white man was destined to inherit North America and that this was his right:

> Friends and Brothers: The people of Europe were the first men who landed upon these shores. As soon as they established colonies, they claimed the sovereignty of the soil by the right of discovery. All the country which was conquered belonged to the conquerors. The Cherokees, the Creeks, and almost every other Indian tribe, powerful and numerous as they were, took sides against us. All shared the same fate. All became subject to the Government afterwards established, under the title of the "United States of America." The Delawares surrendered their sovereignty at the Treaty of Fort Pitt; the Six Nations at Fort

Stanwix; the Creeks at New York; the Chickasaws at Hopewell; and the Cherokees at Hopewell, in 1785, and so on.[24]

American officials succeeded in negotiating removal treaties with the southern tribes. Two treaties, sometimes three, were signed with each of the Five Civilized Tribes who had estimated populations of eighteen to twenty thousand. The removal of these people west of the Mississippi, which became known as the "Trail of Tears," was a massive undertaking and is considered a classic, disgraceful display of the mistreatment of Indian people. The provisions contained in the Treaty of Doaks Stand with the Choctaws was typical of promises made to Indians for removal. The treaty provided "each warrior a blanket, kettle, rifle gun, bullet moulds and wipers, and ammunition sufficient for hunting and defense for one year; said warrior shall also be supplied with corn, to support him and his family for the same period . . ."[25]

Although the federal government initially negotiated treaties with Indians to further American interests, the treaties have become today the mainstay of Indian rights. By establishing treaties with the Indian nations, the United States government acknowledged the sovereign rights of Indians according to the international law of one foreign nation signing a treaty with another.[26] Under the Constitution, treaties are the highest law of the American nation.[27] The question of Indian sovereignty in the white man's eyes is thus a legal one.

Indian treaties with the United States brought into public debate the question of sovereignty for the Red Man. The legality of Indian sovereignty came under attack in the United States court system when two cases involving the Cherokee Nation arose. In *Cherokee Nation v. Georgia* in 1831, the Supreme Court held that the Cherokees were an "independent" nation, meaning that the Cherokees exercised sovereignty. Chief Justice John Marshall's decree in this case was a landmark decision, setting a precedent for all tribes. One year later, in *Worcester v. Georgia*, Chief Justice Marshall reversed his earlier position and stated that the Cherokees were a nation dependent on Georgia and, hence, the federal government. This reversal left only the treaties as the legal basis for arguing for Indian sovereignty.[28]

The Indian nations lost the exercise of liberty when they were defeated by the United States military. Both Indians and whites understood that war determined sovereignty, and that the defeated nations' freedom to continue to live as before depended upon the conqueror. The Indians' defeat subjected them to the standards of American culture, and hampered their efforts to live in harmony with all things and to continue to live like their ancestors.

While the legal interpretation of Indian sovereignty lay in doubt, the sovereign Indian way of life was disappearing. As the United States military supervised the removal of the eastern tribal populations to the West, the ever-increasing white population threatened to overwhelm Indian America. The annual report of the commissioner of Indian Affairs for 1831 commented:

> Gradually diminishing in numbers and deteriorating in condition; incapable of coping with the superior intelligence of the white man, ready to fall into the vices, but unapt [sic] to appropriate the benefits of the social state; the increasing tide of white population threatened soon to engulf them, and finally to cause their total extinction."[29]

The discovery of gold in California in 1848 and later discoveries in Colorado, Montana and the Southwest caused settlers to rush across the Great Plains. Major General John Pope described the situation:

> People, in incredible numbers, continue to throng across the great plains to these rich mining territories, undeterred by the seasons, by hardships and privation, or by the constant and relentless hostility of the Indian tribes. For several hundred miles along the routes to New Mexico, Colorado, and Montana, the hospitals of the military posts are filled with frost-bitten teamsters and the emigrants, whose animals have been frozen to death, and whose trains loaded with supplies, stand buried in the snow on the great plains."[30]

General Pope then asked,

> By what right are Montana and the larger part of Utah, Colorado, and Nebraska occupied by whites? What right, under our treaties with Indians, have we to be roaming over the whole mining territories, as well as the plains to the east of them, molesting the Indian in every foot of his country, drawing off or destroying the game upon which he depends for subsistence, and dispossessing him of the abiding places his tribes has [sic] occupied for centuries?"[31]

The federal attitude towards the western Indians became hostile. In the early stages of fighting, the Indians won easily. The U.S. Cavalry was not accustomed to the Plains Indians' style of warfare. The nomadic warriors would wheel their ponies to attack the cavalry and then dart away. Federal officials, however, were determined to overpower the Plains tribes. The report of the commissioner of Indian Affairs for 1855 stressed that the Indian had to be taught a lesson on the superiority of white civilization. The commissioner reported:

> To overawe the tribes, to make them know and dread our power, to make them fear and respect us, it is clear and apparent, to my mind, as the noonday sun, that the best and only proper method of conducting our Indian relations is to establish military posts in the heart of Indian country.[32]

Several years elapsed during which the military fought small wars with the Plains tribes and other tribal groups until President Ulysses S. Grant's peace policy and the Peace Commissioners' Act in 1867 called for the employment of a full strategy of peace negotiations. Federal officials tried to meet with the western tribes to discuss peace and other mutual interests but had limited success. Several significant councils took place with the western Indians at St. Louis, Fort Laramie, Little Arkansas, Walla Walla and Medicine Lodge Creek. The latter was probably the largest council held between western tribes and the United States. The councils were spectacular events with important tribal leaders meeting with government and military officials before large audiences of tribal members, soldiers and, occasionally, newspaper reporters. At the grand council of Medicine Lodge in 1867, an estimated six thousand Indians representing the most powerful tribes on the southern plains—Cheyenne, Arapaho, Comanche, Kiowa and Plains Apache—assembled at Medicine Lodge Creek in southwest Kansas during October 1867.[33]

The council was viewed differently by Indians and whites. To the Indians, ceremonial rituals based on their traditional cultures were the main features of the council, even though they discussed military and civil matters. The ceremonial rituals produced a spiritual feeling which enveloped the council. The two sides coming together, joining in peace, received the blessing of the Great Spirit. The white officials acknowledged the formalities of the council with the Indian leaders, but more importantly to them, the council represented an opportunity to discuss Indian and white interests and to arrive at an agreement. The white officials preferred a businesslike atmosphere to the rituals of the Indian council; nevertheless, they observed the formalities of shaking hands with the Indian leaders to welcome them and their tribes and, frequently, presented the leaders with peace medals to remind the Indians of their peaceful intentions.[34]

Indian cultures emphasized the importance of council proceedings. The tribal leaders first went through purification ceremonies before entering the council. The meeting of Indian and white officials symbolized a unison of peace, and their hearts were presumed pure. It would have been offensive to Indian tradition if ulterior motives were displayed by either side, although political aims were pursued indirectly during the council talks. While the actual council proceedings were important to the Indians, the resulting agreement or treaty was the most important part of the council to the white officials. This difference between the Indian and white views of what a council meant and should produce exemplifies the cultural differences between the two sides.

The language barrier between government and Indian officials was also a common problem in negotiations. At Medicine Lodge, seven languages were spoken and misunderstandings frequently resulted. The council depended upon interpreters to convey the messages of the speeches given, and relied upon them to maintain peaceful relations between the two sides. Some disagreement occurred over who should serve as interpreters, but usually the tribes made their own selections. Relating the speech of an Indian leader to the rest of the audience was the most important aspect of the interpreter's role. This took time, and although the interpreter stressed the same points as the speaker did, much of the meaning of the speech was lost simply because there frequently were no exact translations for the words. Moreover, sometimes a speech was translated into two other languages. At Medicine Lodge, for example, the speeches of the Plains Apache were first translated into Arapaho by an Apache speaking Arapaho. Then a Margaret Adams, who spoke Arapaho, translated the Arapaho into English.[35]

Tribal customs determined how tribal speakers were chosen and when they presented their talks. Furthermore, a spokesman would not deliver his speech until all members of his tribe were present. Anything different from the Indian order would likely offend the absent tribal members, thus endangering the success of the council. Tribal leaders were the usual speakers and they were responsible for presenting the tribe's terms. Each speaker told the history of his people and explained the Indian rapport with nature, stating that his and his people's lives were affected by the coming of the white man. Satank, an elderly Kiowa leader, gave one of the most moving speeches in all Indian oratory when he described the vast differences between the Indians and whites and their mutual interests in land. The Kiowa leader spoke:

> The white man grows jealous of his red brother. The white man once came to trade; he now comes as a soldier. He once put his trust in our friendship and wanted no shield but our fidelity. But now he builds forts and plants big guns on their walls. He once gave us arms and powder and bade us hunt the game. We then loved him for his confidence . . . he now covers his face with the cloud of jealousy and anger and tells us to be gone, as an offended master speaks to his dog."[36]

There was a pause to allow the interpreter, Phillip McCusker, to translate the words of Satank. Following the translation, the old Indian lowered his eyes and touched the silver peace medal hanging from his neck. He held the medal and looked at the peace commissioners with sad eyes and continued speaking:

> Look at this medal I wear. By wearing this, I have been made poor. Before, I was rich in horses and lodges. Today I am the

poorest of all. When you gave me this silver medal on my neck, you made me poor.

We thank the Great Spirit that all these wrongs are now to cease. You have tried, as many have done, to make a new bargain merely to get the advantage.

Do for us what is best. Teach us the road to travel. We know you will not forsake us; and tell your people also to act as you have done, to be as you have been.

I am old . . . I shall soon have to go to the way of my fathers. But those who come after me will remember this day . . . And now, the time has come that I must go. You may never see me more, but remember Satank as the white man's friend.[37]

When his speech was over, Satank performed the customary hand-shaking with all of the white officials. Indians, who held their leaders in highest esteem, remembered the talk of each spokesman. Likewise, the white officials respected the Indian leaders; nevertheless, they went along with their plans to bargain for United States national interests. In order to gain their terms, they would agree to the terms of the Indians as they saw fit.

Truth was one of the fundamental elements of treaty negotiations between Indians and whites. Because Native American cultures lacked a written language (until Sequoyah developed one for the Cherokees), Indians depended upon truth as the basis of their oral communication. To the Indians, truth was a chief virtue of their people and it gave the spoken word significant meaning; the simplicity of the Indians' spoken words minimized misunderstandings. Although truth seems elementary and stereotypical of American Indians, it is not merely a romantic way of depicting Native Americans in a traditional sense. Truth conveyed the sincereity of one's intentions.

Conversely, the written word of the white man left the meanings of his words open to interpretation and ambiguity. Frequently, federal officials tried to convince the Indians during the councils that their interpretations were the "real" truth. The Great White Father wanted his Indian children to lay down their weapons and follow the white man's teachings of Christianity and civilization.

What actually transpired during the councils was important to the Indians, but the white man found restrictions only in the *contents* of the treaty provisions. The view that council proceedings were less important than the results enabled white officials to negotiate with Indian leaders to obtain the best results for white interests, as in modern business agreement. The Indian leaders interpreted the white man's behavior as lying, speaking with forked-tongue. The business approach of American officials in the political arena conflicted with the Indians' customary ceremonial approach to the council.

American officials had a very limited knowledge of western Indian cultures. At the Medicine Lodge Council, the federal and military officials understood little about southern plains tribal cultures, and even less about the differences among the Kiowa, Comanche, Arapaho, Cheyenne and Plains Apache tribes. The organization of the council camp was important to the tribes attending. Once a year when all the Cheyennes gathered for the Sun Dance and the Council of Forty-Four met for tribal business, each band of the tribe had a designated position in the camp circle. Although this tradition may have seemed inconsequential to white officials, such formality identified the band and showed their status as a part of the whole tribal community.[38]

The majority of the Plains tribes' bands were composed of military societies of ranked warriors who had designated duties. The "akacita" society of the Teton Sioux and the "Black Mouths" society of the Mandans served as the camp police to maintain law and order during their tribal meetings. Tribal designations and other cultural aspects of the council among the various tribes had to be taken into consideration by government officials during the council meetings.[39]

Gift giving also played an important part in the council meetings. It is interesting that Indians and whites viewed this act of hospitality differently. American officials accepted the fact that by giving trinkets and goods to the Indians, they would gain their favor and also impress upon the Indians the advantages of Americanization. Giving gifts helped to break language barriers and eased whatever uneasy feelings there may have been. Because the American officials were the host, Indians expected gifts, especially when they learned that the United States government generously gave goods to the Indians. If the situation was reversed and the Indians were the host, it would be safe to assume that they would generously give gifts and food to their guests.

The host-guest aspect of the council was an element of treaty making that the whites well understood. By the time of the Medicine Lodge Council, it was common practice for the U.S. Army to issue food and gifts to the Indians. In treaty negotiations, federal officials were often concerned that there be sufficient provisions given to the Indians to insure a happy initial relationship. Senator Edmund Ross of Kansas stated that feeding the Indians was much cheaper than fighting them.[40]

In return the Indians expressed respect for the American officials, addressing them as "Brothers," "Elder Brothers" and "Fathers." Raymond DeMallie, a noted anthropologist, pointed out that the white officials could have used the kinship term Brother even more to their advantage if they had understood that one brother could hardly deny the other anything he requested.[41] The Indians expected the whites to be generous and they were. At Medicine Lodge, the Indians received blankets, cooking utensils, food and pistols; the latter, however, proved to be of poor quality, sometimes misfiring and blowing apart in the holder's hand.

The final aspect of Indian tradition in the council was the passing of the pipe among the tribal and white officials to consecrate the council with the blessing of the Great Spirit. The smoke of the ceremonial tobacco became a spiritual link with the Great Spirit.[42] The end of the smoking ceremony completed the council and sealed all that was said and agreed upon. Although white officials politely participated in the smoking of the pipe, they did not view it as the sealing of the agreement or treaty. Their final authorization depended upon congressional ratification of the provisions written in the treaty; the treaty was susceptible to change.[43] Many Indian leaders were led to believe that everything they said during the council was enclosed in the words of the treaty, and that by making their mark or touching the pen, they promised to fulfill their obligations under the treaty. Touching the pen led to the legal demise of the Indian nations. It represented the Indian's consent, whether or not he understood the provisions, that he was obligated to act in accordance with the terms of the treaty.

Simply put, the federal officials entered into treaty negotiations in order to secure larger land holdings for white settlement. First, the officials had to confine the nomadic Plains tribes to specified hunting domains. In most cases, the tribes selected their traditional hunting areas and the American officials agreed to their choices. This literally divided the American West into tribal dominions. Next, the officials negotiated new treaties with the tribes when old ones were broken. Often the tribes were forced to break treaties when promised provisions did not arrive from the federal government and when the annuities of food were too spoiled to eat. Most of the Plains Indians' tradition of raiding as part of a nomadic hunting culture was dismissed by government officials.

The Indians' actions for survival were mistaken for hostilities and provoked a bitter response. The Indians themselves were enraged at having to live on reservations with little or nothing to eat. They wanted to destroy the white man and one way was through raids or warfare. Representative James M. Cavanaugh of Minnesota expressed the vengeful reaction of government officials. He stated before Congress:

> I will say that I like an Indian better dead than living . . . I believe in the policy that exterminates the Indians, drives them outside the boundaries of civilization, because you cannot civilize them. Gentlemen you may call this very harsh language; but per-

haps they would not think so if they had had my experience in
Minnesota and Colorado. In Minnesota the almost living babe
has been torn from its mother's womb; and I have seen the child,
with its young heart palpitating, nailed to the window sill. I have
seen women who were scalped, disfigured, outraged. In Denver,
Colorado, I have seen women and children brought in scalped.
Scalped why? Simply because the Indian was upon the war-path,
to satisfy his devilish and barbarous propensities.[44]

Officials in Washington ordered the military to suppress the Plains
tribes. New treaties forced the Indians to give up hunting domains and
move to designated reservations—parcels of land which white settlers
did not want. There, the government officials hoped the Indians would
become Americanized and learn to cultivate the land as the white
farmer did. P. Prescott, superintendent of farming for the Sioux, reported his evaluation of the ability of the nomadic Sioux warrior to
learn to plough a field. He said:

The great trouble with the Indians is in the intellect, which is but
a little above that of the dumb brute, and at whose door will the
fault lie? The mind of the Indian must be cultivated as well as the
body, or else morality, the great forerunner of civilization, is lost
sight of, and all kinds of debauchery remain with the Indians, and
often civilization to an Indian is an injury instead of blessing[45]

This description shows that Prescott and most likely other federal representatives had little knowledge of and no regard for Plains Indian
culture. Farming contradicted the Plains Indian culture of nomadic
hunting, and trying to raise crops on the poor quality land of the reservations made no sense.

The inability and/or unwillingness of the white officials to understand Indian cultures and the Indians' devotion to their own culture
have been the source of the cultural communication gap in the history
of Indian-white relations. The last treaty which was signed with the
Nez Perce in 1868 exemplifies this point. For years the Nez Perce refused to sign any treaty paper. Chief Joseph recalled his 1855 meeting
with Governor Isaac Stevens of Washington Territory. He said, "My
father, who represented his band, refused to have anything to do with
the council, because he wished to be a free man. He claimed that no
man owned any part of the earth, and a man could not sell what he did
not own."[46]

Eight years later in 1863, another council was held with the Nez
Perce. Joseph's father warned his son again, "When you go into council
with the white man, always remember your country. Do not give it
away. The white man will cheat you out of your home." During his last
breaths, Joseph's father spoke the following words to his son, "A few
years more, and white men will be all around you. They have eyes on

this land. My son, never forget my dying words. This country holds your father's body. Never sell the bones of your father and your mother." Joseph recalled, "I pressed my father's hand and told him I would protect his grave with my life. My father smiled and passed away to the spirit-land."[47]

The defeat of the Indian nations made the treaties binding according to the standards of the white man's law. Today, the Indian is forced to negotiate for his rights via white means. The treaties provide for few, but important, federal obligations to Indian people. The promised provisions of a blacksmith, blankets, removal to reservations, corn during the removal period and so forth, have expired as the treaties became outdated, yet the treaties have obligated the federal government to certain responsibilities to the Indians. Federal trust responsibilities over Indian properties remain a treaty obligation which is carried out by the Bureau of Indian Affairs. Reservations, which were considered waste lands that no one wanted, contain rich underground resources—water, oil, gas, coal and uranium—much needed sources of energy. The reservations are held in trust and the United States is supposed to protect Indian land rights and mineral rights.[48] Finally, the human rights of Indian people remain in question. The sovereign status of Native Americans still hangs in abeyance even though the United States-Indian treaties were negotiated when one sovereign nation made a legal agreement with another. These are current issues that are yet to be settled and which exemplify the history of white America versus Indian America.

NOTES

[1] During his research on United States-Indian treaty making, G.E.E. Lindquist was unable to find the popular phrase, "As long as the grass grows and the rivers run." I concur with his finding. See G.E.E. Lindquist, "Indian Treaty Making," *Chronicles of Oklahoma*, 26:4 (Winter 1948-1949): 416-448.

[2] Rufus Putnam's speech to General George Washington regarding the treating with the northwest Indians in the Ohio area is in *American State Papers* (Hereafter *ASP*), Vol. 1 — Indian Affairs, (Washington, D.C.: Gales and Seaton, 1832) p. 319.

[3] For a chronological list of United States-Indian treaties and agreements, see Vine Deloria, Jr., ed., *A Chronological List of Treaties and Agreements Made by Indian Tribes with the United States* (Washington, D.C.: The Institute for the Development of Indian Law, 1973). Deloria's *Behind the Trail of Broken Treaties: An Indian Declaration of Independence* (New York: Delacorte Press, 1974) discusses the legacy of treaty breaking.

Thorough sources for United States-Indian treaties are Charles J. Kappler, comp., *Indian Affairs: Laws and Treaties* (Washington, D.C.: Government Printing Office, 1940-1941); Richard Peters, ed., *United States Statutes At*

Large, Vol. 7 - Treaties between the United States and the Indian Tribes (Boston, Little and Brown, 1846); Samuel S. Hamilton, comp., *Indian Treaties and Law Regulations Relating to Indian Affairs: To Which Is Added an Appendix, Containing the Proceedings of the Old Congress, and Other Important State Papers, In Relation to Indian Affairs* (Washington, D.C.: Way and Gideon, 1826); and *A Compilation of All the Treaties between the United States and the Indian Tribes, Now in Force As Laws* (Washington, D.C.: Government Printing Office, 1873).

[4]"Treaty with the Delawares, 1778," in Kappler, op. cit., pp. 3-5.

[5]Secretary of War Knox to Governor St. Clair, September 12, 1790, *ASP,* op. cit., Vol. 1, p. 100.

[6]Secretary of War Knox to the governor of Georgia, August 31, 1792, *ASP,* op. cit., Vol. 1, pp. 258-259.

[7]Two of the few studies examining cultural dynamics in Indian treaty making are Raymond J. DeMallie, "American Indian Treaty Making: Motives and Meanings," *American Indian Journal,* 3:1 (January 1977): 2-10; and DeMallie's article, "Touching the Pen: Plains Indian Treaty Councils in Ethnohistorical Perspective," in Frederick C. Luebke, ed., *Ethnicity on the Great Plains* (Lincoln, Nebraska, and London: University of Nebraska Press, 1980).

[8]Brigadier General Josiah Harmar to Secretary of War Knox, November 14, 1790, *ASP,* op. cit., Vol. 1, pp. 104-105.

[9]Secretary of War Knox to Governor St. Clair, March 21, 1791, *ASP,* op. cit., Vol. 1, pp. 172-174.

[10]Governor St. Clair to the governor of the Western Territory and to the president of the United States, May 2, 1788, *ASP,* op. cit., Vol. 1, p. 10.

[11]William S. Hatton, Indian sub-agent, to Col. D. D. Mitchell, superintendent of Indian Affairs, October 21, 1850, in *Report of the Commissioner of Indian Affairs,* November 27, 1850.

[12]Charles Thompson to the governor of the Northwest Territory, July 2, 1788, *ASP,* op. cit., Vol. 1, p. 9.

[13]James Wilkinson to the Indian nations living on the Wabash River, n.d., *ASP,* op. cit., Vol. 1, p. 135.

[14]The secretary of war to the governor of Virginia, May 16, 1792, *ASP,* op. cit., Vol. 1, pp. 223-224.

[15]Governor Telfar (Georgia) to leaders and warriors of the Cherokee Nation, November 14, 1792, *ASP,* op. cit., Vol. 1, p. 334.

[16]"Let Us Examine the Facts," by the Cherokee leader, Corn Tassel, in Peter Nabokov, ed., *Native American Testimony: An Anthology of Indian-White Relations, First Encounter to Disposition* (New York: Thomas Y. Crowell, 1978), pp. 152-155.

[17]William Henry Harrison to Secretary of War Eustis, December 19, 1811, *ASP,* op. cit., Vol. 1, pp. 777-779.

[18]A firsthand account of the campaign against the northwest tribes is found in Dwight L. Smith, ed., *From Greenville to Fallen Timbers: A Journal of*

the Wayne Campaign, July 28 to September 14, 1794 (Indianapolis, Ind.: Indiana Historical Society, 1952).

A copy of the Treaty of Greenville is in Kappler, op. cit., pp. 105-107. Two related studies are Frazer Ells Wilson, *The Treaty of Greenville* (Piqua, Ohio: Correspondent Press, 1894) and Samuel F. Hunt, "The Treaty of Greenville," *Ohio Archaeological and Historical Quarterly*, 7 (January 1899): 218-240.

[19]Colonel Benjamin Hawkins to Tuskunugee Thlucco Oche Harjo and every chief of the Upper Creeks, March 29, 1813, *ASP*, op. cit., Vol. 1, pp. 839-840.

[20]Secretary of War Calhoun to Joseph McMinn, July 29, 1818, *ASP*, op. cit., Vol. 2, p. 480.

[21]John C. Calhoun to the Cherokee delegation, February 11, 1819, *ASP*, op. cit., Vol. 2, p. 190.

[22]*Report of the Commissioner of Indian Affairs*, November 19, 1831, p. 172.

[23]Thomas Hinds and John Coffee to Chickasaw council, October 28, 1826, *ASP*, op. cit., Vol. 2, pp. 723-724.

[24]Indian Commissioners Duncan Campbell and James Meriwhether to the Cherokee council, October 21, 1823, *ASP*, op. cit., Vol. 2, pp. 469-470.

[25]Treaty with the Choctaws, 1820, near Doaks Stand on the Natches road in the Choctaw Nation, *ASP*, op. cit., Vol. 2., pp. 224-225. See also "Treaty with the Choctaw, 1820," in Kappler, op. cit., pp. 191-195, for a copy of the treaty.

[26]Indian sovereignty rights are discussed in David H. Getches, Daniel M. Rosenfelt and Charles F. Wilkinson, eds., *Cases and Materials on Federal Indian Law* (St. Paul, Minn.: West Publishing, 1979).

[27]U.S. Constitution, Art. VI, Clause 2.

[28]Brief excerpts from *Cherokee Nation v. Georgia* and *Worcester v. Georgia* are in Francis P. Prucha, ed., *Documents of United States Indian Policy* (Lincoln, Nebraska, and London: University of Nebraska Press, 1975). For Marshall's opinions, see *Cherokee Nation v. State of Georgia*, 29 U.S. (5 Pet.) 1, 15, (1831) and *Worcester v. State of Georgia*, 31 U.S. (6 Pet.) 515, 534 (1832). See also Richard Peters, *The Case of the Cherokee Against the State of Georgia* (Philadelphia: John Grigg, 1831). The cases are discussed in Getches, et. al., op. cit., and in the updated version of Felix S. Cohen, *Handbook of Federal Indian Law* (Charlottesville, Va.: Michie Bobbs-Merrill Law Publishers, 1982).

[29]*Report of the Commissioner of Indian Affairs*, November 19, 1831, p. 172.

[30]Major General John Pope, *Report of the Condition and Necessities of the Military Department of the Missouri*, February 25, 1866, House Ex. Doc. 76, 39th Congress, 1st Session.

[31]Ibid.

[32]*Report of the Commissioner of Indian Affairs*, October 10, 1855, p. 84.

[33]See Alfred A. Taylor, "Medicine Lodge Peace Council," *Chronicles of Oklahoma*, 2 (June 1924): 98-117; Douglas C. Jones, *The Treaty of Medicine Lodge: The Story of the Great Treaty Council As Told by Eyewitnesses* (Norman,

Okla.: University of Oklahoma Press, 1966); and Douglas C. Jones, "Medicine Lodge Revisited," *Kansas Historical Quarterly*, 35 (Summer 1969): 130-142.

[34]A brief history of Indian-white handshaking can be found in John C. Ewers, "The Image of the White Man as a Glad-hander," *The American West*, 19:1 (January/February 1982): 54-60, 69-71. For information about Indian peace medals, see Francis P. Prucha, *Indian Peace Medals in American History* (Madison, Wis.: State Historical Society of Wisconsin, 1971) and Bauman L. Belden, *Indian Peace Medals Issued in the United States* (Reprinted in New Milford, Conn.: N. Flayderman, 1966).

[35]Margaret Adams was thirty-three years old during the Medicine Lodge Council. She was the daughter of a French Canadian trader and an Arapaho mother, who probably taught her the Arapaho language. Jones, *The Treaty of Medicine Lodge*, op. cit., pp. 107-108.

[36]Ibid., pp. 156-157.

[37]Ibid.

[38]For discussions of Cheyenne cultural ways, see George Bird Grinnell, *The Cheyenne Indians: Their History and Ways of Life* (New Haven, Conn.: Yale University Press, 1923); Donald J. Berthrong, *The Southern Cheyennes* (Norman, Okla.: University of Oklahoma Press, 1963); and Peter J. Powell, *Sweet Medicine: The Continuing Role of the Sacred Arrows, the Sun Dance, and the Sacred Buffalo Hat in Northern Cheyenne History* (Norman, Okla.: University of Oklahoma Press, 1969).

[39]For an understanding of the Plains Indian way of life among the Sioux and the Mandans, see Royal B. Hassrick, *The Sioux Life and Customs of a Warrior Society* (Norman, Okla.: University of Oklahoma Press, 1964) and A. W. Bowers, *Mandan Social and Ceremonial Organization* (Chicago: University of Chicago Press, 1950).

[40]Jones, *The Treaty of Medicine Lodge*, op. cit., p. 158.

[41]DeMallie, "Touching the Pen," op. cit., p. 50.

[42]Ibid., pp. 39-40.

[43]A large number of agreements were never ratified as treaties as can be seen in *Ratified and Unratified Treaties with Various Indian Tribes, 1801-1869* (Washington, D.C.: Department of the Interior Microfilm T494, Record Group 48, National Archives). See also Richard Schifter, "Some Problems Relating to Indian Treaties," in *Proceedings of the Conference on Indian Tribes and Treaties* (Minneapolis: Center for Continuing Study, University of Minnesota, 1955), pp. 41-57; and Ralph A. Smith, "The Fantasy of a Treaty to End Treaties," *Great Plains Journal*, 12 (Fall 1972): 26-51.

[44]Speech by Representative James M. Cavanaugh, D-Minnesota, *Congressional Globe*, 40th Congress, 2nd Session, 1868, p. 2638.

[45]Report by Superintendent P. Prescott of farming for the Sioux, September 10, 1856, *Report of the Commissioner of Indian Affairs*, No. 20, Sioux Agency, Minnesota Territory.

[46]Chief Joseph of the Nez Perce, "My Son, Stop Your Ears," January 14, 1879, in Nabokov, op. cit., pp. 162-168.

[47]Ibid.

[48]Contemporary federal obligations to Native Americans and Indian rights are discussed in Wilcomb E. Washburn, *Red Man's Land/White Man's Law: A Study of the Past and Present Status of the American Indian* (New York: Charles Scribner, 1971). Two excellent sources on the legal status of Indian Americans are Getches, et. al., op. cit., and Cohen, op. cit.

IRISH REPUBLICANISM YESTERDAY AND TODAY: THE DILEMMA OF IRISH AMERICANS

Thomas E. Hachey

Department of History
Marquette University

Irish republicanism, or the goal of a free and united Ireland, has been an enduring and often ambiguous dimension of Irish-American life for the better part of a century and a half.[1] The inception of militant Irish nationalism within Irish America is sometimes cited as St. Patrick's Day, 1858, when Michael Doheny and John O'Mahoney, two of the younger refugees from the abortive Young Ireland insurrection of ten years before, founded a secret, oath-bound society in New York. The Fenian Brotherhood, as it came to be known, took its name from the Gaelic term "Fianna," a military force led by a legendary Celtic warrior. A Fenian chapter was begun concurrently in Dublin where it was more frequently referred to as the Irish Republican Brotherhood. Fenianism was distinct from all previous separatist movements in that it drew its support from both the Irish at home and the many Irish emigrants who had settled abroad. The Fenians repudiated constitutional methods and urged the forcible overthrow of British power in Ireland at the earliest possible date. Uncompromisingly committed to the establishment of an independent republic, the Fenian movement's improbable prospects for success were further weakened by the hostility shown to it by the Roman Catholic Church. It was their taking of secret oaths and their belief in a non-sectarian society, separating church from state, which made the Fenians unacceptable to the Roman Church. The result was that the Fenian movement was condemned by the most powerful institution within the Irish nationalist community.[2]

Fenians adamantly refused to embrace any specific social cause which might distract members from their professed goal of an Irish republic. They spoke instead of the need to liberate the land which had been usurped from its rightful owners by "an alien aristocracy," and expressed vague support for some form of future land reform. This absence of ideology was exceptional in an age when European social thought included Karl Marx's communism, Bukunin's anarchism, and Robert Owen's utopian socialism. The Fenian program, however, started and ended with the liberation of Ireland by means of a violent national revolution. All of Ireland's problems were soluble with a gun, and it was the gun that would drive the British out of the country.[3]

When the American Civil War began in 1861, some Fenians were fearful that the conflict would divert the attention of Irish America from its main goal of Irish freedom. Most of the leadership, however, supported the Union because they hoped for a strong United States as an adversary of British power and imperialism. Fenian recruiters were active in both the Union and Confederate camps throughout the war and, at its conclusion, combat-trained Irish Americans began to drift over to Ireland for the purpose of drilling the Irish for rebellion. In 1866, the American Irish provided the Fenian treasury with almost $500,000 in contributions. The revolutionary blueprint called for American volunteers, money and equipment to help launch an insurrection in Ireland. Once the hostilities commenced, republicans in the British army would then mutiny in order to hamper British efforts to crush the Fenians.[4]

One of the object lessons which the British should have drawn from the Civil War was the potential impact of Irish voting power on American foreign policy. When Canada was used in the war as a sanctuary for Confederates attacking Union targets, Anglophobia in many Northern states reached an intensity unknown since the War of 1812. It was this political climate that encouraged the Fenians to plan their invasion of Canada. The administrations of Presidents Andrew Johnson and Ulysses Grant essentially tolerated the Fenians because their vote was feared. Secretary of State William Seward valued the pugnacity of these Irish-American militant nationalists because of the leverage it gave him in dealing with the London Foreign Office. In the turbulent scramble for power that developed during those early Reconstruction years, the politicians exploited the Fenians, and the Fenians, in turn, did their best to exploit the politicians.[5]

Despite the fact that the Fenian raids on Canada were hopelessly bungled and the Fenian insurrection in Ireland was promptly crushed, these escapades were not entirely without result. The Fenians, after all, did help to convert British prime minister William Gladstone to the view that the Irish question now had "an American dimension" and that constructive measures were required to settle Irish grievances. Meanwhile, Fenian veterans John Devoy and Michael Davitt met in New York during 1878 and fashioned a socio-political movement of astonishing effectiveness known as "the new departure." The significance of the plan was that it brought Fenians, constitutional parliamentarians and agrarian reformers into one camp, and it forged still closer ties between nationalist groups in America and Ireland. This improbable alliance represented the most serious threat to British rule in Ireland since the seventeenth century Cromwellian settlement.[6]

The Irish land war of 1880-81 captured the imagination of the American Irish who, through the agency of some twelve hundred local chapters of the Irish Land League, contributed over $100,000 for their kinsmen in Ireland. State legislatures responded to Irish-American lobbyists by passing resolutions condemning British actions in Ireland, and some advanced nationalists returned from the United States to Ireland for the purpose of joining in what they hoped would be the final battle for Irish independence. When the Americans, along with native Irish nationalists, were jailed without right of trial by jury, prominent members of Congress interceded by pressuring the White House and State Department to seek the release of the Americans of Irish descent. London ultimately capitulated, but only on the express condition that the individuals concerned were to leave Ireland and not return.[7] Later, in 1888, Irish-American political pressure compelled President Grover Cleveland to expel from Washington the British ambassador, Sir Lionel Sackville-West, after he had written a foolish letter which implied that British interests were safe with Cleveland in office.

It is not at all unusual that Irish Americans should have taken such an active role in the earliest development of the Irish republican cause. The goal of Irish freedom provided a binding tie which held the American Irish together, especially the "first-generation" immigrants. For these people emigration from their native homeland had meant a radical loss of community. No matter how enterprising or individualistic he or she might be, the emigrant still missed the emotional support and the sense of solidarity that the village and its customary way of life had provided. Once in this country, the newcomers never could quite reestablish that lost sense of community which had been shattered by the mobile and diverse character of American urban life. But through their fraternal lodges, devotional societies and newspapers, they could create a partial substitute. The Irish nationalist movement was that substitute. "The nationalist movement gave the members of the American community a common bond and a common focus. Who was there with soul so dead he would not say a prayer, shed a tear, and give a dollar for the cause of old Ireland?"[8]

It is true, of course, that the sense of alienation experienced by nineteenth century Irish Americans served to intensify their parochial instincts. In Ireland, native culture had always been associated with a rural environment. The whole nature of Gaelic society was opposed to urban living. Historically, the cities of Ireland had been the strongholds of conquerors and centers for the spread of foreign influence. Danes, Normans and Englishmen made cities the mark of the invader; none was founded by the Irish themselves.[9] In the United States, the Irish reversed this pattern and shunned the farm for the cities. The reasons which prompted this choice are reasonably clear. Economics was a real factor since early immigrants did not have the money to travel and purchase land in the American West. Nor did Irish spade and hoe farmers have the skills to meet the challenges of large-scale tillage in America. Moreover, the lonely and forbidding prairie did not appeal to their clannish and extroverted personalities. In Ireland, small farms were so close together that people could visit over fences and ditches, but in rural America farms were miles apart and such social interaction was rare. This isolation was so unattractive to the Irish that they frankly preferred the cities even if the work was hard and dirty. Beneath those circumstances and propensities, however, there lay a still more profound motivation. The Irish rejected the land for the land had rejected them. Those who came to America in the 1840s had survived not one but a dozen crop failures in less than thirty years. Unlike some immigrants from Europe, they had no recollections of past prosperity to bolster their morale in times of crisis. The Irish immigrants were survivors who had endured an agrarian nightmare, and even the shanties of the urban ghetto did not shake their firm resolve not to repeat that experience.[10]

American cities, however, were no more hospitable to the Irish than they were to later immigrant groups. But the Irish, who in a very real sense were the pioneers of the American ghetto, did have the advantage of knowing the English language and of having dealt with Anglo-Saxon political institutions. They were victims, nonetheless, of the same nativist prejudice which they had come to know and hate under British rule in both England and Ireland. To upper and middle-class Americans, the Irish posed the threat of a barbarian culture; to the native working class they were competition in a tight labor market. Know-Nothing religious and political discrimination contributed to making Catholicism an ethnic identity badge for the Irish in America just as Protestant persecution had made Catholicism a nationalist, if not cultural, delineation in Ireland.[11]

Irish immigrants brought their town, parish and county loyalties with them to the United States, but Anglo-American nativist persecution and the cohesive focus of Catholicism quickly diluted these provincial distinctions. Men from all parts of Ireland worshipped in the same Catholic churches, voted as a bloc for the candidates of Democratic Party machines, and labored together on the railroads and in the mines and factories.[12] This shared experience developed not only a

communal spirit among the Irish Americans themselves, it also cultivated within them a sense of outrage against their real and imagined
oppressors. It was, therefore, in America that the parochial peasant
was transformed into a passionate Irish nationalist.[13]

Many Irish Americans hated England more than they loved Ireland. Despising Britain was a catharsis for Irish-American tensions
and frustrations, a way of accounting for one's failures in life. Britain
was perceived as the source of Irish disgrace and humiliation at home
and abroad. Some Irish emigrants had never reconciled themselves to
physical or spiritual exile from Ireland. They brooded over the opportunities that they had been denied and the ill fortunes that had befallen
them because of English rapacity. Their psychic need for a scapegoat
which would rationalize their lack of success in the United States may
have been the reason behind the oftentimes paranoid reaction that
some Irish Americans had towards all things British.[14]

There were, however, other Irish Americans for whom the cause of
Irish nationalism represented somethng different from love of Ireland
or hatred of Britain. These people had achieved social and economic
mobility, having in some instances advanced out of skilled trades and
into the professional and upper-middle classes. But as a national community, Irish Americans still suffered from a persistent inferiority complex.[15] Status-conscious Irish Americans came to the belief that Ireland's quasi-colonial standing within the British empire accounted for
the low esteem with which the American establishment regarded all
things Irish. They concluded that an independent Irish nation-state
would earn for them the respect of other Americans. And because respectability was such a strong motivation in Irish-American nationalism, the middle class was usually more active in the Irish republican
movement than was the lower class which tended to concern itself with
the bread-and-butter issues of American politics. The better-educated
Irish Americans who came to the United States after 1870, together
with the more accomplished second- and third-generation Irish Americans, were strongly convinced that there was a link between a free Ireland and their success in America. Their psychological need for recognition and social status encouraged these Irish Americans to promote
and sustain a variety of efforts, involving both moral and physical
force, to liberate Ireland.[16]

Perhaps the most sustained and decisive period of the Irish-American effort to involve the United States in bringing pressure upon Britain to help resolve the Irish question was the time between 1899 and
1921.[17] After a period of weakness and schism in the 1890s, both republican and parliamentary Irish-American nationalists were prominently
active in rallies held throughout the United States to denounce Brit-

ain's role in the Boer War.[18] The Clan na Gael, under the leadership of Fenian veteran, John Devoy, sought to promote the view that American interests were incompatible with close Anglo-American relations. In 1907 Tom Clarke returned to Ireland from New York to recruit the more extreme of the emerging new leaders in the Irish Republican Brotherhood, and henceforth Clan money and instructions were channelled through him.[19] A year later, on July 11, 1908, the Irish-American *Chicago Citizen* reflected the growing Anglophobic spirit of that ethnic community, and expressed its expectation that an Anglo-German war might be anticipated with this editorial statement: "There is not an Irishman in America today, in whose veins good red blood is flowing, who would not rejoice to hear that a German army was marching in triumph across England from Yarmouth to Milford Haven."[20]

When war did break out in 1914, it became clear that this was a view shared by a rather substantial majority of the Irish in America. Many of them were openly pro-German and they sharply criticized Irish party leader John Redmond for his pledge of Irish loyalty to the British Empire. The Clan na Gael went so far as to organize and support Sir Roger Casement's mission to Berlin with $10,000 for the purpose of obtaining arms and assistance from the German government. It was not, however, until 1916 that the Irish Republican Brotherhood in Dublin sought to take advantage of England's preoccupation with the war by staging a national rebellion throughout the country. Liaison between Ireland and Germany on plans for the insurrection was managed by the Clan in America.[21] Communications would have been difficult in the best of circumstances, but when the British navy captured the German ship carrying arms to Ireland the entire plan went awry. After quickly crushing an Easter Monday rebellion in Dublin, the British outraged Irish and Anglo Americans alike by executing the nationalist leaders. Yet, in spite of anti-British feeling, the majority of Irish Americans gave their unqualified support to the war effort once the United States entered the conflict in April 1917. Pro-Irish sentiment in America manifested itself that same year when 134 members of the House of Representatives cabled the British prime minister urging settlement of the Irish question.[22]

The war ended in 1918 but the Irish republican movement did not. Supported by the massive Sinn Fein victory in the general election of December 1918, the Irish on both sides of the Atlantic demanded that the Versailles Peace Conference apply President Woodrow Wilson's widely proclaimed principle of "national self-determination" to Ireland. When the British government refused to permit a delegation from Ireland to attend that conference, three prominent Irish Americans were appointed to go in their place by an Irish Race Convention

held in Philadelphia in February 1919.[23] British prime minister Lloyd
George succeeded in also denying the American delegation a hearing at
the conference, but he did permit them to visit Ireland to inspect conditions for themselves on the mistaken assumption that President Wilson wanted him to do this. London was outraged when the three American delegates gave public support in Ireland to Dáil Eireann, the self-
professed parliament of the Irish Republic.[24]

Perhaps the single most notable intrusion of Irish republicanism
into American politics following World War I was the visit of Sinn Fein
president Eamon de Valera to the United States during the period between June 1919 and December 1920.[25] What de Valera hoped to ac-
complish was United States recognition for the Irish Republic and a
loan for Dáil Eireann by means of a bond drive. From the start, however, de Valera was handicapped by his ignorance of American politics
and his unwillingness to share authority with Clan na Gael leaders in
matters which involved Irish Americans. The Irish president, for example, had little patience with John Devoy's and Daniel Cohalan's
campaign to discredit the League of Nations as a British plot. De
Valera regarded such conduct as an unnecessary distraction from the
one important issue of Irish independence and, on at least one occasion,
he accused Clan na Gael leaders of hating England more than they
loved Ireland.[26] It was this unseemly rivalry in 1920 between the native Irish and the Irish-American nationalists which destroyed all hope
of getting either the Democratic or Republican party conventions to
endorse the call for United States recognition of an Irish republic.[27]
The split between de Valera and Cohalan became permanent when the
Irish president unsuccessfully attempted to seize control of the Clan-
dominated Friends of Irish Freedom and then went on to establish a
rival Irish-American organization of his own. Irish-American votes ultimately did help to defeat the Democratic presidential candidate in
1920, but the new president, Warren G. Harding, was no more in favor
of an Irish republic than Woodrow Wilson had been. Indeed, Harding
even expressed his personal regret to the British ambassador for the
difficulties which the Irish problem had created for Anglo-American
relations.[28]

What de Valera did succeed in doing in America was to raise five
million dollars for Irish relief. Nevertheless, there is some evidence that
the funds from America, though larger than ever before, were insuffi-
cient to sustain an effective fighting level for the IRA in Ireland, and
that the shortage of money was one reason for the Anglo-Irish truce in
July 1921.[29] During the negotiations which followed, the British insisted upon partition on the reasoning that Ulster could not be forced
into a Dublin parliament against its will. But in order to satisfy Irish

opinion in the United States and in the dominions, London proposed that two parliaments should be established in Ireland. Paradoxically, one of the most controversial features of the Northern Ireland government which Britain devised, namely the Stormont parliament, was in part due to Irish America. It was the need to satisfy Irish opinion in the United States and in the dominions which prompted Britain to propose that two parliaments be established in Ireland. It could thus be made to appear the the London government was offering home rule to the whole of Ireland, or rather self-determination to both Irelands.[30] The Protestant majority in Ulster preferred political integration with Britain and, at least initally, viewed the establishment of a separate Northern Ireland parliament with suspicion and resentment.[31]

Irish-American nationalist agitation diminished notably after the July 1921 truce between the British and Irish forces. Most Irish Americans regarded the truce as an admission of defeat by the British, particularly after Sinn Fein candidates scored yet another impressive victory in the general election of 1921.[32] The signing of the Anglo-Irish Treaty in London on December 6 of that year was, therefore, as momentous an event for the Irish Americans as it was for the Irish at home. The former, in particular, thought it to be an acceptable settlement even if it offered something less than a republic and reaffirmed provisions for the exclusion of a large part of Ulster. This attitude was indicative of the fact that Irish Americans had never been terribly conscious of the essential differences between such concepts as home rule, dominion status, or national independence. They were baffled when civil war broke out in the South in 1922 since they believed that the struggle for Irish freedom had been won with the establishment of the Irish Free State.[33]

Irish-American jubilation turned to a mood of disillusionment and, eventually, to one of disgust as the pro-treaty IRA and the anti-treaty IRA fought one another with more bitterness than had been shown earlier toward their British enemy. Both sides sent deputations to the United States to propagandize for their respective positions, encouraging rival Irish-American groups to join in the malice and vituperation. The pro-treaty *Gaelic American* charged that de Valera, "that half-breed Spanish-American Jew," was encouraging civil war in Ireland, while New York's anti-treaty *Irish World* labeled Michael Collins and Arthur Griffith, the leaders of the "Irish Freak State," contemptible traitors.[34] The great majority of Irish Americans were embarrassed by such self-defeating tactics since many of them felt that Britain had shown goodwill in granting twenty-six counties the same sovereignty enjoyed by Canada.[35] Others doubtlessly feared that the fratricidal vendetta would be regarded by other Americans as proof of the deficiencies in the Irish character.

During the twenties and thirties, Irish-American involvement in Irish affairs largely evaporated as the American Irish turned their attention to full participation in American life. Moreover, a decrease in physical contacts between the Irish in Ireland and those in the United States served to further diminish any lingering sense of shared community. The passage by Congress of restrictive immigration laws in 1921 and 1924, and the Great Depression of the late twenties and early thirties, sharply reduced the number of Irish emigrating to the United States. Most of the Irish who did leave their country for employment opportunities abroad went to Britain where the cultural and emotional break with Ireland seemed less profound than in America. The decision of post-treaty Ireland to promote a distinctively indigenous form of nationalism, and, more recently, the Irish government's emphasis on becoming a fully-integrated European member of the Common Market, have served to widen the gap between the Irish at home and abroad.[36]

When World War II began in September 1939, Irish premier Eamon de Valera declared that his country would remain neutral. He reasoned that Ireland had no interest in a war that had been caused by big power refusal to protect collective security in the League of Nations, and he insisted that Ireland could not collaborate with Britain while Britain occupied the six counties of Ulster. The outlawed Irish Republican Army, however, saw England's difficulty as Ireland's opportunity, and sought support from both Germany and Irish America for an insurrectionist campaign throughout the United Kingdom. But unlike during the First World War, Irish Americans were unresponsive to the IRA appeal. The strongest anti-British position which any of them was likely to take was endorsing de Valera's policy of neutrality.[37]

Irish-American nationalist activity, which heretofore had been a recurrent motif in the American political mosaic, was no longer a force to be summoned in defense of Irish freedom. Ireland was indeed free, as her affirmation of neutrality so clearly demonstrated. For their part, the American Irish had overcome their identity crisis and in so doing had lost their psychological dependence on Irish nationalism. In the years since World War I, they had begun to move in ever greater numbers from the ghettos to the suburbs. Their gradual assimilation into the mainstream of American society was evidence of the prosperity they had achieved and the respectability they had gained. As dependence on nationality decreased, Irish-American zeal for Irish republicanism diminished proportionately. There would be no monster rallies in the United States for the IRA in 1941 as there had been for Sinn Fein in 1917.[38]

Pearl Harbor brought the United States into the war and Irish Americans began to view Ireland's neutrality with less indifference. British prime minister Winston Churchill immediately took the occasion to appeal to the Roosevelt administration to use its influence with Irish Americans in the hope that de Valera would be pressed into joining the war. The Dublin government responded by involving itself in American domestic politics and enlisting the support of prominent isolationists, many of them Irish-American opponents of President Franklin Roosevelt, for the Irish position.[39] Complicating matters still more was the fact that David Gray, the American minister to Ireland and the husband of Eleanor Roosevelt's aunt, used his close ties with the White House to discredit Prime Minister de Valera whom he disliked intensely. During the summer of 1943, Gray returned to the United States and visited a number of Irish-American communities where he found the tolerance for de Valera's neutrality position wearing thin. Later, in 1944, Gray helped to convince Roosevelt that de Valera's refusal to expel the Axis diplomats from Dublin would expose American troops to danger during the secret and forthcoming D-Day assault on the European continent. When the Irish prime minister refused to compromise his country's neutrality by expelling the German and Japanese ministers, the American press loudly condemned him.[40] Thanks largely to Winston Churchill's abusive public attack against the Irish prime minister at the end of the war, de Valera was given the opportunity to make an eloquent and tempered reply in which he persuasively argued that his pro-Allied policy of neutrality had been the only sensible course which his defenseless country could have taken.[41] Irish Americans, however, were less interested by this date in Anglo-Irish squabbles than they were in such promising post-war opportunities as the GI Bill. It was their future in America, and not Ireland's record in the Second World War, which principally concerned the younger members of this ethnic community.

Irish republicanism made a feeble comeback in the early 1950s when the IRA successfully raided a few British arms arsenals in Northern Ireland. It was also at this time that the IRA attempted to obtain money and arms from other national liberation movements. One of these was EOKA, a Cypriot terrorist organization devoted to seeking *Eenois*, or union, with Greece. EOKA guerrillas, according to one plan, would travel from England to Ireland where they would join up with IRA forces and fight their common British enemy. But the plan never materialized. Very few governments or even revolutionary movements had much to gain from an association with the IRA, which if it had a long tradition of rebellion also had a disconcerting record of failure. Even the money which was sent from its single foreign patron, the Clan na Gael in America, was scarcely enough to keep the IRA campaign afloat.[42]

In the two decades following World War II, many Catholics in Northern Ireland became as uninterested in the IRA as had their American cousins. They began to realize that neither the oratory of politicians in Dublin nor the IRA terrorist activities in Ulster was likely to unite the two Irelands. Moreover, the benefits derived from the British Labor government's welfare state program included free secondary education for all United Kingdom citizens. By the 1950s there was an extraordinary rise in the number of Catholics in Northern Ireland attending universities. Catholic opinion, particularly among the expanding middle class, began to take the view that first-class citizenship in Northern Ireland was a more practical objective than that of a united Ireland. Both this shift in attitude and the work of police forces on both sides of the border contributed to the failure of the subsequent terrorist campaign which the IRA conducted between 1956 and 1962. For all intents and purposes, the IRA ceased to function in Ulster after 1962.[43]

During the mid-1960s, united Ireland became a moot issue for the Irish both at home and abroad as attention was focused on economic and social issues. Even the moribund IRA, operating through the Sinn Fein political party, abandoned terrorist rhetoric in favor of a socialist program calling for decent housing and more social services for the poor. In February 1967, the Northern Ireland Civil Rights Association was founded and, although its objective was to give Catholics full membership in the political, economic and social systems of Northern Ireland, it was a non-sectarian organization which favored Ulster continuing as a part of the United Kingdom. Catholic middle-class moderates joined with socialists, republicans, Protestant liberals and the People's Democracy, a radical student's group from Queen's University.[44] Modeling themselves upon the then prominent civil rights movement in America, even to the extent of conducting freedom marches and singing "We Shall Overcome," the protestors startled and confused Ulster's police and government officials. A Protestant backlash also occurred in which Unionist mobs attacked and beat the civil rights demonstrators. The brutal scences of these ugly confrontations flashed before astonished television audiences in Britain and throughout much of the world. The failure of peaceful protest and the refusal of Northern Ireland's authorities to protect Catholic liberties against Protestant violence allowed the IRA to reemerge in the form of a Catholic defense force. The ascendancy of the IRA meant that Irish nationalism, rather than civil rights, became the vital issue in the Ulster crisis.[45]

During the next four years IRA terrorism and Unionist paramilitary reprisals escalated at an alarming rate, prompting protests from the Dublin government and Irish-American politicians alike. In August 1969, as the Six Counties appeared on the verge of full-scale civil war, the British government sent troops to Northern Ireland. Welcomed as protectors by the besieged Catholics, the army soon became unpopular with this same constituency when it began jailing suspected IRA members and friends while enforcing the law-and-order dictates of the existing Protestant Unionist government. On January 30, 1972, British paratroopers killed fourteen Londonderry Catholic demonstrators in what quickly became known as "Bloody Sunday." Senator Edward Kennedy of Massachusetts led the Irish-American denunciation of this outrage and, in testimony given before a congressional foreign affairs committee, condemned the use of British military force in Ulster. Declared Kennedy, "Fifty thousand Americans died before we learned that tragic lesson in Vietnam and there can be no excuse for Britain to have to learn that lesson now in Ulster."[46] Finally, in March 1972, the British suspended the Northern Ireland government, incorporated the Six Counties into the United Kingdom's political system on a temporary basis, and initiated reforms designed to bestow civil rights on all of its citizens and perhaps pave the way to a united Ireland. But Protestant fears of British motives and Catholic suspicions of British sincerity effectively undermined all hope for any early solution to the Ulster problem. As a consequence, IRA terrorists and Unionist gangs prospered by default.[47]

Irish America proved far less responsive to the strife in Northern Ireland in the 1970s than it had to the cause of nationalist Ireland only fifty years before. One reason is that a large part of this American community is now two generations or more away from any direct experience with Irish life. Another is that most Irish Americans stem from the West or the South and have little familiarity with the tradition of Ulster's communal schism.[48] It may even be argued that Irish Americans have, as a group, become too assimilated in the United States to think much about events in Ireland, despite the interest today in ethnic identity. As Oscar Handlin and other immigration historians have observed, organizations like the Ancient Order of Hibernians or the Sons of Italy have no counterpart in Europe. Nationalist sentiment may be the force that holds such groups together, but their real purpose is to ease the transition of immigrants into American life. They help compensate for a sense of individual weakness by asserting group strength. Contrary to the charge of their critics, such organizations do not create "hyphenated Americans"; they serve to smooth away the hyphen. They promote adjustment to American ways and adoption of

American ideals, rather than retard them. Millions of second- and third-generation Irish Americans had, by the 1970s, moved well away from the initial period of immigrant anxiety and adjustment. As Americans, they had the security to view the Ulster problem from an emotional distance. "For them to enter fully into the passions that convulse Northern Ireland would require a journey into the past they are reluctant to make. They are too involved with the American present and future."[49]

There is, however, another constituency within the Irish-American community which perceives the Ulster crisis in an entirely different way. These are, for the most part, the recent Irish immigrants who provide the hard core support for the IRA in the United States.[50] As with past Irish-American nationalism, the response of Irish immigrants to the events in Northern Ireland communicates the bitterness they feel about the impoverished Ireland they left and their sense of insecurity in America. Because IRA supporters hold the Irish government responsible for the economic conditions that forced them to emigrate, and denounce it as a puppet of British imperialism, these immigrants are unmoved when Irish officials plead with them not to aid IRA activities. Indeed, Irish immigrant support for the IRA reflects a dissatisfaction with their position in the United States. They do not share the values and attitudes of the American-born Irish or participate in their middle-class standing or respectability. The situation in Northern Ireland has afforded them with the means of expressing their own identity in an increasingly ethnic-conscious America. Yet, their attitude is strangely incompatible with their strong law-and-order stance on other American issues. They refuse, for example, to recognize the obvious similarities between black America and Catholic Northern Ireland. They deliberately ignore the socialist pronouncements of the contemporary IRA. And, they purport not to see any obvious comparison between the IRA and political terrorist organizations in other parts of the world.[51]

Irish-born Irish Americans are not nearly as numerous today as they were at the time of the Irish war for independence. There were, for example, some four million such immigrants in 1919, compared with less than 300,000 in 1969. Yet, this immigrant community, particularly in the eastern seaboard states of Massachusetts, New York, New Jersey and Pennsylvania, provide much of the militant thrust behind Irish America's support for the IRA. They are people who are often driven by blind hatred and have no faith in British power-sharing proposals or in any rational political compromise. They have no interest in any minority rights guarantee on the part of the United Kingdom, the United States or the United Nations. They believe that the IRA claim to full sovereignty over Northern Ireland is historically justified and must be accomplished by force of arms. Their perception of Ireland is simplistic, intolerant and ahistoric.[52]

Still, Irish republicanism is often given a wider and more sympathetic hearing in the United States than the relative size or illiberal views of the Irish immigrant community would otherwise warrant. One reason for this has been the carefully calculated tone of the Irish republican campaign in America. As Maria McGuire tells us in her book *To Take Arms*, Provisional IRA fund raisers were instructed to make copious references to the martyrs of 1916 and 1920-1922. They were also advised to promote anti-British sentiment by recalling the potato famine and the Black and Tans, but were cautioned against saying anything praiseworthy about socialism or anything critical of the Catholic Church.[53] American television is another reason for the notable attention given to the Northern Ireland issue in the United States. At the 1981 funeral of hunger-striker Bobby Sands, the IRA ensured that American television crews were afforded fully equipped scaffolding on which to mount their cameras. Viewers in the United States were thereby treated to the dramatic spectacle of hooded Provos at the grave site firing volleys of salute toward an overcast sky. The image conveyed on the television screen was that of a noble tribute to an honored martyr and a rightful cause.[54]

This problem of perception is, of course, a major obstacle for the British to overcome in explaining their own position on Northern Ireland to American audiences. In condemning the atrocities and in suppressing the terrorism of the Provisional IRA, London has failed to capitalize on the fact that the IRA political platform calls for the overthrow of government authorities on both sides of the border, and for a socialist program involving the nationalization of banks and industries throughout Ireland. Instead, the Provos have been permitted to characterize the IRA campaign as a holy war, perhaps even the final chapter in the age-old struggle between the Celt and the Anglo-Saxon. The frequently conservative social thinking of many Irish Americans has, as a result, given way to a romantic idealism deliberately and effectively cultivated by IRA disinformation. Once again, as happened during the 1919-1921 war for Irish independence, Irish republicanism has bested Britain in the propaganda war for American public opinion.[55] Only in very recent times have people outside of Ireland become more discriminating in their assessment of IRA claims.

Contemporary Irish republicans also have been more successful than the Fenians were a century ago in combatting the opposition of the Church to which most of their supporters on both sides of the Atlantic claim allegiance. When the Catholic primate of Ireland, Cardinal O'Fiaich, returned from a visit to the United States in 1981, he condemned recent IRA murders saying: "To cooperate in any way with such organizations is sinful, and if the cooperation is substantial the sin is mortal."[56] But the Irish, who have always had scruples about going against priest and bishop, surmount that scruple by concentrating on the fact that British rule in Ireland is unjust. There thus developed the myth of the gunman, "the freedom fighter," a man committed to the simple ideal of freeing his country from its oppressors, seeking no glory other than martyrdom, faithful in his own way to a church that did not understand him. His blood, and the blood of those who have gone before, will water the seed of freedom which will sprout from the ground and bloom at the moment least expected. Such is the myth and the mystique of the IRA. Its appeal will only be understood when it is recognized that this curious emotional mixture exists in most men of Irish blood and background who have ever identified themselves with the dream of an independent and united Ireland. "As the IRA-man is ambivalent toward his church, so other Irishmen are ambivalent toward him. If they cannot support him, they must do violence to themselves to oppose him."[57] It is a dilemma which continues to inhibit many Irish-American nationalists.

Nevertheless, the terrorist image which has become synonymous with the IRA Provo over the past ten or more years is the single most important reason for the very modest success which the IRA has enjoyed in winning widespread American support for its cause. Neither the IRA's stridently Anglophobic rhetoric nor its patently socialistic mainfestos have alienated people in the United States as much as has that organization's identification with violence and killing. And that general sense of revulsion was and is also shared by some Irish Americans. Appearing before a 1972 congressional subcommittee hearing on conditions in Northern Ireland, New York City resident and writer Jimmy Breslin recounted his own experiences in Ulster and condemned those who collected funds in Manhattan taverns for the purpose of purchasing weapons for the IRA. Breslin remarked, "The idea of raising money on Second Avenue to buy guns so that an 18-year-old in Derry can kill an 18-year-old British soldier, a soldier from Manchester who knows nothing of the reasons for the fight he is in, this notion to me is sickening."[58]

One of the major conduits for smuggling arms from the United States to Northern Ireland in recent times has been the Northern Aid Committee, more popularly known as Noraid, which has some ninety chapters nationwide. Organized in 1970, Noraid is headquartered in a drab second floor office on Broadway in upper Manhattan, sandwiched between a funeral parlor and a bank branch. The United States Department of Justice is presently bringing suit in the state of New York in order to compel Noraid to register as an agent of the IRA. Meanwhile, the Federal Bureau of Investigation has arrested prominent Noraid officials, most of them Irish-born Irish Americans, for conspiring to ship arms to the Provisionals in Northern Ireland.[59] Noraid officials have insisted that the funds raised by their organization have been used mostly to support the families of IRA members interned by British authorities. But United States intelligence sources estimated in 1975 that only 25 percent of the money was spent for such purposes, while fully 75 percent was used for the purchase of weapons and munitions.[60]

United States citizens, including Irish Americans, do not have to depend upon the judgment of their government alone in evaluating Noraid's complicity in providing weapons for the IRA. Indeed, four successive Irish prime ministers have made the same charge. Liam Cosgrave told a joint session of Congress that aid to "relief" organizations like Noraid did not help to resolve the problem of Ulster.[61] Jack Lynch warned American contributors to Noraid that their money, rather than going for the support of widows and orphans, was in fact used to *make* widows and orphans.[62] Garret FitzGerald similarly condemned such American aid to the IRA[63], and Charles Haughey went still further and declared, "there is clear and conclusive evidence available to the government here from security and other sources that Noraid has provided support for the campaign of violence . . ."[64]

Remarks such as these prompted former New York City council president Paul O'Dwyer, a Noraid attorney, to decry the growing rift between the Irish and Irish Americans. O'Dwyer, a distinguished member of the Democratic party in New York, is a native of County Mayo and is representative of that community of Irish-born Americans who identify with the Democratic tradition in American politics, but with the republican tradition in Irish politics. Yet, as Irish cabinet minister Conor Cruise O'Brien observed in a 1976 speech before an American Chamber of Commerce meeting in Dublin, the republican tradition in Ireland is one which has set itself above democracy. And, in direct response to O'Dwyer, O'Brien denied that any rift existed between the Irish and Irish Americans. "I do believe," he added, "that a minority of Irish Republicans are interested in trying to produce such a rift, and to intimidate Irish people with the idea that they cannot afford such a rift."[65]

As more Noraid members were jailed on weapons offenses and as that organization became publicly linked with the Provisional IRA, another group calling itself the Irish National Caucus assumed a more prominent role among Americans concerned with the problem of

Northern Ireland. The group was first formed in 1974 and had as its purpose to make the violation of human rights in Ulster a moral issue for all Americans. By 1979, no fewer than 130 congressmen had signed on with the caucus-sponsored Ad Hoc Committee for Irish Affairs under the chairmanship of New York representative Mario Biaggi. An open schism developed between Irish National Caucus director Father Sean McManus and Noraid leader Michael Flannery when the Caucus proposed hosting a "peace forum" in Washington to which members of both the Ulster Defense Association and the Irish Republican Army would be invited.[66] Nothing came of the plan and, aside from providing further evidence of the divisions within the Irish-American community over the subject of Northern Ireland, the Irish question remained as much on the periphery of American politics as it had been for more than fifty years.[67]

What seems especially ironic, at least at first blush, about the relative impotence of Irish-American efforts to influence United States policy toward Ulster is the fact that some members of this ethnic group are among the most prominent politicians in the country. The so-called "Four Horsemen," Senators Edward Kennedy and Daniel Patrick Moynihan, together with Speaker of the House Thomas O'Neill and former New York governor Hugh Carey, are truly national political personalities whose influence extend beyond their respective constituencies in Massachusetts and New York. These men do not owe their status and power to Irish-American voters, who are increasingly divided in their party preferences and who are often outnumbered by Italians, Jews and other ethnic voting blocs in regions once dominated by the Irish vote. To be sure, Irish domination of political machines in the nation's large cities endured long after the Irish lost their early majority among immigrant groups. But that was because their experience under Anglo-Saxon domination had given them a talent for organization and a gift for survival. Erosion of the political machines began with the establishment of national welfare policies under the New Deal. Even in Chicago, where the late Richard Daley managed to adapt the local Democratic organization to changing conditions, the machine is now a vestigial remnant of what it once was. The "Four Horsemen" fully understand these present-day realities and recognize that there are precious few votes to be gained by tweaking the English.[68]

Irish-American politicians, moreover, have come to appreciate the complexity of the Northern Ireland problem after making a few missteps while promoting the ever-controversial aspirations of Irish nationalism. In 1971, for example, Senator Edward Kennedy somewhat impulsively called for Britain's immediate withdrawal from Ireland

and declared that those Protestants who could not accept a united Ireland "should be given a decent opportunity to go back to Britain."[69] By 1973, Kennedy was affirming that Protestants must have an equal role with Catholics, but he continued to insist that the unification of Ireland under the jurisdiction of Dublin was the only sensible solution to the Ulster crisis.[70] Finally, in 1977, in response to appeals from Dr. Garret FitzGerald and other prominent Dublin politicians, Kennedy, Moynihan, Carey and O'Neill issued a St. Patrick's Day statement which condemned the IRA as the real obstacle to peace in Northern Ireland. These same Irish-American leaders also persuaded former president Jimmy Carter to offer, in August 1977, United States help toward a solution for Ulster. Specifically, Carter promised to encourage substantial American investment in Northern Ireland provided a settlement could be reached between the Protestant and Catholic communities.[71]

Kennedy and his colleagues became increasingly frustrated over the next two years when none of the principal parties took any real initiative toward a reconciliation in Ulster. Meanwhile, successive human rights investigations continued to condemn police brutality in Northern Ireland. The "Four Horsemen" accordingly issued another St. Patrick's Day statement in 1979 which, reflecting their keen sense of betrayal, blamed British insensitivity rather than IRA terrorism as the principal cause for the continuing strife in Northern Ireland.[72] That contention was promptly dismissed as naive by British labor leader Shirley Williams,[73] while a subsequent statement by these Irish-American leaders calling for British withdrawal from Northern Ireland was ridiculed as reckless and irresponsible by Irish labor leader Conor Cruise O'Brien.[74] Nevertheless, the "Four Horsemen," together with President Carter, did succeed in getting London to accept the existence of an "American dimension" to the Irish problem when considering any future resolution of the Northern Ireland conflict. British prime minister Margaret Thatcher best illustrated this fact when she gave the *New York Times*, but not a single British newspaper, an exclusive interview on her proposal for devolution of political power in Ulster one week before publicly announcing it.[75]

But while the "power-sharing" proposals advanced by the British government in recent times have tempered the criticism of some leading Irish-American politicians, these schemes have been sharply rejected by militant Irish-American republican groups. The latter are not interested in the achievement of civil rights for all citizens of a Northern Ireland which remains within the United Kingdom. Rather, they support the call of the IRA for the overthrow of British authority in Ulster and for the unification of Ireland. The majority of Irish Amer-

168 ETHNICITY AND WAR

icans today, however, are disinclined to heed appeals from the IRA as that organization's true character becomes better known. On March 1, 1981, for instance, *The New York Times Magazine* featured a story on international terrorism, and its depiction of the Irish Republican Army is representative of the kind of information regarding Northern Ireland which is presently gaining wider currency among American readers. One excerpt reads:

> The IRA has come a long way since its early days of dependence upon the United States. Fund raising is mostly done at home nowadays, by means of protection rackets, brothels, massage parlors and bank stickups. And the incoming hardware is largely Soviet-made. It took only a few years to make the transformation with the help of the international terror network.[76]

Perhaps, therefore, it is not only their assimilation into the mainstream of American society that has so distanced most Irish Americans from the cause of Irish republicanism. A disillusionment with the nature and methods of the contemporary IRA almost certainly has been an equally restraining factor for these well-educated and sophisticated ethnics. John Brecher, a correspondent for *Newsweek* magazine, made this generational difference rather poignantly in a May 1981 article. Brecher recalled how when three Irish nationalists starved themselves to death in 1920, 100,000 angry Irish Americans poured onto the Boston Common. In May 1981, when IRA hunger-striker Bobby Sands died in yet another act of protest, barely one hundred people demonstrated outside the home of the British counsul general in Boston.[77] While the disparity between these figures does not necessarily represent the true measure of Irish-American concern for the Northern Ireland problem today, it does serve to underscore an essential difficulty for this ethnic community. Irish Americans have discovered that they support an ideal, the unificaton of Ireland, which is the professed goal of an organization that they increasingly feel to be morally abhorrent. It is this dilemma that confronts thoughtful Irish Americans and which accounts to a large extent for the notable absence of their traditional enthusiasm for the romantic aspirations of nationalist Ireland.

NOTES

[1] Irish immigrants to America took a keen interest in the revolutionary role of Wolf Tone in 1798 and in that of Robert Emmet in 1803, as well as in the emancipation and repeal movements of Daniel O'Connell in the 1830s and 1840s. But it was not until the Young Ireland uprising of 1848 that Irish America began to participate in any significant way in the cause for Irish free-

dom. See Charles Tansill, *America and the Fight for Irish Freedom, 1866-1892* (New York: Devon-Adair, 1957), pp. 3-27.

[2]Thomas E. Hachey, *Britain and Irish Separatism: From the Fenians to the Free State, 1867-1922* (Chicago: Rand McNally, 1977), pp. 8-9.

[3]Gary MacEoin, "The Irish Republican Army," *Eire-Ireland*, 9 (Summer 1974):5.

[4]Lawrence J. McCaffrey, *The Irish Diaspora in America* (Bloomington, Ind.: Indiana University Press, 1976), pp. 120-121.

[5]Thomas N. Brown, *Irish-American Nationalism, 1870-1890* (Philadelphia: J. B. Lippincott, 1966), p. 40.

[6]Conor Cruise O'Brien, *States of Ireland* (New York: Vintage Books, 1973), p. 45.

[7]Marjorie R. Fallows, *Irish Americans* (Englewood Cliffs, N.J.: Prentice-Hall, 1979), p. 122.

[8]William V. Shannon, *The American Irish* (New York: MacMillan, 1963), p. 135.

[9]E. Esty Evans, *The Personality of Ireland* (Cambridge, Eng.: Cambridge University Press, 1973), p. 82.

[10]For further analysis of early Irish immigrant attitudes, see Joseph P. O'Grady, *How the Irish Became Americans* (New York: Twayne Publishers, 1973).

[11]For further reading on the political dimensions of Irish Catholicism in Ireland and America, see, respectively, Emmet Larkin, *The Historical Dimensions of Irish Catholicism* (New York: Arno Press, 1976) and David Doyle, *Irish-Americans, Native Rights and National Empires: The Structure, Division and Attitudes of the Catholic Minority in the Age of Expansion, 1890-1901* (New York: Arno Press, 1976).

[12]McCaffrey, *The Irish Diaspora in America*, op, cit., p. 108.

[13]Thomas N. Brown, "Nationalism and the Irish Peasant," *The Review of Politics*, XV (October 1953): 445.

[14]"The children of the famine emigrants grew up in America hating England; they had chosen the U.S.A. rather than the nearer Canada. Their hatred grew out of Gaelic tradition (and their family experience) . . . " O'Brien, op, cit., p. 44.

[15]For sociological analyses of Irish-American perceptions and attitudes, see Andrew Greeley, *Why Can't They Be Like Us?* (New York: Dutton, 1971) and Andrew Greeley, *That Most Distressful Nation* (Chicago: Quadrangle Books, 1973). See also Nathan Glazer and Daniel P. Moynihan, *Beyond the Melting Pot* (Cambridge, Mass.: MIT Press, 1970).

[16]Lawrence J. McCaffrey, *Ireland: From Colony to Nation State* (Englewood Cliffs, N.J.: Prentice-Hall, 1979), p. 90.

[17]The definitive study on this subject is Alan J. Ward, *Ireland and Anglo-American Relations, 1899-1921* (Toronto: University of Toronto Press, 1969).

[18]The United Irish Societies of Chicago actually sent fifty or so volunteers to fight in South Africa in the guise of a Red Cross contingent. See John H. Ferguson, *American Diplomacy and the Boer War* (Philadelphia: University of Pennsylvania Press, 1939), pp. 66-67.

[19]Louis N. Le Roux, *Tom Clarke and the Irish Freedom Movement* (Dublin: Talbot Press, 1936), pp. 73 et. seq.

[20]Philip G. Cambray, *Irish Affairs and the Home Rule Question* (London: John Murray, 1911), pp. 133-134.

[21]Alan J. Ward, "America and the Irish Problem," *Irish Historical Studies*, XVI:71 (March 1968): 74-77.

[22]Fallows, op. cit., p. 122.

[23]The three delegates were Frank P. Walsh, joint president of the National War Labor Board, Edward F. Dunne, a former mayor of Chicago and a former governor of Illinois, and Michael J. Ryan, a Philadelphia attorney and past national president of the United Irish League of America.

[24]War Cabinet Meeting 567A, 14 May 1919 (London: Public Record Office, CAB 23/15).

[25]The most detailed account of this sojourn is Katherine O'Doherty, *Assignment America: De Valera's Mission to the United States* (New York: De Tanko, 1957).

[26]Differences between de Valera and the Clan were particularly acute in matters relating to fund raising. See Patrick McCartan, *With DeValera in America* (Dublin: Fitzpatrick, 1932), pp. 420 et. seq.

[27]For further analysis of this dilemma for the Irish-American cause in the United States, see Thomas E. Hachey, "The Irish Question: The British Foreign Office and the American Political Conventions of 1920," *Eire-Ireland*, 3:3 (Autumn 1968): 92-107.

[28]Foreign Office minutes, 11 May 1921 (London: Public Record Office, F.O. 115/2673).

[29]Dumont (Dublin) to Secretary of State (Washington), 28 September 1920 (Washington, D.C.: National Archives, Records of the Department of State Relating to Internal Affairs of Great Britain, 1901-1929: Political Affairs, State Dept. 841d.00/381).

[30]First report of the Cabinet committee on the Irish question, 4 November 1919 (London: Public Record Office, Cabinet paper 56, CAB 24/92).

[31]J. C. Beckett, "Northern Ireland," *Journal of Contemporary History*, 6:1 (1971) 121. See also the Arthur Balfour memorandum on Ireland, 25 November 1919 (London: Public Record Office, Cabinet paper 193, CAB 24/92).

[32]For further data on the scope of the Sinn Fein electoral victory, see Joseph M. Curran, *The Birth of the Irish Free State, 1921-1923* (University, Ala.: The University of Alabama Press, 1980), p. 52.

[33]Ward, "America and the Irish Problem," op. cit., p. 90.

[34]Francis M. Carroll, *American Opinion and the Irish Question: 1910-1923* (New York: St. Martin's Press, 1978), p. 183. For further information on the

Clan na Gael split over the IRA, see Tim Pat Coogan, *The I.R.A.* (London: Pall Mall, 1970), pp. 104-105.

[35]Most Irish Americans agreed with Michael Collins that dominion status was a firm foundation for the continued expansion of Irish sovereignty. For further comment on this particular attitude, see Tansill, op. cit., pp. 437-442.

[36]McCaffrey, *The Irish Diaspora in America*, op. cit., pp. 152-153.

[37]Traditional Irish hostility toward England, according to one study, was still sufficiently strong to prompt Irish Americans to drift away from the Democratic Party because of President Roosevelt's aid to Great Britain in the early days of World War II. Edward M. Levine, *The Irish and Irish Politicians* (Notre Dame, Ind.: University of Notre Dame Press, 1966), p. 109.

[38]For additional background information on the assimilation process, see Andrew Greeley, "The American Irish Since the Death of Studs Lonigan," *The Critic*, 29 (May/June 1971): 27-33, and Andrew Greeley, "Making It in America: Ethnic Groups and Social Status," *Social Policy*, 4 (September/October 1973): 21-29.

[39]The definitive study for this period is that of T. Ryle Dwyer, *Irish Neutrality and the U.S.A., 1939-47* (Dublin: Gill and Macmillan, 1977).

[40]Portraying Ireland as being infested with Axis spies, the *Dallas Morning News* exclaimed, "Call for St. Patrick! The snakes are back in Ireland." And *New York Times* Washington correspondent James Reston wrote that because of this incident, de Valera would never have quite the same support in Irish America. Quoted in T. Ryle Dwyer, "American Efforts to Discredit De Valera during World War II," *Eire-Ireland*, VIII:2 (Summer 1973): 20-33.

[41]Thomas E. Hachey, "The Neutrality Issue in Anglo-Irish Relations during World War II," *The South Atlantic Quarterly*, 78:2 (Spring 1979): 170-171.

[42]J. Bowyer Bell, *The Secret Army* (Cambridge, Mass.: MIT Press, 1980), p. 320.

[43]McCaffrey, *Ireland: From Colony to Nation State*, op. cit., p. 179.

[44]For an excellent treatment of the origins and development of the People's Democracy Party within the Northern Ireland Civil Rights Association, see Bernadette Devlin, *The Price of My Soul* (New York: Alfred A. Knopf, 1969).

[45]McCaffrey, *The Irish Diaspora in America*, op. cit., p. 155.

[46]Ulrick O'Connor, ed., *Irish Liberation* (New York: Grove Press, 1974), p. 107. A few months earlier, Kennedy had introduced a resolution in the United States Senate calling for the withdrawal of British troops from Northern Ireland and the establishment of a united Ireland. He asserted, "Ireland has given much to America, and we owe her much in return." Quoted in Charles Carlton, ed., *Bigotry and Blood* (Chicago: Nelson-Hall, 1977), p. 117. For the full text of Kennedy's resolution, see *Congressional Record*, 92nd Congress, 1st Session, 1971, pp. 3672-3673.

[47]For further details regarding the British incorporation of Northern Ireland, see John Magee, ed., *Northern Ireland: Crisis and Conflict* (London: Routledge and Kegan Paul, 1974), pp. 133-138.

[48]Donald H. Akenson, *The United States and Ireland* (Cambridge, Mass.: Harvard University Press, 1973), p. 242.

[49]William V. Shannon, "The Lasting Hurrah," *The New York Times Magazine* (March 14, 1976), p. 78.

[50]And within this group, the older generation tends to favor the IRA Provos while many younger Irish immigrants support the Officials. See Gary MacEoin, "Few in U.S. Aid Northern Ireland Causes," *National Catholic Reporter*, 9:38 (October 5, 1973).

[51]Lawrence J. McCaffrey, "The Recent Irish Diaspora in America," in Dennis L. Cuddy, ed., *Contemporary American Immigration* (Boston: Twayne Publishers, 1978), pp. 49-51. See also Jimmy Breslin, *World Without End, Amen* (New York: Viking Press, 1973), in which Breslin's fictional anti-black New York policeman, Dermot Davy, visits Northern Ireland and begins to understand the similarities between the American black and the Ulster Catholic situations. Unfortunately, when he returns home he falls back into previous patterns of behavior.

[52]Raymond James Raymond, "The United States and Terrorism in Ireland, 1969-1981," unpublished paper, pp. 9-12.

[53]Maria McGuire, *To Take Arms* (New York: Viking Press, 1973), p. 119.

[54]Neil Hickey, "The Battle for Northern Ireland," *TV Guide*, 29:39 (September 26, 1981): 8-28.

[55]For the earlier propaganda contest, see Thomas E. Hachey, "The British Foreign Office and New Perspectives on the Irish Issue in Anglo-American Relations, 1919-1921," *Eire-Ireland*, 7:2 (Summer 1972): 3-14; for the more recent Anglo-Irish campaign for American support, see Dennis Clark, *Irish Blood: Northern Ireland and the American Conscience* (London: Kennikat Press, 1977).

[56]*Irish Times* (Dublin: 21 November 1981).

[57]MacEoin, "The Irish Republican Army," op. cit., p. 4. For a more comprehensive study by the same author, see Gary MacEoin, *Northern Ireland: Captive of History* (New York: Holt, Rinehart & Winston, 1974).

[58]"Northern Ireland," Hearings before the Subcommittee on Europe of the Committee on Foreign Affairs, House of Representatives, 92nd Congress, 2nd Session, February 28 to March 1, 1972, pp. 81-82. Several dozen other Irish-American writers, academics and politicians appeared before this subcommittee to condemn the violence in Northern Ireland.

[59]*Wall Street Journal* (October 12, 1981). Among those arrested were Michael Flannery and Joseph Cahill, both of whom were born and raised in Ireland where they had earlier ties with the IRA.

[60]*New York Times* (December 16, 1975).

[61]*The Economist*, 258 (March 22, 1976): 33-34.

[62]*Time*, 114 (November 26, 1979): 92.

[63]*Europe*, 227 (September/October 1981): 4.

[64]*Christian Science Monitor* (November 6, 1980).

[65]*Encounter*, 46:93 (March 1976): 93.

[66]*World Press Review*, 26 (November 1979): 25-28. It is worth noting that a half dozen people associated with Noraid remained on the executive board of the Caucus causing both the London and the Dublin governments to treat the Caucus and Noraid as one.

[67]One student of Northern Ireland has concluded that the failure to focus the attention of the United States on events in Ulster is attributable to the fact that there is no American view of the Northern Irish problem, ". . . but rather a diverse collection of views, often conflicting, often seriously misinformed, of what the problem is, who is to blame and what can be done about it." Ken Heskin, *Northern Ireland: A Psychological Analysis* (New York: Columbia University Press, 1980), p. 17.

[68]For an excellent source on the evolving Irish community within the United States, see Carl Wittke, *The Irish in America* (New York: Russell & Russell, 1970).

[69]*World Press Review, op. cit., p. 28.*

[70]Edward M. Kennedy, "Ulster Is An International Issue," *Foreign Policy*, 11 (Summer 1973): 68-71.

[71]The "Four Horsemen" first obtained the support of former secretary of state Cyrus Vance for a plan involving $100,000,000 in American aid for Northern Ireland at a meeting held on June 9, 1977. No reference was made to any specific sum of money, however, in President Carter's announcement two months later. *New Statesman*, 97 (May 11, 1979): 678-679.

[72]*New York Times* (March 17, 1979).

[73]*New Statesman*, 97 (May 11, 1979): 678-679.

[74]*Harper's* (December 1981): 16-20.

[75]*New Statesman*, 98 (December 7, 1979): 888-891.

[76]Claire Sterling, "Terrorism: Tracing the International Network," *The New York Times Magazine* (March 1, 1981), p. 56.

[77]*Newsweek*, 97 (May 18, 1981): 53.